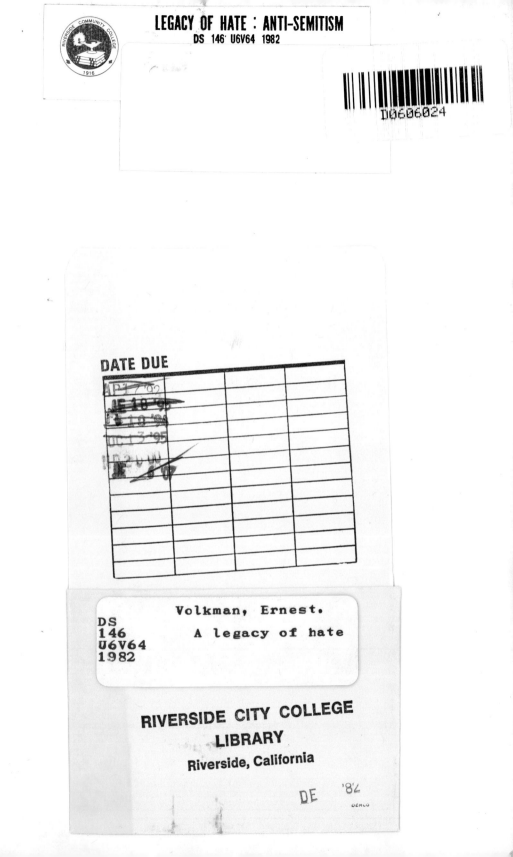

A LEGACY OF HATE

A LEGACY OF

ANTI-SEMITISM
IN AMERICA

ERNEST VOLKMAN

A GROLIER COMPANY

Franklin Watts
New York / London / Toronto / Sydney
1982

Library of Congress Cataloging in Publication Data

Volkman, Ernest.
A legacy of hate.

Bibliography: p.
Includes index.
1. Antisemitism—United States.
2. Jews—United States—Politics and government.
3. United States—Ethnic relations. I. Title.
DS146.U6V64   305.8'924'073   82-2037
ISBN 0-531-09863-X   AACR2

CONTENTS

For Carole, Eric and Michelle
May they never experience this curse

Anti-Semitism makes Jews.
Simon Wiesenthal

A LEGACY OF HATE

PREFACE

Some years ago, when I was working as a newspaperman, I was saddled with the unenviable assignment of interviewing the neighbors of a man who had been accused of being a Nazi war criminal.

Newspaper reporters dread this sort of assignment, for questioning people about Nazi war criminals does not exactly induce the most sociable of conversations. Still, I was not prepared for the near-unanimous reactions I got: their neighbor was being accused only because of "the goddam Jews; it's the Jews who are pushing this." And that represented some of the more mild comments; most of the others were so violently anti-Semitic, they were unprintable.

The memory of that day stayed with me a long time, and it has set off a long personal inquiry to answer the question that first struck me years ago: why do some/all/a few/a lot/so many people hate the Jews?

I must warn at the outset that the final answer is not in this book. Indeed, the answer may not be in any book, for it may lie so deeply within the human soul that we shall never understand it. This book represents some attempt to grapple with the problem; it does not pretend to be the definitive answer. Fundamentally, it is a study of the more modern forms of anti-Semitism in this country, the one place in the world where this ancient disease should not have happened, and where it should not be happening.

A fair number of people aided me in the preparation of this book, and while there is not enough space to thank them all, I do want to cite several who were more than gracious with their time: L. J. Davis; Lawrence Leshnick, formerly head of the European Department of the Anti-Defamation League; Vladimir Sakharov; Budd Schulberg; Kim Greer; Edouard Hayoun; Sergeant Howard Mandell of the Suffolk County Police Department; Marcella Pitts, Council for Educational Development and Research; Judith Banki and Dr. Gladys Rosen of the American Jewish Committee; and Judith Muffs of the Anti-Defamation League. Special thanks to Bob Guccione, publisher of *Penthouse* magazine, for his many kindnesses to me; and Peter Bloch, the magazine's able senior editor. A special medal is reserved for my wife, Carole, who handled the daunting research project this book demanded, and who also shared in the pain of its creation.

And one more special category is reserved for my agent, Victoria Pryor, who never stopped believing.

ERNEST VOLKMAN
Long Island, N.Y.

INTRODUCTION

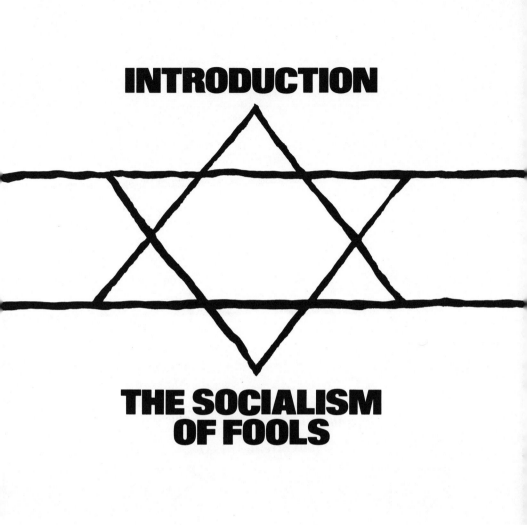

THE SOCIALISM
OF FOOLS

*I prefer having no God at all
than the God of the Jews.*

Julius Streicher, 1937

The *shtetl* of Krasrilovka existed only in the fertile imagination of a Sholom Aleichem (the pen name of Solomon Rabinowitz), but that ramshackle little village, stuck in the middle of some Godforsaken square of mud someplace in pre-Bolshevik Russia, remains one of Jewish literature's great expositions on life among the Jews during that terrible era.

Among other things, Aleichem's fictional little *shtetl* was prototypical, meant to illustrate the absurdity of Jewish existence at a time of bitter tears. In Krasrilovka, the Jewish community considered itself the center of the solar system, an axis on which the rest of the known universe turned. And thus, Aleichem recounted, whenever news reached the *shtetl* of any disastrous event, such as an earthquake in China, the sages of Krasrilovka would debate in the grand Talmudic tradition: *Is it good or bad for Jews?*

Like so much of Aleichem's writings, there is a particular poignancy in his tale of Krasrilovka. While the sight of its sages earnestly arguing over the possible impact of a Chinese earthquake seems absurd, there is a barbed point: for a scapegoat people whose hostile neighbors had blamed them for nearly every misfortune, it was not especially illogical for the Jews of Krasrilovka to wonder if they would be blamed for even the most remote disaster.

The real-life *shtetls* of which Krasrilovka served as a fictional model are all gone now, destroyed in the hurricane of the Holocaust. But their inhabitants' descendants and their traditions live on, among them an abiding concern with events outside their immediate existence—and the attitudes of their fellow non-Jewish human beings, a significant portion of whom are still largely hostile or indifferent.

Indeed, it is possible to tell the history of Judaism by simply reciting one long dirge of anti-Semitism, and as has often been noted, it might be unfair to suspect the Jews of paranoia merely because they are paranoid. But anti-Semitism is a terrible fact of history whose major assumption is that the Jews are fundamentally "other." It is that "otherism" that has been the focus of anti-Semitism for centuries: the Hellenistic anti-Semites, who were infuriated by the Jews' hostility toward the pantheon of Greek gods; the Christian anti-Semites, who were angered by the Jewish refusal to accept the "new light," and modern anti-Semites, who object to what they see as a dangerous sociopolitical entity.

For that reason, anti-Semitism is not an abstraction to Jews, who tend to be alert for the slightest tremors, like the first wavering of lines on a seismograph signaling the approach of an earthquake. Perhaps, as is occasionally argued, the Jews are *too* alert, reading portents where none exist, divining ominous trends that are not trends at all, and misreading the significance of some current events.

It is a bad argument, for few Jews are unaware of the medieval barbarism that always seems to be lurking around the corner. As Arthur Hertzberg notes, "Jews engage in the discussion of anti-Semitism for more than theoretical purposes. We keep retesting the temperature of the waters in which we must swim and the indices of our own strength to survive, because these are everyday matters of the most profound concern."

Then too, Jews are perfectly aware of the fact that modern ideological conflicts are fundamentally religious wars, fought between modern "religions" of competing ideologies. Too many wars, in fact, do ultimately involve old-fashioned religious genocide; for instance, the Indian Partition, Biafra, Bangla Desh. These wars include the slaughter of entire minorities who happen to be in the way. And it is astonishing in modern history how quickly tensions involving minorities can build, then flash into outright genocide, a phenomenon related to how quickly any minority population can get blown about by the shifts in political winds. Consider, for example, the sight of that great twentieth century statesman, Charles de Gaulle, publicly accusing the French Jews of "divided loyalties" on the question of Israel, then turning around and encouraging the very same dual loyalty among the French-speaking citizens of Quebec.

Was de Gaulle an anti-Semite? Probably not, but he was a fervent believer in "political expediency," and there were more crimes committed in this century in the name of that phrase than any other. Taken as a whole, the twentieth century has been called "the century of total war and nationalism." There is a corollary: it has also been the century of anti-Semitism in its worst form as the economic, social, and political patterns of societies have been shattered and reshattered.

This is the world of the Diaspora in which modern Jews live, a world in which they have sought full social and economic integration, living in what they hope are "societies of equals." For the most part, their hope has been achieved since the Holocaust, especially in the United States, the center of world Jewry outside of Israel. Nevertheless, the Jews do not exist in a vacuum, and, more than anybody, they are aware that so long as they are "other," then the threat of a new outburst of anti-Semitism remains.

To be sure, anti-Semitism in its nascent form is always there, the dark thread seemingly ingrained in Western culture. It rises and falls (but is not necessarily synchronized) with the tides of history, sometimes lying quiescent for years, then suddenly breaking out again. Despite a long tradition of scientific study of anti-Semitism, no one has yet been able to discern the unmistakable symptoms of that disease; it will erupt in good times and bad, in times of great prosperity and times of tranquility, in times of quiet peace and times of great turmoil.

All that history teaches us suggests that anti-Semitism exists almost solely because the Jews exist; as long as Jews refuse to disappear as a people, a culture and a tradition, there will be anti-Semitism. That fundamental fact of history remains, whether the Jews are secularized or nonsecularized, assimilated or nonassimilated, united or disunited. Anti-Semitism accuses them only of a fundamental crime: of being permanent aliens—religiously, culturally and politically— everywhere, even in Israel. Anti-Semitism no longer focuses on the charge of deicide, an accusation of which only the Jews of all peoples in history have been burdened, but it concentrates on accusing the Jews of being... Jews.

All of which leads us to the question: is there a new wave of anti-Semitism under way? In order to understand that question, a few definitions are in order.

In the first place, it is important to understand that anti-Semitism is a relatively modern concept. The term itself was first coined by Wilhelm Marr of Germany in 1873. Marr, the first of the modern anti-Semites, wrote a vicious pamphlet called *Der Sieg des Judentums uber das Germanentum* (*Jewry's Triumph over Teutonism*), in which he argued that the Jews had corrupted all standards and idealism in Germany, leading to a dissipated and "Judaized" nation. Marr took the position that individual Jews should not be blamed, and went on to complain that it was stupid to blame the Jews for the crucifixion of Christ. However, Marr accused Jews of a greater crime: dominating the cultural and political life of Germany and corrupting it, a circumstance that could not be altered because they were "a racially determined" group who would not change.

Marr's pamphlet had a tremendous impact throughout Germany and Europe at a time of extensive political unrest and, in retrospect, what he had to say was nothing short of revolutionary. In effect, Marr shifted the classic hatred of Jews from anti-Judaism, which was rooted in religious bigotry, to anti-Semitism (his own term), a broader-based complaint based on race and ideology. The shift was fundamental, for Marr was now accusing the Jews not of religious crimes, but of the more general crime of being a different people—and a dangerous one, at that. In an eerie echo of what was to occur later, Marr predicted that there would be a "last, desperate counterattack" against the Jews' domination of European political life. Marr assumed that counterattack would occur in Russia, where Europe's largest concentration of Jews lived, and his prediction was all too true: three decades after his pamphlet was published, violent pogroms broke out in Russia, exterminating hundreds of thousands of Jews. More importantly, however, Marr's thesis sired the entire modern anti-Semitic movement, and his modernist view of the "Jewish problem" in effect made Jew-hating respectable, by arguing that individual Jews were not despised, only the dangerous movement of Judaism, which had political and cultural power out of all proportion to its numbers. That thesis culminated finally in the gas chambers of Auschwitz, where millions were exterminated by government bureaucrats trying to solve the "Jewish problem."

The gas chambers, of course, did not end anti-Semitism, any more than the death of Adolf Hitler did. From 1945 to the present time, virtually every tenet and manifestation of classic anti-Semitism has repeated itself; Jews are still accused of being usurers, parasites, international conspirators, exploiters, political subversives, destroyers of culture and cowards. Even that long-discredited forgery *The Protocols of the Learned*

Elders of Zion continues to appear in new editions.* Only forced conversions and baptisms, a staple of pre-twentieth century anti-Judaism, no longer seem to exist, but nearly all the beliefs and attitudes held by those who are anti-Semitic continue to flourish.

Anti-Semitism, then, is hatred of the Jews as a people. It should be distinguished from anti-Jewish feelings. People who do not like Jews for one reason or another are not necessarily anti-Semites; there is no compelling reason for Jews to be universally liked, any more than Americans, Chinese, Catholics or Buddhists are to be universally liked. Voltaire, that great humanist, plainly did not like Jews (he regarded them as odd and superstitious), but took pains to note that he thought burning Jews at the stake was uncalled for. Anti-Semites, however, progress over that critical step beyond dislike to pathology, hating Jews for being Jews.

That being the case, is it possible to detect whether there is a "new anti-Semitism" beginning now? Is it possible that the American Jewish community, the world's largest and most powerful—where Jews have achieved the greatest measure of economic and political equality—could be subject to a wave of anti-Semitism that threatens to destroy it? Unfortunately, the answer is yes.

This answer requires some explanation. To begin with, it is important to understand that many of the classic indicators of anti-Semitism that historically have signaled new outbreaks seem to be missing. With the exception of the Soviet Union's "anti-Zionism" crusade and the enmity of the Arab world toward Israel, there are generally no governments encouraging or abetting anti-Semitism. There are, for the most part, few

---

The Protocols, actually a compilation of anti-Semitic writings from the late nineteenth century, claims to be a record of a conclave of Jewish leaders from throughout the world who met in Switzerland sometime around the seventeenth century. During this meeting their leaders plotted to take over the world and destroy all other religions. The "Protocols" were collected and published in one volume by the Czar's secret police and used to justify pogroms against Jews.

physical attacks on Jews; nor are there open manifestations of anti-Semitism expressed publicly or in print. Why, then, do American Jews especially feel a certain anxiety about current events? Why, less than four decades after the Holocaust, is there a growing sense of dread among the Jews that they have now entered a new wave of anti-Semitism?

To be sure, that anxiety would seem to fly in the face of sociological evidence that the Jewish community in this country is still enjoying its Golden Age, defined as the period that began just after World War II, when the horrors of the Nazi era seemed to render anti-Semitism unthinkable (and worse, unfashionable), an age when the last barriers to Jews in the United States crumbled away. Despite national economic slippage, the American economy remains generally robust and the American Jewish community has shared in that bounty, achieving its greatest prosperity. And the most recent Gallup Poll says that 40 percent of Americans have "highly favorable" opinions about Jews, compared with 33 percent in 1975. In terms of political power, the so-called "Jewish vote" remains a critical factor that politicians of both parties dare not overlook.

And yet, the American Jewish community is anxious, an anxiety it has been feeling since 1967, when the Middle East war uncovered some unsettling anti-Zionist trends on the political left, the traditional refuge for Jewish politics. Only a year later, anti-Semitism suddenly popped out of the closet during a bitter schools dispute in New York, center of the American Jewish community, followed by disturbing occurrences at the national convention of the Democratic Party, American Judaism's historic safe haven. The 1968 convention included blatantly anti-Semitic remarks shouted by Chicago Mayor Richard Daley against Connecticut Senator Abraham Ribicoff while Ribicoff was giving a speech to the convention condemning violence by Chicago police against protestors.

Those events, combined with the shock of the 1973 oil boycott, outbreaks of open hostility against Jewish communities elsewhere in the world, the quotas issue and several other problems have all caused a state of uneasiness among Jews. Their instinct, honed by 1,900 years of victimization by prejudice, is accurate: there is a new anti-Semitism afoot. It is not the old anti-Semitism; it is a new and hateful form that in many ways is even more pernicious.

We might call this the "anti-Semitism of indifference," by which I mean an anti-Semitism that seeks not to attack Jews directly, but to assume that the Jews do not even exist, that their concerns and survival are not even relevant questions. There is an historical echo here: in the first debate about Jews in the French revolutionary parliament in September, 1789, Clermont-Tonnerre, a liberal deputy from Paris, uttered the words that were to haunt the Jews of Europe for nearly a century: "To Jews as individuals, everything; to Jews as a distinct community, nothing!" The inherent evil of this sentiment is that the Jews were to be treated as individual citizens on their own merits, with no thought that Jews had any legitimacy in claiming status as a nation or group.

This was the classic opposition to the idea of the corporate Jew, and Jews quite rightly have refused the offer of Clermont-Tonnere—and his political descendants—on the grounds that it amounted to a secular version of Christian demands to convert. What has made America unique for Jews has been its willingness to allow them their separate identity as a group, a circumstance that has allowed American Judaism to flourish as nowhere else in the Diaspora.

American Jews, however, have been detecting a subtle but growing hostility toward the idea of a unique Jewish community in this country. First, there is the official idea that the only groups which have any legitimacy as minority groups in this country are those which have been economically deprived— the implication being, among other things, that these groups will disappear into the American mainstream once their economic deprivations are corrected. This is the central animus behind such things as hiring quotas and welfare programs.

The much-discussed "new pluralism" in the United States means that every minority group will soon enjoy similitude of status, a new version of American equality in which everybody will become "other white," a status to which the Jews have already been relegated by the government's affirmative-action agencies. The fact is that the Jews are no longer a fashionable minority, and it is well to remember that only a scant sixteen years ago a noted cabaret skit in New York City featured the song, "Anyone Who's Anyone Is Jewish This Year."

If the American Jewish community is becoming invisible, then so are some of their major concerns. Increasingly, American government administrations are finding Jewish support of Israel an annoying hindrance, a barrier to the sort of sophisticated power geopolitics they want to play in that area; and that has been combined with open expressions of anti-Zionism, from several points on the political compass, that would have been considered unthinkable even two decades ago.

Anti-Semitism is not a matter of bookkeeping, and there is not much to be gained in merely cataloging the assorted direct expressions of anti-Semitism in this country. Certainly, the growing number of incidents of vandalism against synagogues is cause for concern, but what is more important is understanding the changes in attitudes that lie at the root of those incidents.

Whatever standard is used to measure the new anti-Semitism—the number of vandalism incidents, the rise in Ku Klux Klan and neo-Nazi group membership, growing government indifference, open anti-Semitism by leftist and black groups—the fact is that there *is* a new anti-Semitism. Where it will lead no one can say, although it is not alarmist to say that the lesson of history teaches that every outbreak of anti-Semitism inevitably has a later, tragic echo, as the Jews of Weimar Germany discovered.

Modern America is not Weimar Germany, despite occasional overdrawn attempts to make a parallel, but it is fair to say there are some disturbing similarities. One of the more disturbing ones is the status of the Jewish community. In America, as in Weimar, the Jewish community has enjoyed power and prestige; when the first great wave of anti-Semitism struck in Germany, the Jewish community was divided and confused, was bereft of allies, and finally perished. Regrettably, a similar state of confusion exists today among the modern American Jewish community. Jews are uncertain about the directions of the new anti-Semitism, confused over what to do about it, and at cross-purposes about the loss of their allies on the left and in the black community. Simply put, American Jews no longer seem to know who the enemy is, and in their groping for answers, they have entered what may be the greatest period of danger in their history, especially considering some of the stresses and strains tearing at the fabric of the American Jewish community from inside.

Clearly, the Golden Age of American Jewry has come to an end. It is difficult to say how they will emerge from this latest shadow theatening their existence; each generation of Jews forges the tools of its own survival. The Jews of Sholom Aleichem's fictional *shtetl* would have little difficulty in recognizing the disturbing tremors underfoot today, but it is not easy to hazard a guess on what advice the good people of Krasrilovka might extend to their brethren.

Perhaps this, sometimes attributed to Aleichem himself: "Even a paranoid has enemies."

CHAPTER ONE

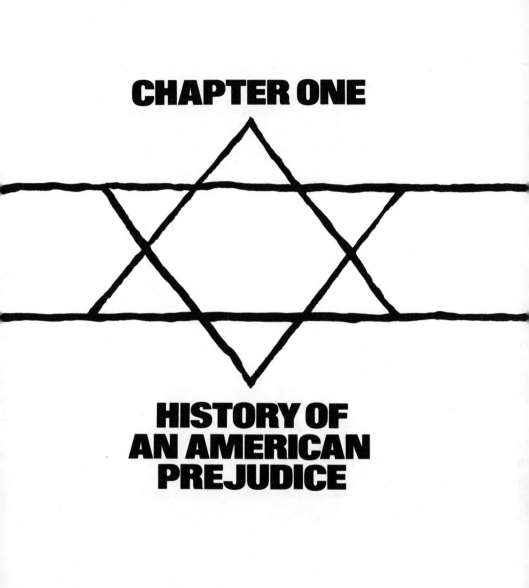

HISTORY OF
AN AMERICAN
PREJUDICE

*We are in the hands of Jews who do
what they please with our values.*

Henry Adams, 1896

Hitler had the best answers to everything.

Charles Manson, 1973

On September 22, 1654, the irascible Peter Stuyvesant, governor of the Dutch colony of New Amsterdam, sat in his office on land now approximately occupied by the offices of the New York Stock Exchange on Wall Street and wrote an angry letter to his bosses in the West India Company.

"The Jews who have arrived today," Stuyvesant fulminated, "would nearly all like to remain here, but learning that they (with their customary usury and deceitful trading with Christians) were very repugnant to the inferior magistrates, as also to the people having the most affection for you...we have, for the benefit of this weak and newly developing place and the land in general, deemed it useful to require them in a friendly way to depart...the deceitful race—such hateful enemies and blasphemers of the name of Christ—be not allowed further to infect and trouble this new colony, to the detraction of your worships and the dissatisfaction of your worships' most affectionate subjects."

The immediate cause of Stuyvesant's anger was the arrival in his colony of twenty-three refugee Spanish Jews from Brazil

who were fleeing the Inquisition. Stuyvesant, a devoted
member of the Dutch Reformed Church, had no use for
Catholics, Congregationalists, and other such aberrations, and
he was less than elated when the Jews arrived. In fact, he was
furious, which is why he wrote the letter to his superiors
demanding they be expelled forthwith.

But Stuyvesant had made a key tactical error; he was
unaware of the fact that Jews were among the board of directors of the Dutch West India Company, and in a carefully
worded letter to their employee in the New World, the board
reminded him that the company was eager to broaden its
business and, since the twenty-three Jewish refugees were traders, the company was not about to send them back to the
Spaniards. Request denied, in effect, and the Jews stayed on in
New York (as the Dutch colony later became known after the
English took it over). Later, they were joined by millions of
co-religionists who helped build New York into the center of
what was to become the Diaspora's greatest and most powerful
Jewish community. Today, a walk northward from Wall Street
passes countless monuments built by those twenty-three Jewish refugees and their successors—great buildings of a mighty
American economic empire that Stuyvesant in his wildest
moments could never have dreamed.

Stuyvesant's attempt to prohibit Jewish immigration to
the New World receives scant attention in most American
history textbooks and, indeed, historiography in general. For
all intents and purposes, the prevailing view is that anti-
Semitism's virus somehow became sterilized the moment Jews
landed on the shores of the New World. One recent work on the
history of American anti-Semitism, for example, begins in
1877, the year that the Jewish banker Joseph Seligman and his
family were excluded from the Grand Union Hotel in Saratoga
Springs on account of their religion. Before then, we are led to
believe, the Jews constituted too small a minority to be
bothered with.

In this alluring vision there is no anti-Semitism to mar the

Eden of early America; there is religious freedom, and Jews have justice and liberty, only to suffer problems late in the nineteenth century as their numbers increased dramatically with the first waves of the great immigrations from Europe. Any incidents before this period—such as the Stuyvesant letter— are dismissed as unusual occurrences that amount to individual and unusual cases.

The problem is that this vision is uniformly wrong. Historically, the fact is that the Jews of America have been experiencing anti-Semitism since 1621, when a handful of Jews landed at Plymouth and began an uneasy coexistence with the Puritan colonists. Anti-Semitism has been an unfortunate part of the American mainstream ever since this country's founding, and any attempt to deny that truth is misleading.

To understand what the new anti-Semitism is all about, it is first necessary to understand its antecedents, and to understand that the American Jewish community has been living with the problem of prejudice from the first moment the New World became reality. There is nothing to be gained from pretending that the mythical version of American history has any basis in reality.

There are two major reasons why this mythical version of the history of Jews in America has persisted for so long. For one thing, in the latter part of the nineteenth century and the early part of this century American Jewish historians sought to demonstrate that hatred of Jews was unpatriotic and a deviation from the American tradition of equality and justice for all. Further, they intended to make the story of Jews in America upbeat, as *The Hebrews in America* (1888) put it, "to show the degree of prominence and influence attained by the Hebrews of the United States." That book represented the official attempt by the American Jewish Historical Society to show that Jews, as they phrased it, "were co-workers in the discovery, settlement and development of our land."

In turn, this attempt to clean up Jewish history in America coincided neatly with the attempts of non-Jewish mainstream historians to clean up American history in general, in the process producing gilded history in which such things as massacres, prejudice and chicanery were neatly swept under the rug. The picture that emerged bore only a faint relation to historical reality: Puritans who had become benevolent Hebraists, George Washington and Thomas Jefferson as philo-Semites, and an assertion that Christopher Columbus himself (not to mention several of his crewmen) was probably Jewish.

In addition, this emerging consensus defining the United States as the "golden land" was picked up and only slightly refined by the progressive historians before and after World War II. Carey McWilliams' *Mask for Privilege* (1948), for example, the definitive study of anti-Semitism in America up to that point, took the position that American anti-Semitism was a by-product of the "triumph of business enterprise," and that Americans before 1877 were "largely free of overt or significant manifestations of anti-Semitism." Oscar Handlin, another prominent historian of that era, even went so far as to claim that anti-Semitism in this country did not really begin until the early part of this century, and that any anti-Semitic incidents before then were "without malicious intent," (whatever that means).

What finally emerged—and what persists to this day in American history textbooks—is a view that depicts anti-Semitism in America as something of an alien phenomenon, attributable exclusively to the "disaffected" in the American mainstream, notably urban "outgroups," and "marginal groups," two of the more prominent clichés of modern sociology. Thus far, this consensus view is surviving an attack by a new wave of historians who find the theories of American exceptionalism not only flatly wrong, but useless, as well. As an outgrowth of the attempt by various American minorities to demonstrate their "real" history—especially blacks, Indians and women—the historians have been examining America's dark side and finding plenty of mud to fling against some of the largest figures in the American pantheon of heroes (the accusation concerning Thomas Jefferson's black mistress is but one example).

In the process, the younger historians have been taking potshots at the consensus historical view of anti-Semitism in this country in general, and how the majority has treated its Jewish minority. As things turn out, the consensus view seems to be based more on wish than reality. The truth is that while anti-Semitism as a term did not exist until the late nineteenth century, anti-Semitism as a fact existed in this country right from the first moment the Jews arrived here. This (thus far) minority historical view concludes that while Jews found more acceptance here than in any other land in the world, their acceptance was not nearly so total as the prevailing historical consensus would have us believe. Americans have never assumed the ideological and nationalistic depth of hatred that has marked European anti-Semitism, but it has always been here nevertheless.

One of the first in the new wave of historiography, Jacob R. Marcus' *The Colonial American Jew* (1970), pointed out that, contrary to the prevailing view that anti-Semitism in the New World was an aberration, in fact anti-Semitism was part of the cultural baggage the European settlers carried with them as they arrived here. In prerevolutionary times, Marcus discovered, there was social prejudice along with many incidents of anti-Jewish violence. "In the colonial era," he wrote, " 'Jew' was still a dirty word, and it was hardly rare to see the Jews denigrated as such in the press." The consistently unfavorable image of Jews as portrayed in the popular press of the day, Marcus noted, was a reflection of the strong anti-Semitism that was endemic to the early American colonists; after the English took over New York, there was at least one violent mob attack against a Jewish funeral and desecrations of Jewish cemeteries were common.

Even the Puritans, those much-romanticized American pioneers, did not extend their doctrine of religious freedom (ostensibly their reason for emigrating to the New World) to

Jews. While devoted to the Old Testament (Hebrew language study was required in colleges by Cotton Mather) the Puritans nonetheless saw their Christian mission as the conversion of Jews to Christianity, and openly held Jews in contempt as "Christ-killers." The triumph of the American Revolution and the Bill of Rights improved the situation of Jews only slightly. The Bill of Rights did not have Jews in mind when it spoke of religious freedom; actually, that provision was concerned only with the Protestants and their assorted warring sects. So while the new United States of America supposedly basked in the glow of religious freedom and tolerance, Jew-baiting was an established part of political mudslinging (John Israel of Pittsburgh had to give up his idea of running for public office because he could not convince voters that, despite his name, he was not Jewish). Further, the young republic had virtually every known manifestation of anti-Semitism, ranging from social and economic discrimination to blood libels and claims that classical Jewish texts were violently anti-Christian. One of the first plays written by an American and produced in America, *Algiers: or a Struggle for Freedom* (1794), written by Susanna Haswell Rowsom, featured a Jewish character who was a forger and who cheated Gentiles because it was "demanded by Moses." The play was very popular, and reflected a strong streak of anti-Semitism in the press and popular arts of the time.

This anti-Semitism was striking even to European visitors, one of whom, a correspondent for a German newspaper, wrote after visiting New York in 1820: "The Jews are not generally regarded with a favorable eye; and 'Jew' is an epithet which is frequently uttered in a tone bordering on contempt. Say what you will, prejudices against the Jews exist here, and subject them to inconveniences from which other citizens of the United States are exempt."

As that anonymous correspondent may have realized, by 1800 Jews were effectively precluded from holding any state or local political offices by the fact that most state constitutions included provisions requiring office holders to believe in the divinity of Jesus Christ, provisions aimed specifically at barring Jews from becoming political leaders. The year 1800, in fact, marks the beginning of several decades that represent the first great wave of anti-Semitism in the United States. This period was marked by a general perception, as reflected in the popular literature and press of the time, that Jews were a dangerous minority who threatened to take over the dominant Christian culture. Consider, for example, the virulent editorial—only one of many—that appeared in the *New York Herald*, one of the most widely-read newspapers in the entire country, on November 18, 1837: "... In the midst of Christians, surrounded by Christian usages, the Jews may conceal these terrible opinions and doctrines—may attempt to beguile and deceive those among whom they live, in order the better to crush all religion under the secret poison of infidelity and atheism, but their Talmuds and Targums are evidences against them."

The author of that hatred, the *Herald* editor James Gordon Bennett, was actually considered pro-Jewish by many of his readers, who also read some of the best-sellers in antebellum fiction. These popular novels featured the classic anti-Semitic motifs, including the "Jew's daughter," the Jewish hunchback, the Jewish criminal and the Jewish pawnbroker. An 1844 best-seller, *The Quaker City or The Monks of Monk Hall*, by George Lippard, featured one of the most notorious villains of antebellum fiction, Gabriel van Gelt, a hump-backed Jewish forger who swindles, blackmails and carries out murders for money. The J. R. Ewing of his day, van Gelt's dialogue is written in what is apparently an odd amalgam of Hebrew and English, remarkably similar to the dialogue spoken by the Jews in the best-selling tales of the prominent American clergyman Joseph Holt Ingraham, which featured "dark-eyed Shylocks," beautiful daughters of Jewish criminals and mysterious Jewish pawnbrokers.

This sort of literature, while reflecting popular prejudices of its time, also grew out of an abiding American curiosity about Jews in the beginning of the nineteenth century. The lure of the exotic led to incidents such as the time that hundreds of people (many from up to 100 miles away) traveled into the city of Cincinnati to look at a small group of Jews who had just arrived. But their initial curiosity soon turned to outright hostility as Americans increasingly came to see the Jews not as exotic creatures, but as an alien force. Charles King (later president of Columbia College) wrote in 1823, "[the Jews are] deficient in that single national attachment which binds the man to the soil of his nativity, and makes him the exclusive patriot of his own country." Even Thomas Jefferson privately said Jews were "morally depraved" and accused them of having no ethics.

As curiosity gave way to xenophobia, the Jews were viewed as Christ-killers, conspirators, radicals and unassimilable barbarians—a transference that led to increasingly violent anti-Semitic outbursts. By 1850, nearly every area in which Jews lived had experienced several such outbursts. In New York City, a rumor of ritual murder caused a mob of 500 men to gather and, led by three Irish policemen, they broke into a synagogue during services, beat up the congregation, then wrecked the building. The curious fact is that these incidents occurred as individual Jews in America were rising to prominence in various fields. But in an American version of classic anti-Semitism, individual Jews who had achieved prominence and power, while often admired and respected on their own merits, were still vilified as members of "that accursed race." It is a peculiarly American symptom of native anti-Semitism that persists to this day in somewhat similar form.

The American Civil War spurred the great industrial boom in the North and created a great explosion in the American economy (at least outside the South), thus creating new opportunities for Jews; it also led to something of a boom in equal opportunity for them. President Lincoln was nearly a philo-Semite, and Jews rose in the ranks of both armies; additionally, for the first time, rabbis won the right to serve as chaplains. But that period is also marked by one of the most famous anti-Semitic instances in American history, an incident begun by a future president.

The incident was the issuance, by General U. S. Grant, in December, 1862, of an order barring Jewish traders from Union Army posts. Known as "General Orders No. 11" it read:

> *The Jews, as a class violating every regulation of trade established by the Treasury Department and also department orders, are hereby expelled from the department within twenty-four hours from the receipt of this order.*
>
> *Post commanders will see that all of this class of people be furnished passes and required to leave, and any one returning after such notification will be arrested and held in confinement until an opportunity occurs of sending them out as prisoners, unless furnished with permit from headquarters.*
>
> *No passes will be given these people to visit headquarters for the purpose of making personal applications for trade permits.*

To this day it remains a mystery why Grant issued this infamous order. The "department" noted in the order was Tennessee, where victories by Grant in 1862 had forced the surrender of Memphis, which immediately caused a boom in the cotton trade because the North was desperate for cotton. So into Memphis poured the cotton buyers—followed by the speculators, smugglers and profiteers. Things got rapidly out of hand in this get-rich-quick atmosphere; at one point, high-ranking Union officers were even involved in the schemes. Grant finally decided to crack down, but why he singled out the Jews, ordering them expelled from the entire Department of Tennessee, makes no sense. Certainly there were Jews among the speculators, but Christians dominated that particular racket. Perhaps Grant, no intellectual giant, was swayed by the Christian speculators, who needed a scapegoat to take the heat off what had become a very nasty public scandal. This is only historical speculation, but it is a fact that the incident was raised during Grant's 1868 campaign for the presidency. Grant said he regretted it, and with the help of Jewish Republicans, he won the White House (his defense was also aided by the fact that President Lincoln had countermanded the order less than a month after it was issued).

Still, the effects of Grant's order lasted well into the Gilded Age after the Civil War, as many Jews prospered in the general American business boom. Rich Jews—many of them calling themselves "Israelites" in an odd attempt to disassociate themselves from the Jewish community at large that still felt the sting of anti-Semitism—built gaudy showpiece temples, the Jewish form of conspicuous consumption, as monuments to their new wealth and status. But the wealthy Jews were treading on dangerous ground, notably territory considered the white Anglo-Saxon Protestants' exclusive domain. Right from the beginning the WASP establishment, normally a great respecter of money, had mixed feelings about whether to welcome the new Jewish parvenus to the ranks of the elite. Generally the reaction was hostile, witness this comment from the *Boston Saturday Evening Gazette* in 1875: "It is strange that a nation that boasts so many good traits should be so obnoxious."

In 1877 came the notorious incident involving Joseph Seligman, who was barred from the Grand Union Hotel in Saratoga Springs because of his religion. Actually such discrimination against Jews was common at the time, but Seligman's case attracted widespread attention because this time the victim was one of the most prominent financiers in the United States. And while Seligman was being barred, another Jew, this one much less well-known, was being blackballed by the New York City Bar Association on the grounds that the association did not want Jews as members.

All this was bad enough, but by the 1880s there were some disturbing indications that the virulent form of European anti-Semitism—exemplified by the 1879 claim of world-famous German historian Heinrich von Treitschke that the Jews were disloyal and a "danger to German civilization"—was beginning to spread to the United States. In 1888 one of the first anti-Semitic tracts appeared in this country, a work called *An American Jew*; it first surfaced in New York and quickly began appearing in other American cities.

By the turn of the century it was clear that American anti-Semitism had entered a new phase; from dislike and discrimination, it had evolved to outright hatred. Coinciding with the new waves of Jewish emigration to the United States (125,000 Romanian Jews had fled their native land to this country in 1878 after a series of repressive measures) the new ugliness of anti-Semitism in effect amounted to a clarion call against the rapidly growing American Jewish population, claiming that the emigrant waves would drown America in Jews. Such overt anti-Semitism was a distinct feature of the so-called "nativist" movement, actually a collection of disparate political groups whose fundamental philosophy could be summed up in the phrase, "America for Americans," meaning Americans who had the good fortune not to be Jewish, Catholic or Chinese, and who had obtained their citizenship before the first great waves of immigration from Europe.

It was during this period that the first of the professional anti-Semites came to prominence. One was the notorious Telemachus Timayenis, a Nazi forerunner who argued that Jews were inferior but nevertheless had a certain genius for crime. The Jews, he claimed in one characteristic attack, "are from an inferior race, degraded by corrupt blood, [their hearts] full of malice, [their] brains full of intrigues and tricks . . . ideas invariably turn by natural law to deceit, usury, theft, counterfeiting, forgery, embezzling, extortion, blackmailing, and above all to fraudulent bankruptcy. This is the field and compass of Jewish inventiveness and skill and genius."

To be fair, Timayenis's views were publicly condemned, and at least one of his publications was banned in Boston. Yet there is some cause to wonder whether his views were condemned on the grounds that they were anti-Semitic, or because they were expressed so violently that they violated the rules of decorum (a possible motive for the banning in Boston). While Boston was banning such anti-Semitism, some Jews in New York walking in a funeral procession for Rabbi Jacob Joseph, were attacked by workers from a nearby printing press factory. The Jews were struck by hot metal, slag and refuse. The incident led to a riot in which police beat Jews with clubs.

It was also the time of another notorious anti-Semitic crusader, Ignatius Donnelly, who claimed that "the aristocracy of the world is now almost altogether of Hebrew origin . . . as merciless to the Christians as the Christians had been to them." Presumably, Donnelly and others of his ilk took some pleasure in a 1908 report by New York City Police Commissioner Theodore A. Bingham, who claimed that while Jews at that time constituted 23 percent of the city's population, they made up 50 percent of New York's "criminal class." Bingham retracted the report after protests by prominent New York Jewish leaders, who discovered the actual statistic: Jews constituted 6 percent of the criminal class in the city, and 16 percent of convicted felons. Why Bingham deliberately distorted those figures remains a mystery.

As this sort of incident indicates, by the time World War I broke out, there was an increasingly vicious streak in the rhetoric against Jews in this country. It was distinctly echoed by the Jew-hatred that littered the pages of *Der Sturmer*, Julius Streicher's Nazi hate-sheet not too many years later. The argument has often been made that a constant recitation of hate, along the lines of the anti-Semitic literature that began to surface in this country at the turn of this century, inevitably has its effect. In its simplest form, the argument says that an endless drumroll of hate ultimately desensitizes its audience to the point of thinking of the targets as inhuman.

This argument is not subject to precise proof, but there is at least one piece of evidence that it might have some merit. That evidence came during what still ranks as the worst anti-Semitic incident in American history.

It began on April 26, 1913, when the body of young Mary Phagan was found murdered in the plant of the National Pencil Company in Atlanta, Georgia. Police determined that Leo Frank, factory superintendent and nephew of the plant's owner, had been the last person to see her alive. He was charged with murder, and in a trial that was a mockery of justice (his defense attorneys were incompetent, as well as the trial judge), Frank was found guilty of murder and sentenced to hang. Throughout the trial, mobs gathered outside the court-house and screamed, "Hang the Jew!" In part, they were whipped into a frenzy by the ravings of Tom Watson, a local populist leader who specialized in anti-Semitism. In his publi-cation, the *Jeffersonian Magazine*, Watson called Frank "the lecherous Jew . . . the lascivious pervert guilty of the crime that caused the almighty to blast the Cities of the Plain . . . every student of sociology knows that the black man's lust after the white woman is not much fiercer than the lust of the licentious Jew for the Gentile."

Not satisifed with that, Watson and other anti-Semites went a step further, inciting mob violence when Governor John Marshall Slayton of Georgia, deploring irregularities in the trial, signed a commutation order changing Frank's sentence to life imprisonment. (For this act of courage, the governor was hounded out of office.) Infuriated, Watson wrote: "The next Leo Frank case in Georgia will never reach the courthouse. The next Jew who does what Frank did is going to get exactly the same thing we give to Negro rapists."

Meanwhile, Frank had been attacked in prison by another inmate and was hospitalized. While recuperating, a mob burst into the hospital on August 16, 1915, and lynched him. Although many of the members of the mob were known, a Georgia grand jury found that Frank had died "at the hands of persons unknown."

The Frank case was a national cause célèbre, and rang an alarm bell throughout the American Jewish community. It had come only a year after the infamous case of Mendel Beilis in Russia. Beilis, the Jewish manager of a brick factory, was accused of ritual murder after a Russian boy was murdered. His trial, immortalized in Frank Kafka's *The Trial*, led to mob violence against Jews throughout Russia and marked the high point in Russia's government-supported pogroms against Jews. (It also led to a massive immigration of Russian Jews to the United States.)

The resurgence in worldwide anti-Semitism, especially in Russia, combined with the shock over the Leo Frank case, stunned the American Jewish community, which was unprepared for the kind of violent anti-Semitism shown in the Frank murder. The case and its repercussions led directly to the founding of the B'nai B'rith Anti-Defamation League, a watchdog group that quickly found itself confronting a major outbreak of American anti-Semitism.

For those who were paying careful attention, the anti-Semitism outbreak which began at about the time of the Frank case and continued through the 1920s was detectable even before it broke out into open violence against Jews. The flood of immigrants, a large proportion of them Jewish, from southern and eastern Europe between 1880 and World War I had overburdened the American social system, which was beginning to show signs of stress and strain. The influx had ignited fears among many Americans about the impact of this flood of humanity upon their country's political and social institutions. It was Theodore Roosevelt himself, after all, who had talked openly about "hyphenated Americans," an uncomfortable popular conception of Jews in the United States. Plainly, there were reactionary forces building in this country, and the increasing anti-Semitism was fundamentally a gut response to what was perceived as the potential danger of hordes of unwashed, foreign-speaking aliens swarming into the United States, threatening to upset a whole series of delicate political and social arrangements.

"For a real American to visit Ellis Island," the Reverend A. E. Patton, a prominent Protestant leader, said in 1912, "and there look upon the Jewish hordes, ignorant of all true patriotism, filthy, vermin-infested, stealthy and furtive in manner, too lazy to enter into real labor, too cowardly to face frontier life, too lazy to work as every American farmer has to work, too filthy to adopt ideals of cleanliness from the start, too bigoted to surrender any racial traditions or to absorb any true Americanism, for a real American to see those items of a filthy, greedy, never patriotic stream flowing in to pollute all that has made America as good as she is—is to awaken in his thoughful mind desires to check and lessen this source of pollution."

The Rev. Patton's comment is a pure expression of nativism, an American political phenomenon that was in direct response to the immigration waves. Combined with the growing American isolationism after World War I, it amounted to a new form of American xenophobia against the "others" in American society—and no better example of the "others" existed than the Jews.

For the first time in American history, anti-Semitic prejudice began to be expressed in European terms, with dark intonations along the lines of "something must be done." And like classic European anti-Semitism, the American version accused Jews of being a dangerous, unpatriotic minority. Even colleges and universities became infected with this virus. Albert Bushnell Hart, the noted Harvard University historian, said that Jews had to choose "between Zion and America," while Phillip Marshall Brown of Princeton claimed that Jews refused their allegiance to any land. (It should be noted that Brown's remarks came in a speech to the American Society of International Law.)

The outbreak seemed to be everywhere. During World War I, the manual used by medical advisory boards in the selection of military personnel included this sentence: "The foreign born, especially the Jews, are more apt to malinger than the native born." In retrospect, this statement may seem thoughtless lunacy, especially in an official government document. But to the Jews it represented another chilling piece of evidence that the United States, the one place in the world thought to be the greatest sanctuary for oppressed Jews (despite social discrimination), had become merely another besieged ghetto. By 1920 it was difficult to argue otherwise. During what the social scientists called the "Return to Normalcy," anti-Semitism became institutionalized. Among hate groups, the Ku Klux Klan was enjoying a spectacular revival, partially on the strength of a pronounced anti-Semitism. Hiram Evans, Imperial Wizard of the Klan, ominously discussed the "problem" of Jews, claiming that they were unassimilable "with no deep national attachment, a stranger to the emotion of patriotism as the Anglo-Saxon feels it." The kind of patriotism Evans and other anti-Semites had in mind was reflected, among other things, in the restrictionist immigration laws that began to win legislative approval. In 1917 they scored their first victory when a bill requiring a literacy test was passed, over Woodrow Wilson's veto—an obvious tactic against the Yiddish-speaking immigrants from eastern Europe. Soon, the restrictionist legislation was broadened even further with a quota system, severely restricting the number of people who could enter the United States each year, especially those from eastern and southern Europe. These two areas just happened to be the major source of immigrants the bigots particularly did not like—Jews and Catholics.

The year 1920 also marked the beginning of restrictive covenants written into real estate agreements that closed large areas of cities and suburbs to those of "Hebrew descent." On a more shrill level, in May of that year, Henry Ford began publishing the *Dearborn Independent*, a newspaper that printed every conceivable staple of contemporary anti-Semitism, including *The Protocols of the Learned Elders of Zion.* Ford was a crackpot, especially on the subject of Jews, and the hate that filled the columns of the *Independent* was some of the most vile anti-Semitism ever to be published in this country. Ford himself was forthright about the purpose of his little newspaper, claiming that Bolsheviks and Jews were the two main threats to the United States, and he was embarked upon a crusade to rid the country of them both. In his view, "Jewish power" attacked the American economy from above through the Rothschilds, while Marx and Trotsky subverted it from below, all at the behest of the "international Jew."

As Freud wrote, "When a delusion cannot be dissipated by the facts of reality, it probably does not spring from reality." Henry Ford and his anti-Semitic hate-sheet illustrated that point perfectly: one of his friends was Rabbi Leo Franklin, who puzzled Ford by refusing to join in his "crusade against the international Jew." It was the same sort of delusion that seemed to afflict the Ku Klux Klan. William J. Simmons, who was mostly responsible for the revival of the Klan in 1915, bristled when asked in a 1921 interview about his group's anti-Semitism. "We are not anti-Jewish," Simmons replied. "Any Jew who can subscribe to the tenets of the Christian religion can get in."

However, there was nothing delusionary about the effects of both the official and unofficial anti-Semitism that swept across America. Nearly 1,500,000 Jews had immigrated to the United States between 1881 and 1914, but there was a greater need than ever for further Jewish immigration. Between 1915 and 1921, over 250,000 Jews had been killed in Russia, either slaughtered in pogroms or dead from starvation and exposure. Violent anti-Semitism had broken out all through the rest of Europe, spurred by political unrest after World War I and a sudden shift to the right in European politics. Yet, the new American immigration laws limited immigration by nationality per year to 3 percent of the number of that nationality in this country as of the 1910 census. A 1924 revision to those laws restricted quotas even further, limiting annual migration quotas to 2 percent and using the census of 1890 as a base. Since the bulk of Jewish immigrants from eastern Europe had arrived here after 1890, the legislation had the practical effect (which was precisely as intended) of reducing the flow of Jewish immigrants to a trickle. Hearings on the bill focused almost exclusively on the "problem" of Jewish immigration.

At the same time, the Jews living in the United States were subjected to a widening range of anti-Semitic prejudices and practices. In 1922, A. Lawrence Lowell, the president of Harvard University, called for a quota system of Jewish admission to "relieve university overcrowding." Although the university trustees rebuffed Lowell's plan, an unofficial quota system was instituted. It spread rapidly to many other colleges, universities and professional schools. Moreover, there was growing discrimination in public associations and accommodations, plus a long list of private groups (many beaches in America at that time had signs reading, "For Gentiles Only").

There were even more serious overtones. In 1928 the rabbi of the Jewish community in Massena, New York, was summoned by the State Police and questioned about the custom among Jews of "offering human sacrifice at Yom Kippur." The question was asked in all seriousness while the police were investigating the disappearance of a four-year-old girl. Fortunately, several hours later the girl walked out of the woods unharmed, just as the situation in Massena began to turn ugly; there was open talk about mob violence against the Jews in the town. Like the Frank case, the Massena situation shocked American Jews as collectively they realized how close Massena had come to a pogrom straight out of the Middle Ages, on the issue nearly as old as the Diaspora itself—blood libel. Jewish organizations seized on the Massena incident, not only to help Jews defend themselves against similiar outbreaks, but also to try to educate Americans about some basic practices of Judaism that would seem unnecessary to teach at a time 400 years after such nightmares as blood libels were supposed to have disappeared from Western culture. But in the year 1928, in what was supposed to be the middle of great advances in science and learning, there were Jews actually trying to explain that Jews did not take the blood from young Christian children as part of the Passover rite, nor did they offer up human sacrifice on the eve of Yom Kippur. (Incredibly, the Jewish organizations discovered, four similar blood libel incidents had occurred at about the same time in other areas of the United States.)

During the 1930s, anti-Semitism in America took another twist, but this time it was not directly related to domestic fears, but to the growing Fascist movement in Europe. In the process, a good deal of homegrown anti-Semitism fell by the wayside. Henry Ford was gone, having quit publishing the *Independent* after narrowly avoiding a libel suit. The Klan was still openly expressing anti-Semitic statements, but had shifted much of its focus onto the blacks, a strategy that tended to attract more Klan recruits in the organization's area of strength, the backwoods South. Discrimination was still a fact of life, but some of it was crumbling before counterattacks by Jewish groups and the inability of anti-Semites to stop the entry of first-generation American Jews into the American economic mainstream. As the American anti-Semites discovered, American culture retained a deep respect for those who had "made it," no matter who they were.

There was still official anti-Semitism, such as the 1932 *Army and Navy Register* article examining why there were not more Jews in the armed forces: "The pay is poor, there is not profit in it, and more, they might be called upon to die for the country of adoption." Surprisingly, perhaps, this sort of anti-Semitism did not find its way into the various postmortems on what had caused the Great Depression in America. There was some talk about "international Jewry" as a cause of the depression, especially among the fanatics, but for the most part, there was too much political infighting (and the simple necessity of

trying to stay alive) for Jews to become the scapegoats. Then
too, the new administration of Franklin Roosevelt had taken
dramatic steps to end the crisis, actions devised and carried
out, to a certain extent, by the first big influx of Jews into the
federal government.

But the shadow that began to lengthen over the American
Jewish community had its beginnings in Europe, where fascism had begun to dominate the politics of the continent. That
phenomenon began to find echoes in this country, spawning a
new variety of American anti-Semitism: uniformed paramilitary groups that were virtual copies of Hitler's *Sturm Abtei-
lung* (Storm Troopers, more popularly known as "Brownshirts"). One of the more notorious of such American groups
was the Silver Shirts, led by William Dudley Pelley, who
averred that his group represented "the cream, the head and
flower of our Protestant Christian manhood." As for goals, in
1934 Pelley announced that his group had only one: "There is
but one issue in the United States, and that is the forcible
removal of the Jew from office." Other such groups included
the Crusaders for Economic Liberty (the "Whiteshirts"), the
American Vigilantes, and a group led by Gerald Winrod, a
fundamentalist evangelist who won a wide following in the
Middle West by claiming that the "international Jew" was
responsible for "the scourge of international Communism."

With their gaudy uniforms, strident rhetoric, virulent
anti-Semitism and occasional show of arms, these groups represented the most sensational expression of Jew-hatred in American history. Their chorus was joined by nonuniformed (yet
equally notorious) anti-Semites such as the gangs of thugs in
New York City who beat up Jews in the streets, and the
infamous Father Charles Coughlin, whose radio audience was
estimated to be about 30 million listeners. Coughlin, a spell-
binding preacher, had begun his broadcasting career with
sermons on social justice, but he soon began making anti-
Semitic remarks. He referred to Supreme Court Justice Felix
Frankfurter and his close association with President Roosevelt

as the "Jew deal," and attacked Frankfurter and the Justice's friends as "Felix and his happy little hot dogs." Coughlin increasingly lost touch with reality, and eventually called for what he termed a "Christian front" that would not fear being called anti-Semitic "because... the term anti-Semitic is only a pat phrase in Communism's glossary of attacks." He went on to say that the authenticity of *The Protocols of the Learned Elders of Zion* was irrelevant since "we cannot ignore the news value of their strongly prophetic nature." Coughlin produced a scurrilous newspaper called *Social Justice*, an ironic name for what was in fact an anti-Semitic hate-sheet; one of its vendors stabbed a Jewish high school teacher, and supporters of Coughlin beat up Jews on the streets in New York after a radio station refused to carry Coughlin's broadcasts.

There were also some other anti-Semitic crackpots, most notably George Van Horn Mosely, a retired Army major general who conspired with several other like-minded men to carry out a Fascist coup to take over the United States government. The scheme never got beyond the conspiracy stage, and when Mosely was called before a Senate committee for questions about the planned coup, he refused to drink water on the grounds that it had been poisoned by Jews. One of his co-conspirators was a man named George Deatherage, a notorious anti-Semite who was head of the Knights of the White Camellia, still another paramilitary anti-Semitic group. Less military was the Gentile Co-Operative Association of Illinois, an anti-Semitic group that published a "Gentile Business Directory" and urged buyers to patronize only stores owned by non-Jews.

But of all these groups, the one that caused the most fear in the Jewish community was the German-American Bund, an organization sprung full-blown from Hitler's Brownshirts. Indeed, the American Bund was covertly financed by Hitler, partly on the promise by its leader, Fritz Kuhn, that the Bund could organize all German-Americans into a fighting force loyal to Germany that would await its "day of deliverance"—

presumably a Nazi invasion of the United States. The Bund inspired fear among Jews not only because of its violent anti-Semitism, but because it seemed to be the best-organized and best-financed of all the neo-Nazi hate groups. Also, the Bund was aiming at a large audience, much larger than any other similar group: the 12 million German-Americans in the United States, many of them first- and second-generation Americans who remained proud of their ethnic heritage,

Throughout the 1930s the Bund tirelessly pursued the German-American community by claiming they were "racially superior" to "polyglot Americans," especially the Jews. The Bund gained control of several German-American organizations, and established summer youth camps for military training and Nazi propaganda. Some military training took place in broad daylight on the streets of Yorkville, the German neighborhood in New York City (and some of the participants used their training to assault Jews on the subways). A flood of anti-Semitic propaganda, most of it produced in Nazi Germany, came into the United States and was distributed by the Bund, while at the same time there was an attempt to take over the American isolationist movement, an increasingly important political faction as the war clouds gathered over Europe.

In the end, Kuhn and the Bund were able to claim 23,000 members out of the 12 million German-Americans he had hoped to recruit. But as nobody needed to remind the Jews, Hitler had started with only seven followers in Germany. Additionally, despite its relatively modest numbers, the Bund had the capacity to frighten: its rallies usually filled Madison Square Garden, and the newsreels of the time carried the unforgettable images of uniformed storm troopers beating hecklers, à la Nazi Germany. It was the sort of thing that led to a popular American cliché of the time, "It *can* happen here."

This was precisely the fear of American Jews as they watched the assorted Brownshirt imitators strutting all over America, ranting about "Jewish conspiracies," and making no bones about their intent to destroy the Jews (in the unlikely event they would ever gain control of the American government). Even as late as 1944, at the height of the war with Germany, domestic anti-Semites were still insisting it was all the fault of the Jews. Gerald L. K. Smith, a notorious anti-Semite, summarized their view of the war, saying. "This is an unnecessary war ... nobody wanted it but the power-mad internationalists operating under the direction of international Jewry." And in 1945, as Americans were shocked by the first pictures out of the liberated extermination camps, American Jews discovered that old habits of discrimination could survive even scenes like those. Dr. Ernest M. Hopkins, president of Dartmouth College, strongly defended the quota system which "regulated" the number of Jews at Dartmouth and other colleges and universities. "Dartmouth College," Hopkins said, "is a Christian college founded for the Christianization of its students."

But some years before these examples of active and casual anti-Semitism took place, the American Jewish community suffered through a prolonged political crisis during which the Jews found themselves not only in the middle, but very nearly made scapegoats. Only the Japanese attack on Pearl Harbor headed off what could have been American Jewry's worst crisis.

In shorthand form, it was known as the "America First debate," which was in fact a momentous political brawl that assumed anti-Semitic overtones. The argument was over whether the United States should get involved in the European war that had broken out in September 1939, after Hitler invaded Poland. The debate, which threatened to tear America apart, was between the so-called "interventionists" and "America Firsters" The interventionists argued that Hitler was a menace to civilization and that only the United States had the power to stop him before he conquered the world; the America Firsters argued that the United States had no business in a European war. The battle was closely fought (the Selective Service Act only passed by one vote in 1940), with President

Roosevelt advocating American aid to Great Britain to stem the Nazi advance, over the objections of the America First movement, which said such aid violated American neutrality laws.

Judged strictly as a constitutional and political argument, there was merit on both sides of the debate. But the America First movement suddenly turned anti-Semitic, in the process creating one of the ugliest episodes of anti-Semitism in American history. Sadly, one of the most prominent America Firsters was Charles Lindbergh, the famed "Lone Eagle" and among the greatest of all American heroes.

Enormously popular with the American public, Lindbergh was an extreme isolationist who used his appeal to try to keep the United States out of war. Lindbergh made a series of bad misjudgments, among them his 1938 trip to Nazi Germany, where he was given a VIP tour of new German industrial centers and shown its burgeoning air force. Lindbergh was dazzled by this show, so carefully orchestrated by the Nazis to impress the gullible, which is what the Lone Eagle turned out to be: he pronounced Nazi Germany invincible in any war, then accepted a medal from Hermann Göring. On returning to this country, Lindbergh began his America First activities in earnest, saying that the United States had to remain strictly neutral in the event of a European war and that there must be total abstention from all European affairs.

This nonsense exposed Lindbergh to ridicule, and interventionists handed out cardboard copies of the Göring medal with the inscription, "For services rendered to the Third Reich." Over the next three years, as the neutrality debate deepened, Lindbergh increasingly was under attack by assorted interventionists, who accused him of either being a fool or a Nazi dupe. (In one radio broadcast, Alexander Woollcott said of Lindbergh, "Have you any doubt—any doubt at *all*—that Hitler would have been glad to pay Lindbergh an immense amount, millions, for the work he has done in the past year?")

Woollcott had hit a raw nerve, for the fact was that the America First movement was steadily accumulating an alphabet soup collection of assorted anti-Semites, who saw the organization as (1) a counterweight to the interventionist movement, which they were convinced was in the clutches of the "Jewish conspiracy"; and (2) a camouflage for their anti-Semitic activities, since they could claim their opposition to intervention was strictly constitutional. More responsible leaders of the America First movement tried to weed out the anti-Semites, but all that effort went for naught when on September 11, 1941, Lindbergh made a speech that sent a chill throughout the American Jewish community.

"The three most important groups who have been pressing this country toward war," Lindbergh said, "are the British, the Jews, and the Roosevelt administration." That was bad enough, but then Lindbergh went on to say, "Instead of agitating for war, the Jewish groups in this country should be opposing it in every possible way, for they will be among the first to feel its consequences. A few farsighted Jewish people realize this and stand opposed to intervention. But the majority still do not. The greatest danger to this country lies in their large ownership and influence in our motion pictures, our press, our radio, and our government."

It is hard to pick out what is the worst aspect of that speech—the crude anti-Semitism, or the thinly-veiled threat to American Jews. Even though many influential Jews were in fact isolationists, Lindbergh's anti-Semitic outburst repelled them, especially his bizarre attempt to make the obvious victim appear the aggressor. In this case, American Jews had plenty of allies, and the interventionists pounced on Lindbergh. How many of them were sincerely repelled by the Lone Eagle's anti-Semitism, and how many were simply using it as a convenient club with which to beat Lindbergh (and the America First movement) over the head, is impossible to say. The fact is, however, that even so fierce an America First supporter as the

Hearst newspaper chain took pains to disassociate itself from Lindbergh's anti-Semitism; America First as a political movement never recovered from that speech of Lindbergh's.

The furor, temporarily obscured the fact that even more ominous anti-Semitism was occurring, including some sponsored by the United States Congress. Senator Gerald P. Nye, a prominent isolationist, had allowed a pro-Nazi unit of the Steuben Society of America (an old-line German group), to send out Nazi propaganda—a good deal of it anti-Semitic slander. At the same time another member of Congress, a midwestern congressman, made anti-British speeches and had them mimeographed and distributed by a registered agent of Nazi Germany.

But the most appalling case involved Congressman Hamilton Fish of New York, who allowed the Silver Shirts to distribute copies of *The Protocols of the Learned Elders of Zion* under this congressional frank, plus pamphlets calling Fight For Freedom (a prominent interventionist group) "The Fight for Jewdom." It turned out that Fish had turned his office into a virtual distribution center for anti-Semitic propaganda; when asked about it, Fish calmly replied, "It doesn't bother me any. . . . There's been too much Jewism going around anyway." (Fish, pleading congressional immunity, declined to appear before a federal grand jury and was defeated in the 1944 elections.)

Senator Burton K. Wheeler, another leading isolationist, didn't send anti-Semitic propaganda from his office, but joined fellow isolationist Senator Nye in complaining about the influence of Hollywood studios in "whipping up war hysteria." Nye read off a list of movie moguls allegedly responsible for this hysteria, then noted that each had an eastern European or Jewish background.

"Why do they want to push us into war?" Nye asked in his speech, referring to Jewish movie executives. "Well, they have interests . . . if Britain loses, seven of the eight leading [movie] companies will be wiped out . . . the quarters and half-dollars of the American movie patrons barely pay for the cost of producing these gigantic movie spectacles. The profits depend on the sales in the foreign market, which is now reduced to England and her dominions." This was classic populist anti-Semitism, but fewer people were listening. In one fell swoop, Pearl Harbor ended not only isolationist vs. interventionist argument, but many of the manifestations of anti-Semitism that trailed behind it.

The enormity of the Holocaust tended to smother anti-Semitism after the war, and American Jews entered what has often been called their "golden age." America was not the same country after World War II, and the changes had the most momentous impact in the Jewish community. Barriers, both official and unofficial, began to crumble, a more aggressive Jewish community exerted increased political power (a key factor in the creation of the state of Israel), and for the first time in over 300 years since first arriving in the New World, the Jews enjoyed full access to the American mainstream. Granted, there were certain hitches along the way. In 1946, the leaders of the Protestant denominations met in Amsterdam and attempted to express their contrition for the murders of six million Jews during the Holocaust. And, while the ovens of Auschwitz and Dachau were still smoking, the churchmen decided that the highest testimony of regard they could give the Jews was to offer them salvation through Jesus Christ. And it was not until 1959 that the National Council of Churches abolished its bureau of Christian Mission to the Jews.

The changes in the relationship between America and its Jews in the years after World War II were nothing short of extraordinary, considering past history. Indeed, it was the general lack of open anti-Semitism in the two decades following the end of World War II that lulled the American Jewish community into the error of failing to spot the symptoms of the new anti-Semitism that began in the late 1960s. To understand how that could have happened, note some of the key deductions the American Jews arrived at on the basis of their experience with anti-Semitism before the end of the war.

1. Anti-Semitism, in however minor a form it appears, must be fought vigorously. Unlike the Jews of Europe, who were awarded their emancipation, American Jews were guaranteed their rights by the United States Constitution right from the beginning, so have to do nothing to "earn" those rights. Forbearance in the face of attacks of anti-Semitism, as was the policy for most of European Jewry, is a failure.

2. Unlike Europe, it will be virtually impossible for American anti-Semitism to gather sufficient force, because hatred is diffuse in this country. Even in its worst days, anti-Semitism in America had to compete with a whole list of other hates, ranging from primitive anti-Communism to anti-Catholicism, to racism.

3. Fundamentally, anti-Semitism on a large scale is antithetical to the American mainstream. Basically, then, it is an aberration whose effects tend to be transitory. More importantly, the American Jews are the first Jews in history to be equipped with a document—the Bill of Rights—that gives them the weapons to fight back (what document could German Jews appeal to?).

4. The American political system, with its unique two-party setup, is resistant to anti-Semitism. The reason for this is the prevalence of close elections, which means that the Jewish votes often play critical roles. Additionally, American politics traditionally aims for a broad support across the political spectrum; a narrow approach based on anti-Semitism or any other form of bigotry cannot possible succeed.

These are all perfectly valid deductions based on the experience of 200 years of various forms of anti-Semitism in this country, but the difficulty is that they do not offer much guidance in the case of new forms of anti-Semitism. And that is precisely what happened in the mid-1960s when, after more than a decade of peace, the Jewish community suddenly found the brunt of anti-Semitism coming from the blacks. It was not only unexpected, but vehement as well, as Jews were caught in the crunch between the blacks' rising expectations and the realities of their status in America. What the American Jews had forgotten was that while Jews were the obsession of Christianity for so many centuries, blacks have been the obsession of Americans. Substantially, the Jews were in a no-win situation: if they helped the whites keep down the blacks, then they would be violating the central inspiration of their own history as a downtrodden minority; if they helped the blacks, they incurred the wrath of whites who resented the Jews for aiding a minority despised even more than the Jews. At the same time, much of the black–Jewish conflict was inevitable, given the rapid changes in society. Blacks migrated into the northern cities where they often settled either adjacent to, or right inside, older Jewish communities. Members of those communities were perfectly happy to support the blacks' struggle for greater equality, but not willing to go as far as social integration.

The other major cause of anti-Semitism in this era has been the question of Israel. Beginning in the late 1960s, those leftist groups committed to the cause of Third World and revolutionary groups began legitimizing the Palestinian cause by claiming that the Palestinians were in fact not only a revolutionary movement, but the victims of oppression, as well. This is an arguable proposition, at best. As we shall see subsequently, the creation of Israel brought American Jews a condition of permanent crisis—and an outbreak of anti-Semitism for which they were totally unprepared.

Their conclusions about anti-Semitism prior to 1965 were no longer of value to them in connection with the three major causes of anti-Semitism that American Jews now faced: black–Jewish relations, the cause of Israel, and the Arab oil boycott, which is actually an offshoot of the Israel question. The seeds of these outbreaks were sown long before they burst forth.

Unfortunately, the plain truth is that the history of anti-Semitism in America up to the present day tells us little about the current problem of anti-Semitism. The only guidance it can offer is that fundamental truth: anti-Semitism in America has been part of the American fabric since the first moment of this country's existence. There are bull and bear cycles, but it goes on, assuming different forms at different times. It is not limited to crazies; if that were the case, there would be no problem.

CHAPTER TWO

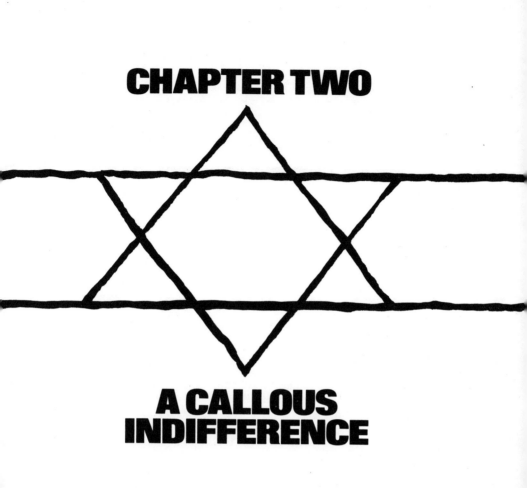

A CALLOUS
INDIFFERENCE

*An anti-Semite is someone who
hates Jews more than necessary.*

old Jewish saying

Sigmund Freud used to tell the story about the European town whose officials once erected a large sign reading, ALL CAMELS WILL BE KILLED BY SUNDOWN TONIGHT. Jews immediately fled the town, and when somebody pointed out to them that they were foolish to leave in view of the fact that they were obviously not camels, one of the Jews replied, "You know that, and we know that, but do *they*?"

The point, of course, is that scapegoat has been Judaism's traditional role for centuries, right from the time Jews were first accused as Christ-killers. From then until the Nazi era, a dangerous pathology in Western culture insisted that Jews had satanic powers, were a race apart that could alter man's destiny. And so, when the great bubonic plague called the Black Death swept over Europe in the fourteenth century, killing a third of the population, Jews were slaughtered by mobs who believed that they had poisoned the wells. The fact that Pope Clement VI tried to stop it by noting that Jews died like everybody else, and that the disease broke out in areas where no Jew lived, made little difference; the mobs in their miserable

anger needed history's classic scapegoats for what they believed
was a divine punishment of some sort.

It would be pernicious to draw a direct parallel between
what happened during the terrible time of the Black Death and
the attitudes of some Americans today—those Americans who
believe that Israel is the direct cause of the oil problem, and
that only a Jewish-controlled media and domination of Congress by an omnipotent Jewish lobby prevents this truth from
emerging. The parallel is not exactly apt, and as historian
Barbara W. Tuchman notes, "People tend to overestimate
history's capacity to repeat itself." By which we understand
that a mass slaughter of Jews, as occurred during the Black
Death and the Nazi era, cannot happen again, and only a small
lunatic fringe fails to understand that the elimination of Israel
tomorrow would not bring back one drop of cheap oil. And,
for that matter, if the Jews of America stopped supporting the
Jews of Israel, the oil problem and Middle East tensions would
hardly disappear.

Prevailing wisdom, in the form of polls and assorted
sociological studies, tells us that the lunatic fringe which
believes in such scapegoating is so small in this country as to be
almost negligible. According to these studies, even with the
occasional highly-publicized instances of scapegoating—an
Attorney General of the United States asserting "Jewish domination" of the Communist movement, and a Chairman of the
Joint Chiefs of Staff claiming that Jews own the media and big
business—the American perception of its Jewish minority continues to grow more and more benevolent. Only a small fraction of the populace, we are led to believe, is either anti-Semitic
or believes in the myth of Jewish domination. So prevailing is
this view, in fact, that few believe that a repetition of the tragic
events that befell French Jews in the Rue Copenic in Paris two
years ago could happen here (a large bomb exploded outside
the main Paris synagogue, killing a score of people). Nor would
its aftermath seem possible here. After French Prime Minister
Raymond Barre said, "This odious attack . . . was aimed at

Jews and . . . struck innocent Frenchmen," storeowners along
the Rue Copenic sent bills for damages to their shops from the
bomb blast to the French Jewish community.

So it cannot happen here. Very comforting, but as we shall
see, there is good cause to doubt the efficacy of those polls and
studies, and it is questionable whether they measure what is in
fact the new anti-Semitism—the anti-Semitism of expediency
or unconcern. And there is some further question whether
these polls and studies are measuring anti-Semitism in the
United States at all.

At first blush,it appears that anti-Semitism in America
has just about been studied to death. A small library of
volumes of such studies could be gathered (work sponsored by
the Anti-Defamation League and the American Jewish Congress in the past decade alone takes up fourteen volumes), so it
would appear that short of reexamining the results periodically
to verify the findings, nothing more fundamental remains to be
done. And it would seem that the general conclusion of all
these studies and polls remains: in the past three decades,
anti-Semitism in the United States has declined dramatically,
to the point where only a tiny minority in this country continues to hold anti-Semitic beliefs and attitudes. Squared up
with the widespread acceptance of Jews in all areas of American society, especially in the professions and the arts, the
results seem to make sense.

But let's take a look at the kind of questions these polls
and studies are asking. One of the most widely reported, the
Gallup Poll, concludes that "positive attitudes" toward Jews
by non-Jewish Americans have increased dramatically in
recent years. One means the Gallup people have used to arrive
at this deduction is questioning its poll subjects about whether
they would vote for a Jewish presidential candidate. According
to Gallup, 46 percent of Americans questioned in 1937 said
they would vote for a Jewish presidential candidate; by 1978
that figure had risen to 82 percent. Another approach is asking
people the range of opinions they hold about Jews. In Gallup's

most recent study on the subject, completed last year, 40 percent of those polled reported "highly favorable" opinions of
Jews, as opposed to 33 percent who had the same response in
1975. (According to Gallup in their 1981 study, only 2 percent
had "highly unfavorable" opinions of Jews.)

A much more elaborate study, this one carried out by the
opinion research firm of Yankelovich, Skelly and White (and
sponsored by the American Jewish Committee), sought to
measure trends in attitudes of non-Jewish Americans toward
Jews from 1964 to 1981. Based on surveys of the opinions of
1,041 people, the study used an 11-item index of negative
statements and attitudes regarding Jews; the report found that
34 percent of those questioned had "prejudiced" opinions of
Jews (as compared with 45 percent in the 1964 survey). Those
who had "unprejudiced" opinions of Jews amounted to 45
percent, compared with 34 percent in 1964. Simplistically,
then, one conclusion is that there has been a shift of about 33
percent in attitudes toward Jews during the past seventeen
years.

The study also examined whether continued economic
problems in this country contribute to anti-Jewish feelings.
Reporting on the results of a question that asked people
whether they worried a lot about losing their jobs because of
the economy (and then correlating their answers with their
basic attitudes toward Jews), the study found that the "prejudiced" group was 1 percent more likely than the "unprejudiced" group to be fearful of job security. Thus, the study
concluded, economic concerns are not correlated with negative
feelings about Jews.

At the same time, the study also examined the attitudes of
Christian fundamentalists toward Jews, finding that 25 percent
of them are "strongly prejudiced" (not significantly different
than the 23 percent of all non-Jews in the study rated as
"strongly prejudiced"). On the opposite side of the spectrum,
39 percent of the fundamentalists were rated as "unprejudiced," compared with the 45 percent of the total non-Jews

rated the same way. Clearly, the Yankelovich, Skelly and White study is saying that (1) neither economic factors nor fundamentalist beliefs have any significant bearing on anti-Semitic attitudes; and (2) levels of anti-Semitic prejudice have been declining at a fairly rapid rate in this country during the past seventeen years. On this latter point, the study concludes that the decline is related to the fact that a younger, better-educated generation has grown to adulthood, and this generation is significantly less biased than older generations.

This would appear to be quite heartening, but there are any number of problems with drawing conclusions from such studies. The most serious problem, of course, concerns whether there is any pertinence to using opinion polls to measure such an emotional issue as attitudes toward Jews. Aside from the question of whether respondents in such a poll reveal their true innermost feelings—virulent anti-Semites tend to be guarded in open expression of their feelings, while people more sensitive to the problem of anti-Semitism tend to confess such bias, however superficial—there is a serious problem: can such surveys detect the new anti-Semitism? Plainly not, considering the way the surveys are constructed and the simple fact that there is no way of knowing whether any of the respondents would even have thought about anti-Semitism unless they were asked. Furthermore, the survey results have no way of moving beyond the question of attitude to determine how many people would *act* upon their prejudices. Or, obversely, how many people found to be "unprejudiced" would do anything to prevent a direct expression of anti-Semitism, or an anti-Semitic act?

The central difficulty with such surveys and studies concerns not so much their conclusions (honestly and professionally reached), but the basis on which the surveys are formulated in the first place. Fundamentally, they address what are considered the three major types of anti-Semitism:

Realistic Anti-Semitism: The result of conflicts among groups, especially on economic questions.

One example would be resentment over Jewish domination of any profession or trade.

Xenophobic Anti-Semitism: Labeling all Jews bad
because of hostility to one Jew. An example would be
calling all Jews crooked because one Jewish druggist
was charged with Medicare fraud.

Chimeric Anti-Semitism: Outright hatred of all Jews,
accusing them of the basest crimes, including ritual
murder and such things as "the international Jewish
conspiracy that controls all money."

Within that framework, the studies generally set out what the
formulators consider to be dominant "attitudes" among prejudiced non-Jews about Jews, including:

1. The Jews all have money and are geniuses at getting it, often by "tricky" means.
2. Jews are dishonest and unethical.
3. Jews are too clannish.
4. Jews are pushy and intrusive.
5. Jews control the mass media, especially television
and movies.

The difficulty is that while these may be popular perceptions
among Jews and social scientists of what they believe are the
dominant anti-Semitic beliefs among non-Jewish Americans,
there is no evidence that these are the only ones. Nor for that
matter, as noted earlier, do the beliefs have much to do with the
new anti-Semitism, which would find such attitudes of no
concern. One problem, then, is a problem of definition: since
anti-Semitism has no commonly-accepted boiling point, simply measuring attitudes tells us next to nothing, since which
attitudes are "important" is important only to those asking the
questions. It does not tell us whether such attitudes are even
relevant any longer.
There are other biases on the questions (or "scales," as the

social scientists prefer to call them), centering on what may be a form of ethnocentrism. Consider, for example, a question on feelings about intermarriage, a common feature of many surveys and studies on anti-Semitic attitudes. Virtually all the studies report a diminution in opposition among non-Jews toward intermarriage with Jews, a development cited as proof of diminishing anti-Semitism among Christians. But if a Christian is intolerant because he or she opposes intermarriages with Jews, then Jews must be equally intolerant if they also oppose intermarriages. The question, however, is not equal to both sides, since the intermarriage question is fraught with many different considerations for Jews than Christians, involving such concerns as group survival, religious legitimacy, and so forth. Making approval or disapproval of intermarriages a barometer of anti-Semitic feeling vastly oversimplifies a very complex problem, and may in fact tell us little or nothing about anti-Semitism.

The intermarriage question is just one of the problems bedeviling all such research. This research, known more formally as survey analysis, is now dominant in sociological investigations, especially in the area of anti-Semitism. The central claim is that those carrying out such analyses are able to transcend their own subjective hypotheses. But as we have seen, that is utter nonsense, for the very selection of the questions (and how the questions are framed) is a highly subjective process, and no matter how innocent the bias in selecting and framing the questions, there is a bias, nevertheless. There is a second, even more serious, problem: assuming that the subjects' reactions in such surveys amount to a primary source of sociological knowledge, as though attitudes were the whole ball game. Or, placed in the context of this book, assuming that attitudes (how people supposedly feel about Jews), as determined by the questioners, in fact define anti-Semitism. Such an approach confuses attitudes with social realities; it is true that attitudes obviously play a role in anti-Semitism, but it is also true to say that Auschwitz was built with bricks, not words.

Does this argue that the small fortune Jewish organizations have spent on such surveys has been wasted? For the most part, yes, for they have lulled the American Jewish community into a false sense of security: there is the conviction that the pseudo-scientific survey analysis they have funded and its results, sifted and resifted like so many shards of pottery from an archeological excavation, represent truth. They represent nothing of the kind, and American Jews are making a serious mistake if they believe that survey analysis, primarily a tool for pulse-taking by political scientists, is any guide to the extent of anti-Semitism in this country. Historically, anti-Semitism has been loaded with contradictions; Jews have been despised for being poor and hated for being rich; attacked as grasping capitalists and denounced for trying to overthrow the capitalist system as Communists; attacked for separatism and criticized for becoming too assimilated. No survey, least of all the ones cited earlier, even begins to address what anti-Semitism—particularly the new anti-Semitism—is all about. For example, what would survey analysis make of the phenomenon of modern Poland, where an outbreak of official anti-Semitism blames "Zionists"—Communism's codeword for Jews—for the country's upheavals? (The present Jewish population in Poland is less than 7,000 people.)

The new anti-Semitism is not susceptible to measurement by the sort of survey analysis method discussed earlier, since it is basically a negative. That is to say, there are virtually no conventional signs of it, attitudinal or otherwise. There are expressions of anti-Semitism, but paradoxically, they are not expressed out of hatred, but because of something even more hateful: simple ignorance. There are in fact two branches of the new anti-Semitism: one can be called indifferent anti-Semitism, which argues in effect that the Jews of America are either an annoying hindrance to larger concerns or simply do not exist as factors in any consideration; and a casual anti-Semitism, in which anti-Semitic statements are made, not out of an animosity, but out of ignorance or an insensitivity to the reactions of Jews. These are, in effect, two sides to the same coin of the new anti-Semitism.

It is this new form of anti-Semitism that has been dominant in this country for at least the past decade. Ironically it is,
to a large extent, the result of the "golden age" of American
Jewry cited in the first chapter of this book. As that chapter
noted, anti-Semitism in its traditional guise was endemic to
American culture right from the moment the first Jews landed
here more than a century before the Declaration of Independ-
ence. It assumed various manifestations right up to World War
II, when the Holocaust and rapidly changing American mores
caused a dramatic change in the way non-Jewish America
regarded its Jews. By the beginning of the last decade, Jews in
America had achieved what Jews elsewhere had never achieved:
full integration and emancipation, with a sharing in the
general American prosperity. But some time before the Arab
oil boycott of 1973, indications began to build that all was not
quite right, and that placid American mainstream in which the
Jewish community had been riding was not so placid, after all.
What has happened is that as the Jews became more a part of
the American mainstream, the more invisible they have
become, at least in terms of the American national conscious-
ness. Aside from becoming victims of their own success, American Jews also appear to have committed that most unpar-
donable of all American sins: they became unfashionable. And
there is an Israeli corollary here: the pronounced shift in how
Americans regard Israel is because Israel's publicized military
successes have transformed that country in American eyes
from David to Goliath. Brave kibbutz settlers fighting off
marauders with rifles is one thing, a military force equipped
with tanks, jet fighters and artillery is quite another, in terms of
American attitudes. By the same token, the shift in how non-
Jewish Americans regard Jews is not because they are any less
anti-Semitic, but because the more Jews succeed and remove
themselves from the status of aggrieved minority, the less
impact they have on the American psyche. And that also means
the less impact Jewish concerns (or even the very question of
Jewish existence as a distinct minority) have.

This is the crux of the new anti-Semitism. Its chief

component—indifference—will be addressed in this chapter, and it should be noted at the outset that there will be no tables of survey analysis cited. But some of the more prominent examples of the new anti-Semitism will make the point.

Early in 1981, as the Reagan administration began to get itself organized, the new Secretary of Health and Human Services (formerly known as the Department of Health, Education and Welfare), Richard S. Schweiker, appointed his executive staff. Now this was a matter of some political import, since assorted Executive Department positions, including Schweiker's staff, are presidential patronage appointments. And, as part of the political payoff to the New Right, a man named Warren S. Richardson was appointed as one of Schweiker's special assistants.

Richardson was unknown to the general public, but he was well-known to the New Right; for the past several years, he had been affiliated with something called the Kingston Group, a coalition of forty top conservative leaders. The group's key member is Paul Weyrich, head of the Committee for the Survival of a Free Congress, a leading New Right pressure group, which among other goals has sought to stamp out "super liberalism" in Congress and the Executive Branch. The appointment of Richardson to Schweiker's staff attracted virtually no interest except in New Right circles, but less than a year later, Richardson had become the center of a full-blown controversy.

For reasons that are still not entirely clear, Schweiker and the White House decided to nominate Richardson for the important post of Assistant Secretary for Legislation in HHS. Presumably, it was part of the White House effort to convince nervous conservatives that it was indeed committed to dismantling some of the liberal legislation that the conservatives find so obnoxious, most especially federal funding for abortion. It was also a politically important payoff to Senator Paul Laxalt of Nevada, who had been pressing the White House to appoint Richardson chief of all White House lobbying operations.

At any rate, it turned out that the White House and Laxalt had overlooked at least one disturbing piece of information in the nominee's background: Richardson had served, from 1969 to 1973, as general counsel and chief lobbyist for the Liberty Lobby, one of the more notorious anti-Semitic organizations in the country.

Founded in 1955 by Willis A. Carto, the Liberty Lobby is one of the more extremely conservative groups in the right-wing spectrum, but differs from most such groups in its frequently virulent anti-Semitism. With a claimed membership of 26,000, Liberty Lobby publishes a newspaper called *The Spotlight* and produces a radio program carried by 500 stations. Carto himself is a longtime anti-Semite and, in 1966, Washington columnists Drew Pearson and Jack Anderson performed the public service of publishing letters by Carto that advocated "repatriation" of American blacks to Africa and praised Adolf Hitler. Here, in one excerpt from a Carto letter, is his view of World War II:

> *Hitler's defeat was the defeat of Europe. And America. How could we have been so blind? The blame, it seems, must be laid at the door of the international Jews. It was their propaganda, lies and demands which blinded the West. If Satan himself, with all of the super-human genius and diabolical ingenuity at his command, had tried to create a permanent disintegration and force for the destruction of the nations, he could have done no better than to invent the Jews.*

It was bad enough that Richardson had worked as general counsel for an organization that spewed such hate, but, it quickly developed, that wasn't the worst of it. Among other interesting items unearthed by Congressman Sam Gejdenson of Connecticut in his drive to defeat the Richardson nomination—a drive also aided by the strong opposition to Richardson by the Anti-Defamation League and the American Jewish Congress—was a 1971 article written by Richardson for the op-ed page of *The New York Times*. The article, critical of American Middle East policy, concluded with this remark: "Liberty Lobby will not tag along with the cowards who would rather countenance another national disaster than brave the screams of the pro-Zionist 'free press' in America."

Confronted with this statement, Richardson publicly disavowed it, then claimed that it had been added onto the article by the Liberty Lobby without his knowledge or permission. Despite his claim that he did not agree with its sentiments, there is no record that Richardson contacted *The New York Times* and requested a correction, nor did he send a letter to the editor disassociating himself from the article.

Richardson had more of a problem explaining away another piece of evidence: a joint interview he had with Curtis Dall, then head of the Liberty Lobby organization, in 1970. The interview, which appeared in the November 1970, issue of *True Magazine*, featured Dall's declaration that Zionism is dedicated to "political and financial world domination," the Rothschild family is head of a "one-world, large-monied group" and also finances both communism and socialism, and that American Jewish financier Jacob Schiff "gave $17 million or more to start communism." Richardson referred to "the international money order," an old right-wing code word for Jews, by which is meant "international Jewish money."

This is all suggestive of some moral squalor, and by April, it was clear that the Richardson nomination no longer had any chance in Congress. Under White House pressure, Richardson withdrew his nomination and then decided to get in the last word. In a letter to Schweiker withdrawing his name from nomination, Richardson claimed that "no convincing evidence" of anti-Semitism had been turned up against him and that he was withdrawing his nomination for "political reasons." In his final statement, Richardson claimed that he was now repudiating Liberty Lobby as "racist, anti-Jewish and morally repugnant," a fact he further claimed to have learned soon after becoming general counsel of the organization. So why didn't he resign? Because, Richardson explained, he needed the job at the time; it paid well and his family had medical bills. He went on to describe his role at the organization as "minor," an assertion at variance with the recollections of other former officials of Liberty Lobby, who recall Richardson as an influential figure in the organization.

No matter. Of more importance was the reaction of the Reagan administration when confronted with the Richardson problem. As mentioned earlier, the White House pressured Richardson to resign, but this should not be taken as evidence of concern over the question of anti-Semitism. In fact, what happened was that the White House was concerned with having to fight a political battle over the Richardson nomination while being confronted, at the same time, with another battle involving the Jewish community over the proposed sale of AWACS (airborne warning and control system) radar planes to Saudi Arabia. In the view of White House strategists, no matter how the Richardson case came out, it would have the practical effect of aligning the Reagan administration with someone perceived by at least two activist Jewish organizations as an anti-Semite. The administration believed it was hardly the best posture for it to take while trying to make the American Jewish community "understand" its desire to sell such planes to a country regarded by Israel (and a considerable percentage of American Jews) as Israel's sworn enemy.

This sort of *realpolitik* by the White House is disturbing for a number of reasons, not the least of which is a notable lack of moral suasion over the question of Richardson's attitude about Jews. More to the point, how was it possible for an administration to nominate, for a high-ranking domestic policy post, a man who at the very least had served an avowedly anti-Semitic organization? That sort of thing isn't supposed to

happen, and yet it did, and it happened because whether
Richardson was or is an anti-Semite simply did not enter into
the thinking of the people who dreamed up the idea of his
nomination. As indicated earlier, the only reason why the
Reagan administration decided not to press ahead with the
nomination was because of its concern over the bigger political
fish it had to fry, notably the question of the AWACS sale. As
counterpoint, Schweiker himself accepted Richardson's withdrawal "with regret" and said that "after careful review . . . no
convincing evidence" had emerged indicating that Richardson
was anti-Semitic (he said nothing about Liberty Lobby).

It remained for Nathan Perlmutter of the Anti-Defamation League and Bertram H. Gold of the American Jewish
Committee to address the more significant questions arising
from the Richardson affair. "Since Mr. Richardson," they
pointed out in a joint statement, "never attempted to hide his
affiliation with Liberty Lobby, in fact listed it in his bio, why
was he selected for nomination to a government post and who
recommended him in the first place?" And Perlmutter, in
something of an understatement, summed up the entire affair
by noting, "There is something amiss."

There certainly was, and lest the Richardson case be considered a fluke, that imbroglio was soon followed by another,
and this one had some even more disturbing implications.

In June of last year, an embittered Ernest W. Lefever withdrew
his nomination as Assistant Secretary of State for Human
Rights, blaming an assortment of human rights groups for
whipping up hysteria against him. Lefever insisted that he was
in fact devoted to human rights—although he maintained a
bizarre distinction between "authoritarian" and "dictatorial"
regimes on the matter—and hinted at dark forces undermining
his nomination. To be sure, Lefever had some credibility problems, including his role in an "objective" study of infant formula in the Third World (which he claimed had no relationship
to a large grant awarded to his foundation by the Nestle

Company, the world's largest maker of infant formula), and his apparent willingness to let countries torture their citizens without protest from this country—provided, of course, that the countries were friends of the United States.

But there was something more troubling about the Lefever nomination, an aspect that received almost no publicity since it transpired behind closed doors in executive sessions of the Senate Foreign Relations Committee. Because the Lefever nomination never came to a full Senate vote, the transcript of what happened in the closed door sessions was not made public. That's unfortunate, because the transcripts would raise, as in the Richardson case, significant questions about the Reagan administration's concerns with respect to the American Jewish community. Indeed, there is some cause to wonder whether there is any concern at all.

Some years before, Lefever had written a book called *Nuclear Arms in the Third World*, one of the growing pile of works produced by conservative authors questioning various American policies. In this case, Lefever was questioning the rigid American bans on proliferation of nuclear technology to the Third World. Apparently very few people had actually read the book, for its content elicited almost no interest as Lefever's nomination hearings droned on before the Senate Foreign Relations Committee. But one member of that committee, Senator Paul Tsongas of Massachusetts, had read the Lefever book and he was not happy with what he found.

Tsongas asked Lefever about a passage in the book in which he argued, "The United States should consider extending a nuclear guarantee to Egypt, Syria and other Arab states" that would deter "the use of Israel's [nuclear] force for military purpose or blackmail."

Taken aback by this assertion, Tsongas asked Lefever if he was actually proposing the threat of American nuclear weapons on behalf of Arab states against Israel. Lefever replied that the section was taken out of context, and that the entire chapter would have to be read in order to show that he was talking about developing a "system for nuclear stability" in which Israel, as well as the Arab states, would be interested. This made little sense, and Lefever began to read long excerpts to buttress his argument. Tsongas and the other senators listened patiently until Lefever read this section: "Modest nuclear assistance to Israel compatible with the non-proliferation treaty is a small price to pay for helping to induce greater nuclear responsibility in a new nuclear state . . ."

At that point Tsongas interrupted the reading. "Now wait a minute," said the senator, who had taken the trouble to follow the reading in his own copy of the book. "Are we reading from the same book?" Yes, but only to a certain extent; it turned out that the actual paragraph did not contain the words "to Israel;" which, as Tsongas noted, changed the entire meaning of the excerpt. Lefever somewhat lamely replied that he had added the words "to Israel" so that his "real meaning" would be clear to those who did not have a copy of the text before them.

This was nonsense, of course, and Tsongas pointed out that the context nowhere implied that the reference was meant to be applicable to Israel. In fact, it was quite clear what Lefever was trying to say, and his reference was to the Arab states, not Israel. Lefever remonstrated with Tsongas about this at some length, finally saying, "No one can pin an anti-Israel label on me for anything that I have said . . . any effort to pin a label on me at this point is without foundation." Truly, another morally squalid performance.

In view of Lefever's later withdrawal from the nomination, all that colloquy would seem academic, but again it raises a disturbing question about the Reagan administration's attitudes. Unless they were deaf, dumb and blind, as conservatives familiar with all the players on that side of the political spectrum they must have been aware of Lefever's views. And if they were, how could they have nominated such a man for one of the most important diplomatic posts in the government? The irony here, of course, is that the nominations of both Richardson and

Lefever, however inimical to the feelings of the American Jewish community, at the same time would seem to refute what some right-wing paranoids have to say about the omnipotence of the Jewish lobby. Possibly, and those seeking additional evidence need look no further than certain events which transpired at the United Nations during the past few years.

Activities at the United Nations tend not to attract much particular attention in the media, unless some extraordinary event occurs, such as on the evening of March 1, 1980, when United States Ambassador Donald F. McHenry voted in favor of an especially nasty anti-Israel resolution in the UN Security Council. With good cause, the American Jewish community was outraged and the Carter administration soon found itself in the middle of a major political controversy. This controversy was accentuated by some curious assertions by administration officials, including the claim that the vote was a "mistake" made by incompetent people at the American UN Mission who failed to understand what the anti-Israel resolution actually said. However, Secretary of State Cyrus Vance refused to disavow the vote, and disgruntled State Department officers leaked stories that Carter and Vance were perfectly aware of what the resolution said, and were now only trying to wiggle out from underneath it because of criticism by Jewish organizations during a time of closely-fought presidential primaries.

Ultimately, it was never determined with much certitude exactly what happened. But the voters apparently decided it was incompetence, and the incident played no small part in their conviction that the Carter administration was incapable of running foreign affairs. And the controversy undoubtedly played some part in the fact that significant numbers of Jewish voters deserted the Democrats that year and voted for Ronald Reagan.

What they failed to realize, however, was that the controversial vote was merely the culmination of at least four years of American drift at the UN, a drift that amounted to a flirtation with what the Carter administration liked to call the "new realities" of Third World politics. And there is one forum where Third World politics is played, almost to the exclusion of anything else: the United Nations. The problem is that such a flirtation came with a price. That price was Israel, and it turned out to be a price the White House was willing to pay.

Almost from the first moment of its existence, the Carter administration appeared determined to avoid what it called "confrontation politics" with the Soviet Union and began advocating a "new dialogue" with Third World nations. At the United Nations, for years an American diplomatic side-show because of that organization's dominance by Third World nations and its pronounced bias toward Israel, things changed rapidly. The American ambassador to that world body was given enhanced status (his name soon appeared in second place on the State Department's directory under the secretary of State's name), and the new effort to "improve north-south relations" began. However much the United States wanted to carry out its new dialogue about economic aid and development projects, Americans soon discovered that the Third World mainly wanted to talk about Israel. More specifically, many of the Third World nations wanted to talk about the destruction of Israel, including how to end American support for that country.

The Carter administration, however, seemed unable to understand that it was carrying out a dialogue with the deaf; it was operating in a forum that in 1975 had declared that Zionism was "racism." Under such circumstances, what dialogue was possible? The fact was (and is) that the majority of Third World nations regard Israel as an enemy—and the United States as equally perfidious for its support of that enemy. And so when Somalia, the principal sponsor of that Zionism-equals-racism resolution, broke with the Soviet Union in 1977 and came to the Americans seeking a new deal, the White House gave it to them—and there was no mention of Somalia's role in siring that anti-Israel resolution. The signal could not have been more clear to Third World nations in the UN, and a whole new round of anti-Israel mischief began there, abetted by an increasingly silent American mission. True to their word about ending confrontations at the UN and elsewhere, the United States was not about to engage in the sort of confrontations that in 1975 led then-American ambassador Daniel P. Moynihan to publicly denounce the Zionism resolution in the most scathing terms.

Instead, the Americans sat on their hands while a series of events took place that should have aroused the strongest U.S. protest. One was the final resolution of the summit meeting of the "nonaligned nations" in Havana, Cuba, in September 1979, which included this statement: "The heads of state or government reaffirmed that racism, including Zionism, racial discrimination, and especially apartheid constituted crimes against humanity and represented violations of the United Nations Charter and of the Universal Declaration of Human Rights." Another incident took place at the June 1980 meeting of the Organization of African Unity, when Israel was referred to in the group's official documents merely as "the Zionist entity." Clearly the American silence was a signal that, contrary to previous American policy, Israel was now fair game.

The clearest signal came on March 22, 1979 when to the shock of its ally Israel the United States abstained on a UN Security Council resolution that directed the formation of a three-member commission to "examine the situation relating to establishments in the Arab territories occupied since 1967, *including Jerusalem.*" (Emphasis mine.) The potential mischief of that resolution centers on the highlighted phrase, and it seems extraordinary that any American delegation would abstain on it; the fact is that Jerusalem is disputed territory, and even the closest reading of Middle East history would not be persuasive that Jerusalem was ever anybody's guaranteed territory. For some reason, the American delegation chose to overlook the fact that Jerusalem was a city divided between Israeli and Jordanian sectors right up to 1967, when Israel took

over the Jordanian part. Thus, any intelligent definition of
"occupied territory" would at best be concerned with the
Jordanian-occupied part of the city, not the entire city. (Which
in any event is the capital of Israel; how any nation's capital can
be considered occupied territory makes no sense.)

The American abstention was a disaster for Israel, which
found itself bereft of its major ally. Worse, because of American supineness, the anti-Israel bloc at the UN—the nations
with whom the United States was now having the "dialogue" so
that we could get on their "right side"—became emboldened
and shortly formulated another resolution on Israel, this one
affirming that the Fourth Geneva Convention "is applicable to
the Arab territories occupied by Israel since 1967, including
Jerusalem," and that Israel must, "as the occupying power,
abide scrupulously by the 1949 Fourth Geneva Convention."
The resolution was insulting, since the Fourth Geneva Convention, approved by the nations of the world after World War II,
specifically prohibits nations from deporting or murdering
indigenous populations and settling the territory with their
own nationals—as Nazi Germany did in Poland, where millions were deported or slaughtered at death camps such as
Auschwitz. However insulting, the United States went along
with the resolution.

Which brings us to March 1980, when that three-member
commission formed a year earlier finished its work and
reported to the United Nations on its findings. And what
findings. The commission found that Israel was in "flagrant
violation of the Fourth Geneva Convention," and that "all
measures taken by Israel to change the physical character,
demographic composition, institutional structure or status of
the Palestinian and other Arab territories occupied since 1967,
including Jerusalem, or any part thereof have no legal
validity...."

The resolution in the Security Council for which the United States voted accepted these findings, which amounted to
comparing Israel to Nazi Germany and calling Israel an outlaw

state. It is only fair to note that at the very moment this lunacy was being debated in the UN, Iran was defying international law by holding American diplomats hostage, Libya was trying to destabilize Chad, and Russian helicopter gunships were slaughtering villagers in Afghanistan—not to mention the Vietnamese invasion of Cambodia. Later, Secretary of State Vance would try to convince the American people that the United States' vote for the resolution did not imply acceptance of the odious findings of the three-member UN commission, an assertion that had no basis in fact. The resolution clearly states, in its second paragraph: "2. *Accepts* the conclusions and recommendations contained in the above-mentioned report of the commission...." (Emphasis mine.)

What could be clearer? Yet when Vance testified before the Sentate Foreign Relations Committee, he tried to insist that nothing had happened in the UN, and that the United States never accepted the report's conclusions. When Senator Paul S. Sarbanes of Maryland asked Vance if he thought the word "accepts" meant the same as the word "receives," Vance replied: "You do correctly understand."

That proved to be too much for Senator Moynihan (an ex-United Nations ambassador and student of the English language), who then informed Vance that the word "accepts," especially in the context of a United Nations Security Council resolution, could not possibly be confused with the word "receives." Vance said that the United States Mission to the United Nations told him that the two words are virtually synonymous in UN diplomatese, an explanation that rang hollow, considering Vance's reputation as one of the nation's shrewdest international lawyers.

In any event, the damage had been done. Taken as a whole, the American record was shoddy. Its "new look" diplomacy, in the name of beginning a dialogue with Third World nations, abandoned Israel in the process—despite the solemn vows of President Carter that he would never do any such thing. The fact is that on nine substantive votes concerning the Middle East in the Security Council from January 1979, to August 1980, the United States abstained seven times. (The only American veto during this period was against a Tunisian resolution calling for creation of a Palestinian state, a resolution even the Arab "front-line states" considered nearly frivolous.)

And there was yet more damage to be done, even after the Carter administration's chagrin following the March 1980 vote. In December the UN General Assembly approved five resolutions on the Middle East, all of them strongly critical of Israel, and spurred by an openly anti-Semitic speech from the Jordanian ambassador. (Among other things, he accused Jews of being a "cabal, which controls and manipulates and exploits the rest of humanity by controlling the money and wealth of the world.") The American delegate made no response to this vitriol, and wound up abstaining on a resolution declaring that Israel was in violation of the Geneva Convention. No greater monument to the new government's official indifference toward its Jewish citizens exists than this silence in the face of overt anti-Semitism.

The Jewish community to a certain extent felt misled, not only by Carter—who had also flirted with the Palestine Liberation Organization and promised Saudi Arabia advanced American military technology as a bribe for continued Saudi oil production—but also by Ronald Reagan, whose campaign rhetoric espoused renewed American support for Israel. Reagan was only in office a short while when his administration made it clear that, irrespective of former pledges to the American Jewish community about Israel, it was also determined to woo Saudi Arabia. To that end, the administration proposed selling to the Saudis more advanced military equipment, including several airborne radar planes and advanced armament for F-15 fighters, while the United States was building $24 billion worth of military installations in Saudi Arabia.

The American Jewish community is increasingly nervous about that policy. It is aware that Saudi Arabia continues to be

the most important arms supplier and fund raiser for the
Palestine Liberation Organization, so there is something of a
contradiction floating among the pieces of Reagan's policy.
The contradiction was painfully evident during an appearance
by White House aide Fred Ikle last May before the American-
Israel Public Affairs Committee, the official pro-Israel lobbying organization on Capitol Hill.

Ikle (the administration's point man on the sale of radar
planes to Saudi Arabia), on the one hand promised strong
American commitments to Israel, but also warned the committee that opposition to the plane sale "could jeopardize" the
American-Israel relationship. Then, in a thinly-veiled warning
to American Jews, he said, "I hope you will weigh what is to be
gained over the long term. . . . We must not fear differences
between ourselves. But we must be vigilant to assure that these
do not become divisions."

Committee members were somewhat put out by this warning, and no wonder, for relations between them and the White
House have been steadily deteriorating for years. In 1978,
when American Jews reacted bitterly over sale of F-15 fighters
to Saudi Arabia, Carter aides privately complained about
being "squeezed by the Jews." A similar pattern developed in
the early days of the Reagan administration, and White House
counsellor Edwin Meese has been quoted as reacting bitterly
over a "campaign by the Jews" to balk arms sales to Saudi
Arabia.

All this tension is really a symptom of a larger problem,
the continuing annoyance felt by the White House over what is
regarded as the irksome problem of the American Jewish
community. Plainly put, in the view of a growing number of
government officials, the Jewish community and its fervent
support of Israel is a hindrance to the sort of sophisticated
geopolitics they want to play in the Middle East. This view,
especially pronounced since the 1973 oil embargo, argues that
America's long term interests are better served by a reorientation of U.S. policy in favor of the Arabs, and that continued

support of Israel only alienates our Arab "friends" who hold the key to the future in the Middle East. (Besides, they have all that oil.)

Put in its simplest form, it is better known as "Arabism," a term its proponents do not like, preferring instead "realism," or some similar term. Especially prevalent among many career Foreign Service officers in the State Department, Arabism in its plainest form takes the position that Israel is ultimately expendable in the name of greater American interests in the Middle East. Their worst criticism is reserved for the American Jews who pressure the White House to "tilt" U.S. interests toward Israel, thereby "warping" American Middle East policy. The depth of their anger at American Jews can be gauged by the remarks of American Ambassador to Saudi Arabia Robert Neumann last July when, following Israel's air strike on Iraq's nuclear reactor, he pressed the State Department to condemn Israel and block further shipments of U.S. arms. Instead, Secretary of State Alexander Haig made relatively conciliatory comments, criticizing the raid but nevertheless expressing sympathy over the threat to Israel from an Iraqi atomic bomb. These comments, Neumann said, made him "want to throw up." Neumann went on to suggest that Haig harbored presidential ambitions and was therefore wooing American Jews.

Neumann was fired for such indiscretions, but he was only one of the Arabists in the State Department. A considerable body of Arabists also exists outside the State Department within the foreign policy establishment, whose organizations and publications for some years have been marked by dozens of articles and studies discussing what they see as the necessity for a new American policy orientation in the Middle East— meaning a more pro-Arab policy. One prominent feature of all these discussions is the question of what to do about the American Jews and their fervid support of Israel, as though this were some sort of annoying blister to be excised. Perhaps the leading Arabist in the establishment is George W. Ball

(Under Secretary of State, 1961-1966), who has consistently espoused a "stronger attitude" by the United States toward Israel. In a 1980 article for *Foreign Affairs* magazine, the bible of the foreign policy establishment, Ball argued that the close relationship between America and Israel deprived this country "of freedom of diplomatic action on issues that deeply affect its national interest." He went on to assert that the "American Jewish lobby" contributes "in a major way to the constrictions imposed on American freedom of diplomatic action toward Israel." In substance, Ball's thesis is that the only way a permanent Middle East peace can be achieved is by American pressure on Israel—pressure that cannot be exerted because of support by American Jews for Israel. Ergo, American Jews are primarily responsible for the failure to achieve Middle East peace.

This is an interesting modern twist on the old scapegoat theory, and the question arises whether Ball, an intelligent man, actually believes it. Apparently he does, judging by an article he wrote about a year later for the *Washington Post*. This time Ball called the American-Israel relationship "lopsided," and advocated a cutoff of American aid to Israel every time the Israelis embarked upon a "military adventure," such as the bombing of the Iraqi reactor or attacks on Palestinian guerrilla bases in Lebanon.

There is an apparent growing trend that seeks to blame America's Middle East difficulties—only part of which are attributable to its relationship with Israel—exclusively on the American Jewish community and its support for Israel. Even so intelligent a congressman as Paul McCloskey of California somehow fell prey to this new scapegoatism. In a speech last July to the Admiral Kidd Officers' Club in San Diego, McCloskey said, "We've got to overcome the tendency of the Jewish community in America to control the actions of Congress and for them to force the President and the Congress to be evenhanded." In a subsequent press conference McCloskey added: "We have to respect the views of our Jewish citizens, but not be controlled by them." The San Diego chapter of the Anti-Defamation League rightly termed such views "arrant nonsense" and "an insult to the Jewish community."

Actually, his views are far more than that—they are dangerous. Nobody disputes the fact that Israel is far from perfect in its foreign policy, and indeed there is a great deal to criticize in the way that policy is sometimes conducted. But to turn the problem on its head and blame American Jews because Israeli policy is intransigent or inconvenient, or because the Middle East is a mess, is scapegoatism of the worst order, and can reach truly ominous proportions. Witness this statement by Senator James Abourezk of South Dakota, contained in an article he wrote in 1978: "If and when the day comes that our oil supplies are shut off or we find ourselves in a nuclear confrontation with Russia or we are forced to send American troops to the Middle East, it will not be difficult for the public to find who was reponsible for a generation of foreign policy mistakes." Abourezk also said, "The Israeli lobby uses threats of political reprisal. It generates hate mail to target politicians, and even bomb threats are used to prevent speeches critical of Israel from being given."

Aside from the fact that there is hardly a shred of truth in these remarks, they contain a disturbing animus, focusing on American Jews as somehow responsible for so complex a problem as Middle East diplomacy. This attitude can even creep into normally balanced news accounts; consider the 1977 article in *Time* magazine, which casually asserted, "Israel's dependence on the United States has grown to staggering— and probably unhealthy—proportions." Further along in the article, discussing the necessity of President Carter acquiring "greater leverage" over Israeli Prime Minister Menachem Begin, the article concludes that such an eventuality will not occur because of "the influence of the Jewish lobby...."

None of this is to say, of course, that the Arabists in the State Department are anti-Semites, nor for that matter could such an accusation to be leveled at so distinguished a public figure as George W. Ball, or Congressman McCloskey, or Presidents Carter and Reagan, or even so bitter an enemy of Israel as (now ex-) Senator James Abourezk. But what they say and do amounts to expositions of the new anti-Semitism, all the more pernicious because it is a virtual certainty that none of these men have the slightest trace of the classic anti-Semitism. Equally certain would be their violent protest if anyone were to accuse them of being anti-Semites. But they are realistic and expedient men, proud of their American political pragmatism. It is a blind pragmatism that has grown increasingly myopic on the question of Israel and the role American Jews play.

If these were only isolated incidents, there would be enough cause for concern, but the fact is that they must be judged along with a long series of other incidents occurring outside government that amount, again, to a callous indifference to the feelings of American Jews. Taken together, they would fill several volumes, but to cite just a few of the more onerous ones:

• It took four years for the anti-Defamation League to convince the New York State Education Department that it should approve high school courses on the Holocaust. State officials dragged their feet on the request, first made in 1977, in effect arguing there was no real need for such a course. Their letters to Jewish leaders often referred to the "Jewish Holocaust," as though the murder of six million Jews by the Nazis (and seven million non-Jews) was some sort of private argument between Hitler and the European Jews.

The state's foot-dragging was odd, considering the fact that not only do the country's largest concentration of Holocaust survivors live in New York, but the state also has this nation's largest Jewish community. And the approval came only after the state's lieutenant governor intervened.

• After the "Sixty Minutes" television program broadcast a critical piece on Israeli policies on the West Bank, Jewish newspapers in this country criticized the way in which the program was put together, accusing the program's producers of distorting facts and biased reporting methods. Barry Lando, producer of the program, wrote a detailed letter of rebuttal, and concluded it by saying, "Why are Jews so fearful of taking an honest look at Israel and its policies?" The question assumed that American Jews are incapable of making intelligent judgments about Israel.

• Any mention of Israel has been eliminated from literature published by British Airways and Sabena, the Belgian airline. The action was described last year by a British Airways spokesman as "commercial realism" and part of an effort to attract more passengers from the Arab world. It attracted hardly a ripple of attention in this country, least of all from travel associations, who continue booking on Sabena and British Airways.

• British officials distributed a booklet last year in this country, listing "alternative holidays," including a "vacation in a mock Nazi death camp." According to the brochure, "for about 30 pounds (about $70) you can join the ranks of forty paying prisoners of war at a chillingly realistic concentration camp, complete with barbed wire, searchlights, watchtowers and fifty guards in SS uniforms." The price, the brochure noted, "includes accomodation in barracks, meals of gruel and stale bread." A vigorous protest by the American Jewish Congress compelled British authorities to withdraw the brochure from circulation, but up to the time of the Jewish protest, the British had not received a single objection.

• For some years, the Hilton Hotel chain did not list Israeli Hilton hotels in its brochures and advertising material that might circulate in the Arab world on the grounds, as a Hilton official explained, that the company did not want to "flaunt" its Israeli activities to the Arabs. Hilton did not get around to listing its Israeli facilities until 1980.

• A book published last year on the reminiscences of a notorious Mafia killer contained the sensational revelation that in 1947 Menachem Begin attended a conclave in the United States headed up by Jewish gangsters who raised money for arms that were supposed to go to Jewish underground guerrillas in Palestine. (Begin at that time was head of the Irgun, then the most radical of the Jewish underground factions.)

The revelation attracted strong media attention, including a segment on "Sixty Minutes." But it turned out that nobody— least of all the publishers of the book that contained the revelation—bothered to check if it was true. It wasn't; in fact, Begin never set foot in the United States until 1948. In 1947 he was in hiding, disguised as an Orthodox rabbi while British authorities, who had a $20,000 price on his head, searched throughout Palestine for him. He was hardly in a position to take a trip to the United States, even if he wanted to.

Despite the fact that the publicity was highly damaging to Begin personally, and caused some embarrassment for American Jews—they have been using him to raise money for such causes as Israel Bonds and the United Jewish Appeal—no correction was ever issued.

CHAPTER THREE

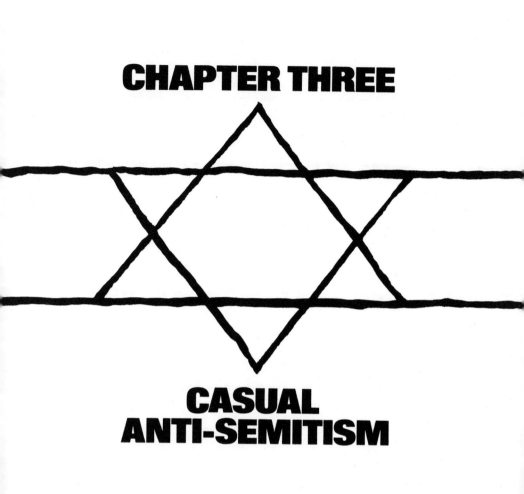

CASUAL
ANTI-SEMITISM

*For the Jew, the whole history is
packing bundles and getting away.*

Arthur Miller

A short while after Hitler took power in Germany, a German Social Democrat (and a Jew) fled to England when he began hearing rumors he was about to be killed by the Gestapo.

The English Fabians gave him a warm welcome and expressed much sympathy for his plight. The refugee took all this in quietly, but when one Fabian began talking about his particular agony as a Jew in Germany, he suddenly burst out, "No, I'm sorry, I am not a Jew." He then explained he had been born Jewish, but in 1924 had formally resigned from Judaism in a letter to the Jewish community of Berlin. The Fabians pondered this for a moment and then one of them said, "Oh, I see. The Jews are a club."

There are any number of lessons to be drawn from this little anecdote, not the least of which is the absurdity of anyone resigning from Judaism. It is a horrible absurdity, since Hitler drew no such fine distinctions about Jews; apostate or devout, young or old, assimilated or nonassimilated, they were shoved into the gas chambers. Their crime was being Jews, period. As the German Jews discovered (many of them showed their Iron

Crosses won in World War I service, insisting as they entered
the gates of Auschwitz that there had been some sort of horrible mistake), no one on that particular seat of judgment cared
what kind of Jews they were.

Modern anti-Semitism has never made such distinctions,
nor has the question even seemed relevant to it. In this modern
anti-Semitism of indifference, as we have seen earlier, Jews
simply do not count. It does not matter what they do or say or
do not say, or what they care about; Jews represent an increasingly invisible minority that is often seen as a hindrance to
larger, more important concerns. Among these concerns are
the new geopolitics of American Middle East policy and, on
the domestic front, the advancement of "economically deprived
minorities" (a category which does not include the Jewish
minority, which is apparently presumed to be wealthy).

For the most part, Jews in America have not yet fully felt
this indifference. Partially, that's because indifference is difficult to measure in the seemingly endless rounds of studies and
reports of which the Jewish community leadership is so fond,
but also because it tends not to show up on the fever charts
(indications of outright hostility and discrimination) which the
Jewish community uses to measure how the non-Jews regard
the Jewish minority in its midst. But while there is declining
evidence of classic anti-Semitism, a circumstance that has led
sociologists and others to conclude that attitudes of non-
Jewish Americans toward Jews has altered radically, there are
also continuing, open expressions of anti-Semitism—some of
it from the most unlikely quarters.

There would seem to be, then, a paradox: if anti-Semitism
is supposedly disappearing, why are there so many instances of
open expression of anti-Semitism? Because it is what we might
call casual anti-Semitism, a new form that is most often
expressed by people who claim no animosity toward Jews. For
the most part they're telling the truth; whether they are making
such statements in the name of "truth" or "objectivity" or
"realism" or "historical fact," they very seldom have malicious

intent. Again, the reason is that casual anti-Semitism is expressed either out of ignorance or because there is simply no awareness that such a statement might be considered in the least anti-Semitic. Centrally, this sort of thing is a function of the American Jews' growing invisibility. No greater example of this casual anti-Semitism exists than the disturbing attempt to disprove one of the touchstones of modern Jewry, the Holocaust.

The Holocaust has, for quite some time, been an especially sensitive matter in Jewish-Gentile relations, since it raises a number of questions of non-Jewish complicity in that great crime. The questions center not only on the role of other religions and what they did or didn't do to stop it—the argument over the Vatican's role is only one example—but also concern the actions of the Allied powers. There is plenty of grist for debate here, including the decision by the U.S. Office of War Information in 1944 to avoid mentioning executions of Jews by the Nazis on the grounds that such publicity would be "confusing and misleading if it appears to be simply affecting the Jewish people." Nevertheless, despite often acrimonious arguments on these questions, there had never been a serious attempt to deny that the Holocaust even took place. Until recently, only a tiny lunatic fringe advanced the crackpot idea that the Holocaust was in fact a myth dreamed up by Jews to further their plans for world domination.

But at the present time this insanity is no longer restricted to diehard Nazis; it has gotten a respectful hearing in American academic institutions, and the amount of material being produced on this gross revisionism is lengthening. How that came about is at once puzzling and disturbing.

Shortly after World War II, Nazis and neo-Nazis alike began to propound the idea that Hitler was blameless for the war, having been provoked into it by "English warmongers" and the Poles. This was a crackpot twist on the revisionist thesis advanced by the distinguished British historian A. J. P. Taylor, who argued that the war was actually a mistake, the

end result of a series of diplomatic blunders made by all sides—
a thesis not highly regarded by other historians. The lunatic
fringe seized on this thesis as "proof" of the perfidy of the
Allies, and it was but a short step from there to a deduction that
if everybody had lied about Hitler, then they probably lied
about the genocide against the Jews, too.

Still, the first expeditions into the Holocaust revisionism
were cautious, generally conceding that some sort of Holocaust had taken place, but claiming that whatever happened
was "provoked" by powers outside Germany, compelling
Hitler to take action against the "Jewish Fifth Column" in his
country. This is the sort of classic anti-Semitism long familiar
to Jews—blaming the victims for the crime. But by the beginning of the 1960s, it was clear that the ancient libel was assuming a new dimension.

In 1961 an American named David L. Hoggan published a
book in Germany (no American company published it), called
*The Imposed War: The Origins and Originators of World War
II*. Essentially, the book was a radicalization of the Taylor
thesis, arguing that Hitler was the only European leader of the
prewar era devoted to peace. While advancing that argument,
Hoggan claimed that Hitler had treated the Jews of Germany
"more generously" than the government of Poland treated
Polish Jews. That was the first indication that some perverse
rethinking was going on among the lunatic fringe, underscored
by the publication, a year later, of a pamphlet called "Blasting
the Historical Blackout." Written by the American isolationist
Harry Elmer Barnes, it supported Hoggan's thesis, but went on
to add, in connection with the Holocaust, that such crimes
were "alleged." Worse, it turned out that Barnes had joined up
with radical libertarians and had written a foreword to a book
published by the Libertarian Book Club. (In 1966, two years
before his death, he wrote an article for a libertarian journal
claiming that "atrocities of the Allies" were far worse than
"alleged extermination in gas ovens" by the Nazis.)

The sudden convergence of the hopelessly muddleheaded

Barnes and the libertarian movement, perhaps the hottest American political movement in the past two decades, should have rung alarm bells. It was a clear indication that Holocaust revisionism was coming out of the closet—in fact, was becoming very nearly respectable.

In 1964 the first tentative efforts by Barnes and Hoggan to deny the truth of the Holocaust resulted in the publication in France of a book called *Le Drame des Juifs Europeens*, by Paul Rassinier. An ex-Communist, Rassinier had been imprisoned at Buchenwald, an experience which somehow led him to conclude that no atrocities went on in Nazi concentration camps, and if any Jews were killed, they were murdered by Jewish *Kapos* (camp trustees). Rassinier claimed that of the 6,000,000 Jews said to have been murdered by the Nazis, precisely 4,416,108 of them were actually alive, and the remainder were killed by persons unknown, none of them German. Barnes enthusiastically praised this gruesome arithmetic in the pages of *The American Mercury*, the journal founded by H. L. Mencken which had fallen on lamentably hard times since his death and became an anti-Semitic hate sheet. Barnes praised Rassinier as "courageous," and said that the author:

> ... *lays the chief blame for misrepresentation on those whom we must call the swindlers of the crematoria, the Israeli politicians who derive billions of marks from nonexistent, mythical, and imaginary cadavers, whose numbers have been reckoned in an unusually distorted and dishonest manner.*

Barnes sought to give the Rassinier book wide circulation, and ultimately suceeded in getting a Maryland neo-Nazi outfit to publish it under the title *The Drama of the European Jews*. The book has since gotten fairly wide circulation, but nothing compared with the circulation of a far more odious tract, also inspired by Barnes. Called *The Myth of the Six Million* by an anonymous author, it was published at Barnes' instigation by an outfit called Noontide Press. That organization is a subsidiary of the Liberty Lobby (the group whose activities played a role in the Richardson affair mentioned in the previous chapter), which also funds *The American Mercury*.

The Myth of the Six Million, like Rassinier's book, threw all caution to the winds and flatly insisted that there had been no genocide and that the gas chambers did not exist. Any information to the contrary, the small (119-page) book asserted, was part of the "big lie" dreamed up by Jews, presumably as part of their master plan. No one knows for sure how many copies of this book are in circulation at the moment, but since it is currently a staple of the far right and has been translated into several foreign languages, the total probably is somewhere around one million-plus. First published in 1969, it figured in a court suit in 1973 over profits, a good clue that the book is enjoying brisk sales.

The impact of that book, however, is not solely because of its apparently wide circulation, but because it was the progenitor of a whole new wave of Holocaust revisionism. It led, for example, to the publication in England of a pamphlet called "Did the Six Million Really Die?" which relied heavily on *The Myth of the Six Million*. Authored supposedly by Richard E. Harwood (actually a pseudonym for Richard Verrall, an official of the National Front, the British neo-Nazis), it liberally sprinkled phrases like "revisionism" and "historical review" to give the book a gloss of reasonableness, a practice that soon found its way into a long string of successor publications.

The Myth of the Six Million also led, in 1976, to the publication of a book titled *The Hoax of the Twentieth Century*, published by the very same outfit in England that had produced the Harwood/Verrall pamphlet. Significantly, the 1976 book was written by a quiet professor (of electrical engineering) at Northwestern University. The professor, Arthur R. Butz, claimed that the European Jews had not been "exterminated and that there was no German attempt to exterminate

them." His book was replete with academic jargon and para-
phernalia, and attempted to "prove" that authors of works
claiming that a Holocaust took place were "extermination
mythologists." His "proof" included what he considered to be
incontrovertible evidence that all the Jews who were supposed
to have died were in fact still alive, carefully hidden from view.

The Butz incident ignited widespread attention, for here,
for the first time, someone not of the known lunatic right had
published, with all the academic imprimatur his professorial
position implied, an ostensibly "academic" work "proving"
that the Holocaust was a lie. More interesting was the reaction
of Northwestern University, whose provost, Raymond W.
Mack, said that the Butz work was "contemptible," but went
on to defend academic freedom which, he noted, gave Butz the
right to publish whatever he chose. Perhaps, but it did not seem
to occur to Northwestern that equally cherished standards of
academia were being trampled in the process, including truth,
research and facts. Northwestern did sponsor a symposium
featuring several experts on the Holocaust, which amounted to
an eerie equal time forum, intended to demonstrate that
Northwestern was indeed committed to the fundamental academic principle of historical truth. Still, the mere fact that a
major university first shrugged off the fact that such hatred had
been produced by one of its tenured professors, then belatedly
sponsored a symposium (presumably as a sop to the strong
Jewish protest on the Butz issue), speaks of a gross insensitivity—and not a little moral myopia.

Butz's book has since become another staple in the anti-
Holocaust movement, distributed in this country by several
outfits (including Noontide Press) and reprinted in a number
of foreign editions. The publication of the Butz book in France
brought forth one Robert Faurisson, a literature professor at
the University of Lyons. In 1978, Faurisson began publishing
articles claiming that "the alleged gas chambers and the alleged
genocide are one and the same lie . . . which is largely of Zionist
origin." One of those articles was published in *Le Monde*, one

of the world's most distinguished newspapers, a circumstance that caused an outcry in France. The university suspended him, and that in turn set off an extensive debate about academic freedom in the French university system.

Normally, *l'affaire Faurisson* would be of peripheral interest to this study, except that among the people who leapt to his defense was Professor Noam Chomsky of MIT, considered among the world's greatest linguistics experts. Chomsky's position was, in effect, that he could be ranked an agnostic on the question of whether Faurisson was right, but that it was more important to him to "defend his right" to publish. Chomsky also said he was unconcerned about any charge of anti-Semitism that had been leveled against Faurisson (and, by extension, Chomsky himself), since he found the term anti-Semitism to be "vague."

It is difficult to know where to begin with Chomsky, except to wonder how a man of such considerable academic attainments could become so blind. Aside from the question of whether Chomsky understands what anti-Semitism is all about, there remains the question of whether he has even bothered to read the sort of stuff Faurisson and his ilk have been producing. The best summary, in fact, was provided by Faurisson himself in a pamphlet titled "Conclusions After 30 Years of Research by Revisionist Authors." Produced in 1980, and distributed in this country by Liberty Lobby, it sets out these five "conclusions":

1. The Hitler gas chambers never existed.
2. The genocide of the Jews never took place. In other words, Hitler neither gave an order nor permission that anyone should be killed because of his race or religion.
3. The alleged gas chambers and the alleged genocide are one and the same lie.
4. This lie, which is largely of Zionist origin, has made an enormous political and financial fraud possible, whose principal beneficiary is the state of Israel.

5. The principal victims of this lie and fraud are the German people (but not the German rulers) and the entire Palestinian people.

Chomsky is also apparently unaware of how this poison has spread beyond the borders of America, its birthplace. In Australia, for example, the publication of Butz's book compelled the secretary of the Melbourne Council for Civil Liberties to distribute several hundred copies of the book and to make speeches calling the Holocaust a "gigantic lie" created by "Zionist Holocaust propaganda." Alarmed at the possible impact such hatred might have on Australian schoolchildren and other Australians whose lack of knowledge on modern history might lead to its acceptance as historical truth, the Melbourne Jewish community and the West German embassy joined forces to produce an exhibit on the Holocaust.

But back in this country, there was still worse to come. At about the same time as the Australian uproar, American Warren B. Morris, Jr.—holder of a doctorate in history from Oklahoma State University—wrote a book called *The Revisionist Historians and German War Guilt*. It set out to decide which group was correct on the question of the Holocaust—the revisionists or the traditionalists. In Morris's view, the Holocaust had come down to an argument between two competing academic schools of thought, with such traditionalists as Holocaust historian Lucy Dawidowicz vying against revisionists like Faurisson. Morris concluded that the revisionists had failed to prove their case, but he nevertheless praised them for "forcing historians to reconsider their evaluation of Nazi policy toward the Jews," which has "done a very valuable service to scholarship."

They had done nothing of the kind, yet the Morris book received the complete panoply of academic welcome by way of a respectful review in the June 1980 issue of *American Historical Review*, journal of the American Historical Association, the leading professional organization of American historians. Publication of that review in one fell swoop gave the whole anti-Holocaust movement a respectability that seems astonishing, considering the kind of material it was producing. As a result, pseudohistorians were soon popping out all over the place, producing such odd minutiae as detailed studies on exactly how many Jews were gassed at Auschwitz (was it one million? Two million?) and whether Hitler knew anything about concentration camps (he didn't, because there weren't any).

This sort of Holocaust-cheapening led to the creation of something called the Institute of Historical Review, a legitimate-sounding organization that is in fact a front group funded by the ubiquitous Liberty Lobby, designed to offer cover to the anti-Holocaust revisionists. It convened a "Revisionist Conference" in 1979, repeated annually since then, which featured the reading of papers by several attendees—Faurisson and Butz among them—arguing that photographs of concentration camps were all fakes and that no Jews were killed in the Holocaust. If one did not listen to the content, the conclave had all the trappings and appearance of a typical academic conference. It even had an elder sage as opening day speaker—in this case, a man named James J. Martin. For the uninitiated, Martin was described as "dean of historical revision scholars." In fact, he is director of Ralph Myles Publishers, one of the growing number of small firms that have been specializing in printing "revisionist" works. A protégé of the grandfather of all this ghastly business, Henry Elmer Barnes, Martin also has connections with the libertarian movement. The Cato Institute, the prime underpinning for the libertarian movement, including its political party, in 1980 published a collection of Barnes's essays with a foreword by Martin.

Since then, the Institute has gone on to bigger and greater things. It announced a $50,000 contest, the winner being the first person to *prove* the existence of gas chambers and concentration camps. The announcement was contained in a special mailing to 12,000 professional historians and scholars, all of whose names, it turned out, had been obtained by the purchase of the mailing list of the prestigious Organization of American Historians. The Organization later conceded that it had made a mistake (which it blamed on an office foul-up), and apologized to its members and the Anti-Defamation League, whose vigorous protest brought the matter to public attention.

The contest offer was withdrawn after a California businessman who is a survivor of Auschwitz (his mother and two sisters were killed at the camp) moved to collect the $50,000, while simultaneously suing the Institute for $17 million. One hardly knows whether to laugh or cry over something like this terrible contest, but it is a sobering experience to read the masthead of the Institute's magazine. It's sprinkled not with fools, but with holders of PhDs—such as Dr. James J. Marin, formerly of the University of Michigan; or Dr. Reinhard K. Buchner, a physicist at California State University, Long Beach. Moreover, the magazine—every issue of which contains assertions such as that Zyklon B cyanide gas was used not to kill Jews, but to disinfect their clothing—now has over 3,000 subscribers, including a few libraries.

It is possible to argue that, given the size of the magazine's circulation and the limited public appeal of what the Institute has to say, there is really little cause for concern. But the important fact is that an activity that was once confined to a tiny handful of fanatics has now been expanded into something of a minor industry, replete with pseudo-academic trappings. And more disturbing is the sort of near-respectful hearing such anti-Semitism has been receiving. In the case of the Organization of American Historians, for example, only a few of its 12,000 members protested when they received in the mail copies of the latest claims that no Jews died at the hands of the Nazis. Indeed, the Organization wound up forming a committee and assigned it the task of studying the magazine to determine "the credentials of the contributors and the use of evidence." What possibly could have been the point of this academic exercise? To find that the contributors to the Institute's magazine had failed to use a sufficient number of footnotes when claiming that Jews at Auschwitz died from typhus? And what if such articles met the technical standards of the Association? Would the Association then find them at least academically sound?

It is hard to imagine the Association or any other group of scholars devoting such hair-splitting to a magazine sponsored by the Ku Klux Klan which would assert that no blacks were ever lynched, that slavery never existed, and that blacks were driven from their happy existence on plantations by Union propagandists. Instead, we find something of a madhouse, with a respected organization of historical scholars debating how many angels are dancing on the head of the pin, somehow forgetting their primary scholastic duty to the cause of historical truth. And in the case of the anti-Holocaust revisionists, that duty was to denounce the Institute and its evil works loudly and clearly, then make sure the Organization had no connection with it. The issue was never the Institute's right to publish. Such ravings are protected by the First Amendment— but so is the Organization, whose First Amendment rights include a minimal scholarly duty to denounce hatred, falsity and base calumny whenever it is published, especially when it is published in the guise of scholarly pursuit.

In the final analysis, trivialization of the Holocaust—or denying its very existence—debases Jews by trivializing the one experience that is central to all modern Jewry. From the first moment that the Holocaust began, the Nazis sought to trivialize it by referring to it as "the final solution," or calling the uprooting of entire Jewish communities "resettlement," the terrible movement of thousands of people in jammed cattle cars "transport." The Nazis sought to trivialize it not only to hide their terrible secret, but because they were perfectly aware of the fact that they were confronting an immutable historical truth: they were destroying the thousand-year-old civilization of European Jewry. American Jewry is an offspring of that European Jewish community, and is keeper of the flame of memory in their name and in the name of history. American Jews have assumed that the historical truth of what befell their European ancestors is so huge and undeniable that nothing could ever prevail against it. That turns out to be not necessarily so, but even more disturbing is the fact that there is no great outcry against this perverse revisionism. There is, for the most part, silence, a silence that seems to say the Holocaust amounted to some sort of private argument between Judaism and Nazi Germany (and as though seven million Christians did not also die in the Holocaust). As historian Lucy Dawidowicz discovered, there seems to be a great deal of indifference at work. Invited to debate Faurisson on a radio program, she refused on the sensible grounds that such a debate would dignify the Frenchman's ravings. She was thereupon accused of being unwilling to debate "controversial" matters.

Is the Holocaust "controversial," presumably in the same category with such public issues as gun control and abortion? That is hard to imagine, yet it should be judged in the larger context of Holocaust-cheapening, an ongoing attempt to commercialize that horrendous event. One example is the brisk trade in memorabilia associated with concentration camps. Others seek to capitalize on the growing sadomasochistic trend, with death camps used as a fixed locale for such fantasies; the pornography trade has been making small fortunes from such movies as *The Golden Boys of the SS* and *Ilse the She-Wolf of the SS*. (It has also crept into the soft-core market: *The Night Porter*, Liliana Cavani's 1975 film that reduced the Holocaust to the story of the sadomasochistic relationship between an SS officer and a virgin victim, was highly successful, and was rereleased last year.)

This death camp chic is bothersome enough; of more concern is the infiltration of Holocaust-cheapening into what are supposed to be mainstream historical works. The biggest offender is the British historian David Irving, author of nearly a dozen works on various aspects of World War II (his *The Destruction of Dresden* and *The German Atomic Bomb* are classics in this field). But beginning several years ago, Irving's work began to assume a disturbing anti-Semitic tinge. In 1977 his study of German strategic direction during World War II, *Hitler's War*, made the astonishing assertion that Heinrich Himmler was solely responsible for the murder of Jews, and that Hitler knew nothing about it—the implication being that if Hitler did know, he would have stopped it. While Irving averred that he was no anti-Semite, his assertion nevertheless provided some grist for the anti-Holocaust revisionists, who were able to cite the conclusion of a recognized historian as another piece of evidence for their claims. Moreover, Irving added fuel to the fire by publicly offering $1,000 to anyone who could prove that Hitler knew of Auschwitz—a disturbing echo of the $50,000 prize offered by the revisionists to anyone who could prove that the Holocaust happened.

Irving's claim that he is not an anti-Semite is seriously called into question by another of his books, published last year. Called *Uprising!* it is supposed to be the history of the 1956 Hungarian revolution, but the book contains a number of slurs, including the claim that up to 1956 Hungarian Communism was a "Jewish dictatorship," and that before World War II Jews had "overrun the more lucrative professions." He labels most of the key figures in the book either Jewish or non-Jewish, as if that had anything to do with it, and says at one point that a Jewish leader had "the tact of a kosher butcher" and "velvety eyes." He also claims that "Jewish intellectuals cowered in their flats" during the fighting in Budapest. Interestingly, there was almost no mention of this strong trace of anti-Semitism that is woven throughout the book in reviews, the one glittering exception being the review in the *London Observer*, which correctly headed its review "A Bucketful of Slime."

The fact that Irving's pronounced anti-Semitism caused virtually no interest in the media should not be surprising, for if there is one component of contemporary civilization that has demonstrated a notable indifference to anti-Semitism, and has often been the vehicle for casual anti-Semitism, it is the media.

There are more than enough examples to make this point, but one of the most notorious is worth some examination: the case of Truman Capote. For some years now, Capote has been insisting that there is a "Jewish Mafia in American letters," a large conspiracy that dominates writing and publishing, and which aims to publish works of "approved" Jewish writers. The conspiracy, Capote has alleged, extends to magazines and newspapers, whose book review sections are part of the same conspiracy. This nonsense has been expressed in many of America's major media outlets, including "The Johnny Carson Show." In an interview with *Playboy* magazine, Capote said that "anti-Semitism has nothing to do" with his charges. That is not so, and for proof, consider this excerpt from the Andy Warhol interview with Capote in *Rolling Stone* magazine:

> *ANDY: No, but you were talking before about Neil Simon's plays. I think about them, too. They are terrible. Why are they popular?*
>
> *TRUMAN: Well, this is something I don't mind saying, and I've said it in a thousand interviews and on "The Johnny Carson Show." The truth of the matter about it is, the entire cultural press, publishing . . . criticism . . . television . . . theater . . . film industry . . . is almost 90 percent Jewish-oriented. I mean, I can't even count on one hand, five people of any importance—of real importance—in the media who aren't Jewish. I can't. If those people could have done me in, they would have done me in like nobody's ever been done in. But they couldn't do me in. They would have done me in, because I not only wasn't Jewish and wasn't in the Jewish clique, but I talked about not being part of it. I've said for years: "Here's this goddammed Jewish Mafia working tooth and tong on*

the New York Review of Books, *the* New York
Times, *whether they're doing it consciously or not."*
And mostly they're doing it consciously. I'm not in
the least bit frightened by them.

ANDY: But that's good, too.

TRUMAN: In the sense that it has consistency? It's not
a good thing. It's a bad thing.

ANDY: But it's funny, because they're the ones that
buy your books and go to the plays. . . . They really
care. Why don't the other people care?

TRUMAN: You're so wrong.

I have quoted this excerpt at some length in order to show its
nearly breathtaking prejudice, replete with all the classic tenets
of anti-Semitism: a vast conspiracy, the clannish Jews, the
domination of a particular profession. It is similar to the sort of
things Capote has been saying in many other forums, including
this quote from an article about him that appeared in *New
York* magazine: "On the urban intellectual Jewish writers:
'Very talented, very powerful, and very parochial. I call them
the Jewish Mafia. They exclude too many good writers.
They're afraid of me. I can manipulate beyond their reaches. I
never would play the game. Styron is accepted because if ever
there was a goy Yid, it's Bill Styron."
      There is not too much point in analyzing why Capote, an
intelligent man of great talent, has come to believe such prattle.
Presumably, it does not stem from resentment, since Capote's
successful writings have made him quite wealthy (of the two
interviews mentioned, one took place at Capote's vacation
home in Palm Springs; the other took place at his expensive
New York apartment). More to the point, why was there no
outcry when Capote's anti-Semitism was published? Why was
there no committee or group of fellow writers strongly criticizing such views, views echoing the terrible sort of anti-Semitism

directed against the Jews of Weimar Germany (who were accused of dominating and perverting German culture)? Why didn't Andy Warhol, who ought to know better, interrupt Capote's fulminations and say, "Look, Truman, this anti-Semitism is garbage; you're full of baloney. Where's your proof?"

Those things did not happen because, simply, nobody cared enough. No one disputes the fact that anti-Semitism has occasionally broken out in the literary world, but even Ezra Pound, toward the end of his life, saw the light and described his violent anti-Semitism as "a suburban prejudice." (In much the same way, Ernest Hemingway moderated his own anti-Semitism late in his life.) But that's not the point; the anti-Semitism of Pound and Hemingway was confronted head-on, and became blots that have stained their reputations to this day. One wonders if the same thing would happen today; it is possible to imagine a future obituary of Capote that would omit any mention of the author's anti-Semitism.

The dynamic that makes this indifference to casual anti-Semitism work is the conviction that anti-Semitism is no longer a social disease, but some form of social gaffe, similar to slurping one's soup. What is extraordinary is not the amount of casual anti-Semitism that is expressed today, both privately and publicly, but the fact that such expressions, especially the public ones, usually do not meet with the sort of disapproval that would be expected even a generation ago. The problem can be seen as two sides of the same coin: on the one hand, an almost fashionable anti-Semitism; on the other, a deafening silence.

Earlier, it was noted that the media, especially, is the respository for a good deal of the contemporary casual anti-Semitism (the term media meant to include also the arts). Television is an especially sensitive barometer on this matter, since it is most subject to outside pressure by racial, religious and ethnic groups on its programming practices. Judged by that standard, the American Jewish community must be regarded by the television industry as very nearly invisible. That is the only conclusion possible after considering the decision to cast Vanessa Redgrave—widely regarded by Jews as an anti-Semite for her anti-Zionism and fervent support of the Palestine Liberation Organization—as a concentration camp inmate in *Playing for Time*, a play written by Arthur Miller. The play was based on the real-life story of a Jewish French woman who performed with an orchestra of Auschwitz inmates, its melodies designed to convince Jews they were in fact being "resettled," rather than being led to the gas chambers.

The notion of casting a perceived anti-Semite in such a role seems the height of insensitivity, but there are even more extreme examples. One was the highly offensive staging of Shakespeare's *The Merchant of Venice* on public television. The Shylock character not only was made up with an oversized hook nose, but also spoke with a pronounced Yiddish accent. Aside from gross historical inaccuracy—obviously, Yiddish was not spoken in sixteenth century Venice—there is cause to wonder why the show's producers went out of their way to produce an anti-Semitic stereotype. The question is especially relevant, considering the fact that the particular production was used by schools across the country as part of their English programs. One can only wonder if the producers, in a staging of *Othello*, would have the Moor portrayed as a shuffling minstrel man.

By the same token, there is cause to wonder what could have been running through the minds of the producers of *Jesus Christ Superstar*, one of the more popular shows among young audiences. When it first opened on Broadway in 1971, Christian groups condemned the show on the grounds of "vulgarity," although they said little about its anti-Semitic parts, including a line that called Jews of the time "vultures." Jewish groups were much more upset at what they considered to be gratuitous anti-Semitism sprinkled throughout the play. They were concerned with the perpetuation of the myth of malevolent Jews demanding Christ's death, but their criticism of the play failed; critics complained of censorship, especially when the American Jewish Committee circulated a study by Christian theologians citing many historical inaccuracies in the production. Jewish groups became even more upset when they got a look at the 1973 movie version of the play; for some reason, the authors decided to add a few lines not in the stage version. One had Pontius Pilate saying, "You Jews produce messiahs by the sackful."

The worst case of insensitivity to Jews, however, occurred on an episode of the "Sandy Duncan Show" television series. Titled *Play it Again, Samuelson*, the episode featured just about every Jewish stereotype in the book. The story line featured a Jewish couple named Samuelson filing a phony lawsuit against the Sandy Duncan character. The Samuelsons were portrayed as frauds and connivers who spoke with pronounced Jewish accents. A number of Jewish viewers protested, and they would have been even more upset had they learned that as originally written, the script had an Italian couple. The couple's ethnicity was changed to Jewish after the producers decided that Italians would protest too loudly. Much the same mentality underlay the production of the movie version of Philip Roth's *Portnoy's Complaint*, where the novel's comic characters became transformed into mock stereotypes.

The anti-Semitism that marks some instances is a casual one, expressed or written almost offhandedly, without the slightest recognition that such statements—which seem to have been expressed more privately in the previous decades—might be offensive to Jews. A few examples:

● A large ad in *The New York Times* was headlined, JEWS CONTROL CRIME IN THE UNITED STATES. The ad, for a book by author Hank Messick on the life of Meyer Lansky, was criticized by the Anti-Defamation League, which pointed out that the book says nothing about Jews controlling crime. An executive of Putnam's which placed the ad, replied to the complaint by saying, "There are crooked Jews in America, and if you read Hank Messick's *Lansky*, you will learn something about some of them."

• A profile of Henry Kissinger in the *Village Voice* was headlined, "Portnoy in Tall Cotton, or Making It on the Potomac." The article ridiculed Kissinger's nose and accent, and called him a fawning sycophant and implied that he is ashamed of his own Jewishness.

• The *Parkersburg* (West Virginia) *News* featured a guest editorial by Austin W. Wood, executive vice-president and general manager of the Ogden Newspapers chain, which noted that Kissinger is "of German-Jewish descent." Wood further noted that Kissinger was part of a "colony" of Jews in New York. "It may very well be," Wood wrote, "that Mr. Kissinger is behind a great many of our troubles all over the world."

• An edition of the *Family Farmer*, official publication of the National Farmers Organization, contained an article about a prominent Jewish grain dealer. "Here is a gent," the article said, "that has made himself a billion dollars many times over dealing in food product that hungry people had to have to stay alive. Of course, first he had to snare the production away from the 'family farmer' at a fraction of its value. I wonder if that is how those birds got themselves into so much trouble in Europe back about World War II."

• The chaplain for a professional football team, asked why only Christian denominations were represented at pregame chapel meetings, replied, "Jews own the teams. This is for playing personnel."

• *National Lampoon* carried an article called "Children's Letters to the Gestapo." Written by Michael O'Donoghue, also a writer for the "Saturday Night Live" television show, the article contained such "letters" as these:

Dear Heinrich Himmler:
How do you get all those people into your ovens? We can hardly get a pot roast into ours.

Dear Mister Himmler:
I am Rolfe. When I grow up I want to kill sheenys and wear big boots like the Fuhrer.

• A full-page advertisement in *The New York Times*, purchased by a prominent businessman and leading Arab sympathizer, claimed that the United States was a "dancing bear, responding dumbly to the commands given it directly by the government of Israel and indirectly through a potent Fifth Column which operates here in America and which gives blind obedience to the Zionist credo that all Jews everywhere owe national loyalty to Israel."

• After two professors at C. W. Post College made violently anti-Semitic remarks at a faculty meeting ("You Jews, now I begin to understand Hitler," one was quoted as saying), the college president issued a letter of rebuke, despite a faculty recommendation that the professors be fired.

• A number of local elections around the country last year were marked by open expressions of anti-Semitism, including New York City, where one candidate accused Jews, especially Mayor Edward Koch, of "dominating" the city. In Glen Cove, New York, a candidate for mayor sent out letters to voters in which he said the city's politics were under the control of "our Mediterranean brothers and sisters," barring "Nordic and Slavic Americans."

• A review of *The Garden of the Finzi-Continis*, the Vittorio DeSica film about the destruction of Italian Jews, which appeared in The *Christian Century*, concluded by saying, "Yes, the Jews were gored and ejected from their homes and they in turn gored the Arabs and ejected them from their homes to establish a Jewish homeland."

• A number of popular music groups wear swastikas as adornments, and there are various Nazi themes in their music or on their record album covers. One American rock group, The Dictators, proclaims, "We are the master race!" and Blue Oyster Cult has a quasi-swastika emblem. Rock star Marianne Faithful has a large swastika in her home; in one interview, she acknowledged that Jews were upset about it, but added, "Jews don't mind upsetting people, but they do mind being upset."

This list could go on at some length, but there is not too much to be gained by an endless recitation. The point is clear: a lot of casual anti-Semitism has been openly expressed in the past few years. A good deal of it is simply mindless, and while that might serve as an explanation for the casual anti-Semitism of people such as rock stars, editorial writers and producers, it will not fit a more important category of people—national leaders, who ought to know better.

The most prominent example, of course, has been former President Nixon, whose tapes of his private Oval Office conversations revealed a bigoted man. Initially, the White House tapes turned over to assorted congressional committees contained no bigotry; they were carefully sanitized of any such references, the gaps filled with the mysterious "characterization deleted." But as more complete transcripts emerged, it turned out that Nixon had a pronounced anti-Semitic bias. For example, complaining about a pending Securities and Exchange Commission investigation into a secret $200,000 campaign contribution, Nixon said, "Those Jewboys (in the SEC) are all over everybody. You can't stop them." Nixon's ire was directed at two SEC lawyers, both Jewish, who were doggedly pursuing the illegal contribution, despite the best efforts of the White House to balk them. Nixon was also livid, in the early days of the Watergate investigation, about his inability to forestall the efforts of three Justice Department prosecutors. Actually, two of the prosecutors were Jewish, but Nixon thought all three men were Jewish and complained about "stopping those Jews over in the U.S. Attorney's Office." At another point, Nixon recounted his difficulty about "sitting down there with a bunch of Jews."

One of the uglier aspects of Nixon's anti-Semitism was the attempt by his aides to cover it up. White House Assistant Leonard Garment, a Jew, was upset when he heard rumors that the tapes contained anti-Semitic utterances; he confronted other White House aides, including Alexander Haig, all of whom assured him that Nixon was not anti-Semitic and had not made any anti-Semitic remarks. Garment was infuriated when he later learned that the tapes did contain anti-Semitic remarks, including Nixon's claim that "a network of Jews in government and the press...keep each other informed." Nixon later said that allegations that he was anti-Semitic were "without proof," and cited his appointment of Henry Kissinger as Secretary of State as evidence. Meanwhile, White House aides sought to convince newsmen that Nixon was just one of the boys, conceding that he occasionally made racial and ethnic epithets in private, but these "were not meant seriously and were made in the spirit of good humor among friends." (But since the anti-Semitic remarks were made to non-Jewish friends of Nixon, one wonders what Jews would have thought had they heard them; would they have realized that Nixon was speaking only in "the spirit of good humor"?)

Also ugly was the pronounced anti-Semitism of former Vice-President Spiro Agnew, whose bias differed from Nixon's in that it was stated publicly. Shortly after he left office in disgrace following a *nolo contendere* plea to a tax evasion charge, Agnew began a serious flirtation with Arab business interests as part of his new international business career. And the man once regarded highly by the Jewish community in his home state of Maryland began expressing an expedient anti-Semitism, attacking "Zionist imperialism" and accusing the American media of "pandering to the Zionist cause." (He subsequently wrote a novel in which pro-Israeli zealots conspire with an American vice-president to take over the United States.)

This proved to be big box office in Saudi Arabia and other Arab countries, but earned the criticism of American Jewish organizations. Agnew accused the organizations of being "too sensitive," and claimed that the American press was "unduly influenced by Zionist opinion.... All you have to do is look around and see who owns the networks, who owns the *Washington Post... The New York Times....* As you look around in . . . the big news business you see a heavy concentration of Jewish people."

Agnew has insisted, "I am not a bigot," when the question is raised whether such views are anti-Semitic. He is probably telling the truth when he says that; like almost all of the modern casual anti-Semites, he feels no personal animosity toward Jews. They are, however, inconvenient obstacles to his vision of bigger and greater commercial relations with the Arab world.

Undoubtedly, it was the same syndrome in operation when in 1974 General George S. Brown of the Air Force (and Chairman of the Joint Chiefs of Staff) complained in a speech about "Jewish influence" in Congress. The strength of that influence, Brown complained, was due to American Jews: "They own, you know, the banks in this country, the newspapers. Just look at where the Jewish money is," This was appalling, all the more so because Brown himself—as everybody who knew him seemed to agree—was not an anti-Semite. But Brown, who directed the airlift of critically needed American military supplies to Israel in the 1973 war, is ambivalent about Israel, and has expressed privately the fear that too much American military hardware was being sent there, which might someday lead to the United States being drawn into a Middle

East war. In Brown's view, the equation was simple: Israel is a close ally of the United States almost exclusively because of the pressure American Jews exert on Congress. Thus, American Jews are responsible for the fact that the Israeli-American alliance is too close.

Such casual (but not hate-inspired) anti-Semitism has broken out in various corners of the federal government, particularly during the past several years. There was, for example, the letter dispatched by a Treasury Department official to the International Longshoreman's Union complaining about federal legislation designed to prohibit American companies from participating in the Arab boycott. The letter specifically complained about a provision of the proposed law that would reveal publicly the names of American companies which had been charged with participating in the boycott. Such a provision, the letter complained, would "lead to harassment [of the company] by certain New York interest groups." That was a clear reference to Jews, and again, the barbed point was clear: Jews are responsible for the potential decline in United States-Arab trading.

A more lunkheaded, but equally casual, anti-Semitism was expressed some years ago by William Saxbe when he was United States Attorney General. During a press conference on the problem of terrorist groups in this country, he avowed that a new breed of terrorist had replaced Communist front groups as the main threat to internal security. This shift was due in part, Saxbe explained, because of "the change in the Jewish intellectual, who in those days was very enamored of the Communist Party." When Jewish groups protested the remark, Saxbe swore he was not an anti-Semite, then sought to clarify his previous statement. He only made things worse; the change in attitude of American Jews toward the Soviet Union was due to "issues of importance to Jews," Saxbe explained, then went on to say that considering the Soviet Union's support of Arab nations and its oppression of Soviet Jews, the

appeal of communism to "Jewish intellectuals" has just about
disappeared. Saxbe complained that newspapers had "taken
out of context" his remarks at the previous press conference, a
procedure he described as "something of a zinger."

What can be made of Saxbe's mishmash? Substantively,
not much; what he had to say defies all laws of logic and
history, and amounts, apparently, to some sort of conviction
in his mind that Jews were primarily responsible for the Communist Party, a romance that ended when Soviet Communists
began oppressing Soviet Jews and supporting the Arabs
against Israel. Or perhaps not; it is very difficult to say. However, whatever Saxbe was trying to say, it amounted to bias.

One lesson that can be drawn from all these episodes is
that it is hardly accurate to say—as a fair number of people
cited in this book seem to be saying—that the Jews in this
country form a sinister, single intercommunicating entity
whose mysterious ways are beyond comprehension, but whose
vast power over economics, the wellsprings of media and God
knows what else, is unparalleled. If there are so many people
running around saying things against the Jews, then how could
Jewish power be so vast? This implies that there is logic to
anti-Semitism, but of course, as history teaches, there isn't.
What lies behind all anti-Semitism—whether an anti-Semitism of indifference, or the casual variety—is an anxiousness
about Jews, an odd fear deep in the American psyche that Jews
have the power to cloud men's minds. Jews seem to sense this
anxiousness instinctively, which is one of the reasons why they
were perfectly content to see President Ford rebuke General
Brown for his anti-Semitic remarks. More drastic action, such
as demanding Brown's resignation, would have proven the
very "Jewish power" that Brown was criticizing in the first
place.

It remains for us only to consider a matter that may not seem
especially germane to the discussion at hand—the question of

Anne Frank. Her diary, printings of which now run into the many millions, remains one of the great documents of humanity. And yet it is important to remember that the diary was first published almost unnoticed in France after attempts to get it published in the United States failed (almost all American publishers rejected the diary as unpublishable). Finally, a British edition was published and, following serialization of part of the diary in *Commentary* magazine and a front-page review in *The New York Times Book Review*, an American edition finally came out—and became a huge best seller.

But the story is not yet finished.

A stage version of *The Diary of Anne Frank* won the Pulitzer Prize for drama in 1956, and has been revived in hundreds of productions ever since. Most people who saw the play, however, did not realize that there had been a significant change from Anne Frank's own words, the words she carefully wrote each night in the semi-darkness of her family's tiny attic refuge. She had written:

> *Who made us Jews different from all other people? Who has allowed us to suffer so terribly up till now? . . . If we bear all this suffering, and if there are still Jews left when it is over, the Jews, instead of being doomed, will be held up as an example. Who knows, it may even be our religion from which the world and all peoples learn good, and for that reason alone do we suffer now.*

But in the stage version of the diary, this poignant monument to Anne Frank's faith does not appear. Instead, there is this line: "We are not the only people that've had to suffer . . . sometimes one race, sometimes another." What is said in the stage version, of course, is very different from what Anne Frank had said; the line was never written by her, and was inserted into the play to substitute for her declaration so that the play would not appear too Jewish.

But the story is not yet finished.

Last year, nearly forty years after Anne Frank died in the Nazi gas chambers for the crime of being Jewish, the foundation that was organized in her name came under fire for its statements claiming that "no Jews, only people" were killed by the Nazis. The Anne Frank Foundation, headquartered in Amsterdam, also got in trouble for allowing a unit of the Palestine Liberation Organization to use the Anne Frank House as a meeting site.

The director of the foundation described it as a "nonsectarian organization."

CHAPTER FOUR

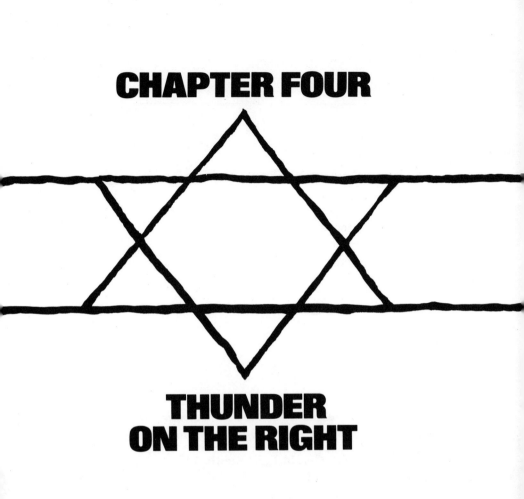

THUNDER
ON THE RIGHT

The Watergate noise is designed to preoccupy the American people while the Jews conspire to bring us toward fulfillment of an international conspiracy.

Gerald L. K. Smith, 1973

Like a lazy dog snoozing in the sun, the tiny hamlet of Reedy, West Virginia, sprawls around the crossroads in the hill country. It is quintessentially small-town America; the people are preoccupied with crops and other such vital local concerns. Few of them are aware that their little town is the nerve center of the entire worldwide Nazi movement.

At first glance, this seems impossible. There are no jack-booted storm troopers in Reedy, no swastika flags, no rallies of uniformed men, no shrill diatribes against the Jews (indeed, there are no Jews at all in Reedy). There are only a few scattered businesses and homes around the crossroads, and Reedy's population of about 350 moves in the slow, unchanging rhythm that is the hallmark of small-town America.

But look closer. Here is a small white bungalow; in front a sign says, "Dietz Realty." Inside, the owner of Dietz Realty, George P. Dietz, a thin, balding man, likes to call himself "the farm broker" to local clients. But in a large showroom behind his front office is Dietz's real passion.

One entire wall of that showroom is almost completely covered by crates packed with copies of *Mein Kampf,* plus other Nazi works. The other walls are lined with shelves filled with other books and pamphlets—*Jewish Ritual Murder, The Hitler We Love and Why, Positive Christianity in the Third Reich,* and *The Protocols of the Learned Elders of Zion.*

Except for a nearby building that houses a print shop, this is the only overt sign of an operation called Liberty Press, which is in fact the central locus for the effort to keep Hitler's legacy alive. From Dietz's press spews a steady stream of pamphlets, books, pictures, leaflets and other material, almost all of it anti-Semitic. The material is sent all over the world, and West German authorities claim that about 95 percent of all Nazi and anti-Semitic literature in their country originates in Dietz's print shop (such material is illegal in West Germany).

Through a monthly publication called *The Liberty Bell,* Dietz serves as theoretician of the worldwide disparate Nazi movement, printing such articles as "The Jewish Associates of Benedict Arnold" and extensive correspondence from supporters in various countries in Western Europe, Latin America, the Middle East and Africa. One correspondent, in what may have been admiration for a recent article in Dietz's magazine speculating on a Nazi stronghold in Antarctica guarded by an aged Adolf Hitler and a "last battalion," told Dietz that he should run for president of the United States. If that event should come to pass, the correspondent wrote, "I want to serve on your firing squad."

The Liberty Press catalog now lists over three hundred titles, ranging from recordings of Nazi war songs to anti-Semitic tracts—in four different languages. One large-selling item is a portrait of Hitler with a caption that wonders when he will return "to lead his people." It is unclear which people the caption is referring to, but presumably they are among the anonymous donors to another Dietz enterprise, raising money to help defend accused Nazi war criminals. It was Dietz who set up the Hermine Ryan defense fund, which underwrote costs of

defending Hermine Braunsteiner Ryan. She was convicted last
year in a West German court following a four-year trial on war
crimes charges; a guard at the infamous Majdanek concentration camp during World War II, Ryan was accused of beating
Jewish children to death.

Dietz violates no American law by his fund-raising, nor is
any law broken when he prints anti-Semitic hate literature, as
West German officials discovered when they tried to convince
their American counterparts to put Dietz out of business.
Jewish groups, along with Nazi-hunter Simon Wiesenthal,
accuse Dietz of running the biggest anti-Semitic propaganda
mill in the world, but neither those criticisms nor death threats
from such organizations as the Jewish Defense League have
deterred Dietz in the slightest. If anything, business is better
than ever, with printings now running an estimated 650,000 in
circulation.

It is possible to be sanguine about a man like Dietz. After
all, he may be organizationally the nerve center of the world
Nazi movement, but that movement is diffuse and not worth
taking seriously. And as for his publications, anybody with a
printing press and the protection of the First Amendment can
print hate; the fact that it is lunatic means that few will take any
of it very seriously.

But Dietz and his operation must be judged in a larger
context: there is now a strong resurgence of right-wing extremism in this country, whose virulence has spread outward to a
number of foreign countries. The resurgence, somewhat unexpected since it broke out following a long dormancy, has a
central force: anti-Semitism. And, combined with the right
wing's other unexpected development—paramilitary violence—that means this resurgence is a very disturbing development, indeed.

The resurgence can be split into two distinct parts. First,
there is what might be called the traditional right, including the
Nazi movement, the Ku Klux Klan and other such extremist
groups. Second, is the so-called New Right, a loose coalition

of assorted conservative groups on the right section of the political spectrum; they are by definition "respectable," focusing their attention on so-called "family" or "morality" issues. Both movements are enjoying something of a boom, and while the extent of that boom (and its grip on the electorate) is in question, there is no doubt that right-wing politics of all stripes, supposedly laid to rest during the liberal consensus of the past two decades, are now an important fact of life.

It is also a fact of life that anti-Semitism has served as a central stimulus for all kinds of right-wing political reaction. Essentially, the right-wing resurgence is a status revolt, the rebellion of what social scientist Ben Wattenberg calls the "unyoung, unpoor and unblack... middle-aged, middle-income, middle-minded." Economics is only part of it; they resent the fact that important social questions are decided by others—the "others," of course, often meaning Jewish liberals. Adherents of the right deeply resent the "social engineering" they feel has come to rule their lives (and in their view wrecked the country), which amounts to official disapproval of the traditional values they have long held as sacred. The unrest over such issues as sex education, abortion, school textbooks and the broad umbrella of "family" is an important symptom of that phenomenon.

Ironically, much of this unrest is a function of the success of American Jews. Their disproportionate role in a number of intellectual fields has made them highly visible targets of the frustration that grips the right wing. To the violent segment of the right wing, the Jews' "control" of commerce and media is the single cause of the country's troubles; end this "domination" and the United States can return to the mythological "good old days" of no crime, maximum personal freedom, uncomplicated foreign policy, cheap oil, a sound dollar, and strong families. To the intellectuals of the new right movement, the problem in their view is not nearly as simple as that, although they maintain that America's failure is chiefly a failure of its liberal intellectual leadership, a leadership dominated by Jewish intellectuals. Therefore, an important reason for "America's decline"—a favorite right-wing phrase—is the fact that there are too many Jews in the upper echelons.

In an important sense, the reactions of these two segments of the right-wing resurgence amount to traditional anti-Semitism and the new anti-Semitism. The difference, however, is largely academic; the fact is that it is anti-Semitism they're both talking about, and it may be hairsplitting to note that extremists in the right wing want to push Jews into gas chambers, while the other segment merely wants them to disappear, somehow.

It all means a fundamental antipathy toward Jews, and while Jews may feel a great deal of alarm about the rise of Nazi groups, they at least can recognize their traditional enemies: Nazis, neo-Nazis, Klansmen and others of that ilk do not betray any subtlety when they make it clear they want to destroy the Jews. But it is a much more difficult matter to understand what such code words as "return to traditional values" and "an end to secular humanism" mean, and to understand that they represent merely another form of authoritarianism. And authoritarianism and anti-Semitism walk hand in hand, for all American right-wing politics has a central dynamic: *somebody* is responsible for our moral decay, or rampant crime, or economic disaster, or whatever the current bugaboo. Almost always, that somebody is the Jews. This anti-Semitism among the right is a recurrence of a process that is long familiar: a rekindling of dark sentiments deeply rooted in the past, the fear of the Jewish pariahs.

In its modern form, it takes the guise of anti-elitism and anti-intellectualism, refined into a conspiracy theory. This form reached its most prominent stage during the sudden political rise of George Wallace, whose fulminations against "pseudo-intellectuals" stirred strong reactions among the alphabet soup of right-wing organizations and supporters who briefly gathered under his banner during the late 1960s. In Wallace's view, the pseudo-intellectuals were college professors, heads of foundations, leading editors and high-ranking bureaucrats in Washington who were united in a gigantic conspiracy to destroy the country. Never once did Wallace say "Jews," but none of his disciples failed to understand what he really meant, especially when he attacked "Eastern money interests" which, he claimed, had deliberately sabotaged public opinion polls against him.

Despite Wallace's attempt to mute the pronounced anti-Semitism of his political organization—known as the American Independent party—Jew-hatred was a prominent feature of the group right from the beginning. In 1967, when the party was being formed, one of its original founders was Floyd Kitchen, a Missouri right-winger whose extremist credentials were exceeded only by another progenitor, Asa E. ("Ace") Carter, an acknowledged ex-Ku Klux Klan member who had founded an anti-Semitic group called the North Alabama Citizen's Council and distributed *The Protocols of the Learned Elders of Zion.* Kitchen became one of the party's national directors and Carter wound up as adviser and speech writer to Wallace.

During the 1968 presidential campaign, it was clear that Wallace's national political structure was riddled with anti-Semites. In Texas, for example, Vance Beaudreau, a member of the state party's executive committee, had previously been active in the American Nazi party and had once served as a bodyguard for the American Nazi leader George Lincoln Rockwell. In California the party secretary in Los Angeles turned out to be a field representative of the Christian Nationalist Crusade, one of the most anti-Semitic right-wing organizations in the entire country. In a study of the Wallace organization in twenty-two states, the *Wall Street Journal* found that a "sizeable majority" of the key political posts were held by members of extremist groups, most of them anti-Semitic. The head of the Wallace organization in New York was quoted as saying he tried to screen out "rabid extremists" from the group, especially its slate of electors, but conceded that a number of them had infiltrated the party. Not that he felt unduly concerned about the development, "as long as they don't wear hobnailed boots and stomp people."

Yet, Wallace's 1968 campaign was generally free of any overt expressions of anti-Semitism. Partially, that was a tribute to Wallace's political acumen since he was able to forge a right-wing coalition, while at the same time keeping some of its more rabid members quiet, at least for the duration of the campaign. One tactic was Wallace's shrewd decision not to hold a national convention, an occasion that would almost certainly have generated the irresistible impulse on the part of some extremist groups to use the event to propound their ideas before a large national television audience. He was also shrewd in deciding that his party would not field local candidates, which not only eliminated a major potential for trouble—one can imagine some of the characters who would have wound up in local races in certain areas of the country—but tended to focus media attention on Wallace himself, a tactic that worked.

Wallace and the political movement he headed became known as "the politics of resentment," an overused political cliché of the time, which tended to obscure what Wallace and his American Independent Party were really all about. They were a coalition of right-wing extremists, a disturbingly high percentage of them anti-Semitic, who were able to mute their extremism and capture the allegiance of a large number of Americans who were disturbed at the stresses and strains tearing at the body politic.

Wallace's party received nearly 10 million votes (or about 13 percent of the total vote) in 1968, but his near-assassination during the 1972 campaign took the steam out of his movement. By the 1976 campaign, with Wallace virtually retired from politics, his party reverted to the sort of overt anti-Semitism he had tried so hard to keep hidden. The party made the mistake of holding a national convention, whose tone was set by the keynote speaker. There was great danger from "atheistic political Zionism," he declared, which he called "the most insidious, far-reaching, murderous force the world has ever known." The convention began to sound like a Nazi party rally, and ran rapidly downhill. It wound up nominating for president no less a figure than Lester Maddox, whose claim to fame at that point was his policy of keeping black customers from his Georgia fried chicken establishment by threatening them with ax handdles. (Maddox attempted to create a new American political tradition by distributing souvenir miniature ax handles to potential voters.)

Maddox led the American Independent Party to an electoral disaster, and by the 1980 campaign the party was moribund, having been co-opted by the New Right of computerized mailing lists and sophisticated economic theories that eventually resulted in the election of Ronald Reagan. Still, upon reflection, what Wallace accomplished was nothing short of extraordinary. He had forged the coalition of the right wing that everyone said could never be forged, and had managed to conceal what had been up to that time the right wing's electoral Achilles' heel—overt racism, especially anti-Semitism. And it is well to remember that a shift of votes in only a few precincts prevented Wallace from causing a major electoral crisis; in the event of a near dead heat between the two major parties, Wallace and his party would have occupied the fulcrum of power. It is sobering to think what Wallace's political price would have been for the release of his electors to guarantee a Republican or Democratic victory.

With the departure of Wallace from the national political scene, the assorted groups that had gathered under his wing set out on their own. It was widely assumed that without a legitimate political umbrella under which to operate, and a general electoral mood that was distinctly anti-extremist, the right wing extremists would fade into near-obscurity on the political fringe. But that is not what happened. In fact, the extremists have returned bigger and stronger than ever, marked by a pronounced anti-Semitism that includes outright violence against Jews. Take a close look at some of the more prominent extremist movements:

The American Nazis

The post-World War II American Nazi movement is the creation of one man, George Lincoln Rockwell, a failed and embittered magazine illustrator who hit upon the idea of bringing Nazism out of the closet. There were, of course, small Nazi cells in this country after the war, but they operated in darkest secrecy; walking around in public in a storm trooper uniform and swastikas was unthinkable.

Rockwell decided that was bad strategy, and as he later recounted in his autobiography, "At once, I had the answer! By being an OPEN, ARROGANT, ALL-OUT NAZI, not a sneaky Nazi—but a Nazi—with the swastika, storm troops, and open declarations of our intentions to gas the Jew-traitors..."

In 1958 Rockwell founded the American Nazi Party, and commemorated the event by leading a small group of Nazis in picketing the White House with signs that read "Save Ike from the KIKES!" Over the next nine years, until his death at the hands of a disgruntled follower in 1967, Rockwell deliberately confronted the American Jewish community with a series of provocative acts, including anti-Semitic speeches, pornographically anti-Jewish tracts, and appearances in heavily Jewish neighborhoods while dressed in Nazi regalia. Surrounded by a small band of loyal followers, he spent much of his time in a Virginia farmhouse he described as the party's headquarters. (At the entrance a Jewish prayer shawl was used as a doormat.) Rockwell tried to create a worldwide Nazi movement under his leadership, and actually succeeded in convening a "world conference" of Nazis in 1962 in England, which created a "World Union of National Socialists" with Rockwell as "World Leader" (one British newspaper headlined this development, "The New 'World Führer'—Elected by 27 Idiots!")

But that grandiose-sounding effort came to nothing, as did all of Rockwell's efforts in this country to create a large national Nazi movement. Despite his flamboyance and flair for publicity, Rockwell nevertheless was careful: on the streets, his followers were unarmed and he was insistent that the American Nazis not carry out violent acts against the Jews or Jewish institutions. At its height, Rockwell's movement was never able to attract more than about five hundred hard-core followers.

Rockwell had badly misread the American temper, and never quite understood that he could not tap into the reservoir of anti-Semitism in this country because his movement appeared too "foreign." No matter the accent, Rockwell's Nazi movement fundamentally appeared to most Americans as a stepchild of a German political phenomenon, and there was no way storm trooper politics would ever fit into even the more extreme tributaries of the American political mainstream.

Rockwell's successors made the same mistake. Matt Koehl, a former Rockwell lieutenant who suceeded the American führer in 1967, changed the American Nazi Party's name to National Socialist White Peoples Party, in an attempt to capitalize on growing black-white tensions in this country. That didn't work, nor did Koehl. Lacking even Rockwell's modest leadership abilities, he couldn't hold the party together, and in 1970 it split into several factions. They briefly reunited in 1973 to carry out a series of provocative demonstrations during the Arab oil embargo, blaming the Jews for the gas lines, but again, their storm trooper regalia and virulence only alienated even those Americans who agreed that the Jews were primarily responsible for the oil embargo.

With that, the American Nazi movement again split into bitter factions, and by the end of 1974 it was considered dead, for all practical purposes.

But without warning, the Nazi movement suddenly rose from the dead in 1980, accompanied by a change in tactics: violence. Membership grew to over 2,000 (hard-core), with another estimated 4,000-5,000 sympathizers, scattered among 13 different groups, some of which for the first time advocated violence against Jews. Further, in another change of tactics, several of the Nazi groups began to make forays into electoral politics.

The electoral gambit was first inspired by Koehl, whose National Socialist White Peoples Party remains the most noted of the American Nazi groups. He has built the group's membership to around 700, one of whom carried out the party's first foray into politics in 1976 during a mayoral primary in Milwaukee by winning 4,764 votes (about 5 percent of those cast). At about the same time, a Nazi candidate for city alderman in Chicago got 2,064 votes (16 percent of the total), while Nazi candidates in Houston and North Carolina got 975 votes and 424 votes, respectively.

While these electoral ventures have generated some media attention, much more publicity has been focused on a Nazi group competing with Koehl's outfit, the National Socialist Party of America, based in Chicago. Although the group is small (only three dozen uniformed followers), it is led by a man named Frank Collin, who is the son of a survivor of the Dachau concentration camp. It was Collin's group that tried to hold a march of storm troopers in 1978 in Skokie, Illinois, a Chicago suburban community where a large number of concentration camp survivors live. Collin welcomed the furor this proposal aroused, although he was less happy over the publicity surrounding the fact that John Hinckley, Jr., the man who shot President Reagan, was once a member of the group (it was explained that Hinckley had been thrown out of the group "because he was a nut," an explanation that seems improbable).

Collin was originally a member of Koehl's organization, but broke away during the great Nazi scattering in 1970 to found his own group. Another breakaway was Robert F. Brannen, who has since founded the National Socialist Movement, based in Cincinnati, Ohio. Brannen has worked assiduously to forge ties between the Nazis and other extremist groups, especially the Ku Klux Klan, an effort that has met with some success, as we shall see later in this chapter. Brannen's effort is the spearhead of a new propensity for violence by some of the younger Nazi leaders in this country, exemplified by the National Socialist Liberation Front in Los Angeles. Another splinter from Rockwell's old party, the Los Angeles group was founded by Joseph Tomassi, who was murdered in 1975 by one of his followers during an argument. Tomassi advocated "armed guerrilla struggle against the Jew power structure," and to that end recruited the most violence-prone Nazis, including many former convicts. The group bombed a socialist group's headquarters in San Diego, and police in Louisville, Kentucky, forestalled a plot by Tomassi's organization to assassinate 106 prominent citizens of that city, most of them Jews.

There are no firm estimates on the membership of the Tomassi organization, although it is believed to be the fastest-growing Nazi organization in the country. It now claims branches in Boston, San Francisco, Detroit, Saint Louis and San Diego. Its message of violence has become appealing to the new wave of young Nazis attracted to the cause, and there are growing indications that the entire Nazi movement is becoming more violent. Some of the violence at this point is simple vandalism—Nazis smashing out windows of a San Francisco synagogue—but there are more ominous instances. One was the rampage of a crazed Nazi in New Rochelle, New York, in which he killed five people before turning the gun on himself. And in Chicago, one of Collin's Nazis forced a Jew to inhale cyanide, killing him, then committed suicide by the same method.

Nazi groups sometimes like to claim that these acts of wanton violence, including the shooting of President Reagan by an official former Nazi group member, are committed by demented members without sanction. Possibly, but harder to explain are the instances of another ominous development, the

Nazi links with other extremist groups to carry out violence. Consider, for example, the case of a group of Americans arrested last year on charges of trying to invade the Caribbean island of Dominica with a mercenary force to topple the government. According to press accounts, all the Americans were Ku Klux Klan members recruited by disaffected elements in Dominica to carry out a coup. But that is not entirely accurate. A closer look at the thirteen people arrested in the plot reveals that six of them were members of Nazi groups— and three of *that* group were Canadian extremists newly recruited to help their American counterparts.

The Dominica incident represents the tip of what may be a large iceberg. Increasingly, Nazis are aligning themselves with other extremist groups, finding common cause with the new anti-Semitism of such groups as the Ku Klux Klan. Indeed, many of the distinctions between the two groups are becoming hazier. For example, the National Socialists Movement has not only forged close links with Klan groups, but other racist groups, as well. Still other Nazi groups have changed their names to sound more attuned with the "struggle of white people" against blacks and Jews. Prominent examples of that trend include the United White Peoples Party in Cleveland, which has advocated a "white confederacy," the American White Nationalists Party of Columbus, Ohio, and the White Power Movement, headed up by George Dietz, the central figure in this development, whose activities were outlined earlier in this chapter. (It should also be noted that the Nazis have even forged links with the homosexual community; the Nationalist Socialist League, with branches in Los Angeles, San Francisco and other cities, is for homosexual Nazis only. It now has over 200 members.)

The Ku Klux Klan

Like the American Nazi movement, the Klan was considered a barely breathing fossil only a few years ago, supposedly relegated to the dustbin of history because of the final crumbling of racial barriers in the South. But after a long period of dormancy, the Klan re-blossomed in the late 1970s. It was not the old Klan; the sheets and hoods were still there, but the members were younger and more violence-prone, the leadership generally more sophisticated, and the organization has been organizing successfully throughout the country and overseas, including the U.S. armed forces. And one other significant change: the Klan has become much more anti-Semitic.

The new Klan now has an estimated 12,000 members (it has grown by about 25 percent in the last two years alone), with another 25,000 "affiliated" members in a number of Klan-type front groups, such as "gun clubs," and so forth. They are fractured among a dozen factions, the two main ones being the United Klans of America based in Alabama, and the Louisiana-based National Knights of the Ku Klux Klan. The United Klans, especially, have been in the forefront of the group's new anti-Semitism; its head, Robert Shelton, publishes *Fiery Cross*, which is usually laced with virulent anti-Semitism. One Shelton staple is a statement that American institutions are "undermined by a world Zionist conspiracy of kike Jews."

Much of the Klan's violence, once reserved for blacks and civil rights activists, is now directed at Jews. Consider these examples, all of which occurred in just the past eighteen months:

• In Evansville, Indiana, two Klansmen spray-painted swastikas and slogans ("Death to Jew Dogs!") on tombstones in a local Jewish cemetery. One of the men vandalized a synagogue and wrecked a Jewish delicateseen.

• In Ada, Oklahoma, a cross was burned near the town and signs exhorted the townspeople to "stop the Jew anti-Christ!" Klansmen also distributed anti-Semitic literature to local schoolchildren.

• In Nashville, Tennessee, three members of the Confederate Vigilante Knights of the Ku Klux Klan were arrested on charges of planning to bomb a synagogue and several Jewish-owned businesses.

• In Catonsville, Maryland, a Klansman was arrested as he was about to bomb a local synagogue.

More disturbing has been the Klan's marriage with the Nazi movement. The most prominent example of that alliance is in North Carolina, where the Klan joined forces with two groups, the Nazi National Socialist Party of America and the Neo-Nazi National States' Rights Party, to set up a paramilitary training camp. Members of all three groups practice guerrilla warfare and fire semiautomatic weapons; the Nazis call the training "storm trooper training" and those who go through it become members of the "SD." (The choice of initials is no accident; Nazi Germany's secret police was called SD, meaning *Sicherheitsdienst*, or "secret police," of which Gestapo, or *Geheime Staats Polizei*—Secret State Police—was the most notorious branch.)

Klan graduates of this camp become members of the organization's "Security Guard," and wear gray uniforms and storm trooper boots. This is apparently to set them apart from the "SD" graduates, who wear black shirts with swastika armbands in commemoration of their achievement. Camp graduates were among the six men charged with that shooting of Communist Workers Party leaders previously mentioned.

The Klan-Nazi link in North Carolina has now gone a step further, with the recent formulation of a formal alliance, known as the "United Racist Front." The alliance is not merely a paper entity. One of the Klan activists who ran the paramilitary training camp says he'll run for a sheriff's post later this year, another has announced he will run for governor in 1984, and another recently announced himself as candidate for mayor in Winston-Salem. The candidacies were no doubt spurred by the experience of Harold Covington, at one time director of the National Socialist Party of America, who got 54,000 votes last year during his race for the state attorney general's job in North Carolina.

There are at least a half-dozen other Klan-Nazi military-type training camps throughout the country, including one in east Texas that featured "special training" for a new paramilitary arm of the Klan in Texas called the "Texas Emergency Reserve." About 500 men are estimated to have been involved in the training, including some active-duty soldiers from nearby Fort Hood.

These camps are symptoms of a larger phenomenon at work here, the conviction among members of the Klan and Nazi organizations that Armageddon is just around the corner, and only a well-trained paramilitary force will be able to "uphold the American way." The two groups have been able to find common cause after a lengthy period of estrangement, not only because of their joint conviction about impending doom in this country, but also because they have found a common enemy: the Jews. With few exceptions, the Klan's targets since at least World War II had been the blacks, mainly over the issue of segregation. But with the end of segregation and the coming to power in the South of black political leaders, the new Klan found it was confronting new dangers, notably school busing for integration, affirmative action plans and other developments that caused deep fears among the lower rungs of the white socioeconomic classes. And while some of that fear (and anger) still centers on the blacks, the bulk of it is now aimed at what is perceived as a mysterious, faceless entity that grips the White House, Congress and the federal courts in its powerful grasp, an entity seen as part of a master plan to dominate the world and undermine the white race. And that mysterious entity, the Klan discovered, is the "Jewish world conspiracy." (Didn't the Jews dream up "civil rights"? Aren't many judges Jewish? Don't Jews control all the money?)

Those fears are being translated into the new wave of

violence being carried out by both the Klan and the Nazis, or sometimes a combination of both. The U.S. Department of Justice reports that cases involving the Klan or Nazi groups increased nearly 200 percent last year, ranging from arson to murder. (Two Klansmen in California were convicted of shooting a black man; they claimed they shot him because they could not find a deer to shoot.) These statistics, however, do not include a wide range of harassment activities, such as the Jews in Rhode Island who received death threats from the Klan and found their homes splattered with eggs and smeared with swastikas.

The Klan's new emphasis on anti-Semitism partially explains its remarkable growth outside the South, the group's traditional bedrock of support. At the moment, there are Klan organizations in twenty-two states, a large percentage of them in areas where there are few blacks or where there are no outstanding black–white tensions. One popular Klan outfit is called the Aryan Knights of the Ku Klux Klan, a Texas-based faction that emphasizes attacks on Jews. Its publication, *Aryan Views—White Folks News*, is probably the most popular Klan literature in circulation; the paper often features boxed messages reading, "Jew Communists say integrate, rob, rape, riot, kill."

The Aryan Knights' literature is being distributed worldwide, and is to a large extent responsible for the dramatic growth of Klan organizations in other countries. Canada, which has a nearly nonexistent racial problem, nevertheless has a booming Klan movement that has grown so rapidly that last year the Canadian Jewish Congress felt compelled to form a large coalition of over 100 organizations to fight the Klan. There is also a burgeoning Klan movement in Great Britain. In Germany, authorities recently discovered that the Klan had managed to recruit nearly 1,000 Germans as members, and was making strong efforts to sign up American servicemen stationed there. Further, West German officials revealed, the

Klan was trying to cement an alliance with the large German neo-Nazi movement.

Other American Right-Wing Groups

Any listing of the American lunatic fringe (excepting the Nazis and Ku Klux Klan) must begin with the bizarre organization known as the National States' Rights Party of Georgia. Although its membership is estimated at about 600 members, the party's publication, *Thunderbolt*, claims a circulation of nearly 15,000, which seems to be a somewhat inflated figure. In any event, the significance of the party lies not in those figures, but in the fact that although it is the most avowedly anti-Semitic organization in the United States, the party's candidate for political office has received over 40,000 votes in at least one election—despite a platform calling for extermination of the Jews.

The National States' Rights Party was formed in 1958 by Jesse Stoner and Edward Fields, two Georgia right-wingers who created the new entity by joining together a number of extremist hate groups including the Columbians, an outfit that used the Nazi SS symbol and ran afoul of the police after stockpiling large amounts of arms and explosives threatening Jews with extermination. (Stoner himself, in 1946, had announced formation of the Stoner Anti-Jewish Party, which proposed making Judaism a legal offense punishable by death.)

For the past twenty-four years, Stoner and Fields have presided over the party, spewing out a long stream of hate directed primarily against Jews (although the party also wants to deport all "aliens," defined as anyone not a "white Christian American"). In 1971 the party began operating from a new headquarters in Marietta, Georgia, and a year later Stoner became the focus of a national scandal. He decided to run in the Georgia Democratic primary for the United States Senate, a campaign that featured the worst of Stoner's anti-Semitism. He again advocated making Judaism a crime punishable by

death, and in one television interview called Atlanta Mayor
Sam Massell a "Christ killer" and "Jew gangster." The radio
and television ads for his candidacy were along much the same
line, adding that blacks wanted integration because "the
niggers want our white women."

This hatred moved both the Anti-Defamation League and
the NAACP to petition the Federal Communications Commission to block Stoner from the air. The FCC refused on the
grounds of free speech, setting off an argument that had
national implications. In the debate over free speech, however,
just how many voters actually found Stoner's anti-Semitism
appealing was a matter that got lost in the shuffle. As it turned
out, Stoner got 40,675 votes, or about 6 percent of the total.
That amount seems small when judged in the context of the
overall total, but there is something very disquieting about an
avowed anti-Semite winning that many votes. And what
Stoner had to offer the voters was pure *hatred*, as his statement
issued just before the election demonstrated: "Every Jew who
holds a position of power or authority must be removed from
that position. If this does not work, then we must establish
[the] Final Solution!!!"

Stoner and his party, who have continued their forays
into Georgia politics, are not known to be involved in any
actual physical violence against Jews. The same cannot be said
for a number of other groups of the extremist right.

All of them have a common ancestor, The Minutemen, a
collection of armed right-wingers who gathered together in
1959 and formed an "organized underground army" that stood
ready to wage war against what they were certain was an
imminent Communist takeover of the United States. Under the
leadership of Robert DePugh, The Minutemen were strong in
the Middle West and West, and at one point claimed a membership of over 25,000, including many policemen and members of the armed services. They spent much of their time
training in military tactics and building up large caches of
explosives and arms for the coming battle.

The problem with The Minutemen was the group's belief that "liberals"—classified as anyone who did not share their fanatical beliefs—were "traitors" and had to be dealt with in order to prevent the Communists from taking over. The Minutemen became avowedly anti-Semitic, attacking Jews as "fifth columnists" preparing the United States for the Communist takeover. By the mid-1960s, The Minutemen had become notorious for committing attacks on the "traitors," including dynamitings and shootings. (Those incurring Minutemen wrath first received a card with a rifle crosshairs design.)

Finally, the federal government cracked down: DePugh was arrested on kidnaping and weapons charges, and by 1970 The Minutemen as an organization had been pretty well destroyed. But in the same year some members of the organization formed a new group called the Secret Army Organization (SAO). It picked up right where The Minutemen left off, carrying out burglaries, bombings and snipings throughout the Southwest against "liberals," and other perceived enemies. Again, as with The Minutemen, the SAO seemed to find that a high proportion of its liberal enemies were Jews. (It was an SAO conviction that virtually all Jews were liberals, meaning that almost all of them were enemies to be exterminated.) The group's hatred even extended to President Nixon, who became the subject of "Wanted for Treason" posters put up by SAO members in several states after he had announced his policy of détente with the Soviet Union and China.

The SAO was destroyed in an extensive law enforcement crackdown in 1972 after the group blew up a theater in San Diego, narrowly missing killing several city officials. Some SAO members drifted into a new organization called IDENTITY, another secret right-wing underground group. Run by the New Christian Crusade Church of Glendale, California, IDENTITY and its members use coded instructions, dead-letter drops and other tight security procedures to balk police and FBI infiltration. IDENTITY is not believed to have carried out any armed attacks, but spends most of its time "preparing" for "the final battle" by stockpiling arms.

Most of the old SAO membership joined a much more violently-inclined extremist group, the Posse Comitatus (named after the federal law that prohibits the use of federal troops to enforce civilian law). Posse Comitatus has enjoyed amazing growth since its founding in 1969 by H. L. (Mike) Beach. The group now claims over 400,000 members, although law enforcement officials place the total closer to 10,000. Beach's function, primarily, is to oversee the group's several dozen local chapters. Charters for chapters are granted upon payment of $21 in dues and the signatures of seven men. After the charter is granted, what the chapter does is entirely its own business, in line with Beach's decentralization theory (and to make the filing of conspiracy charges against him that much more difficult).

The Posse Comitatus's national leadership does publish a newspaper, called *National Chronicle*, which sets out the group's principles—and its pronounced anti-Semitism. In a 1976 issue, for example, Posse Comitatus made its position unmistakably clear. "It will soon be dangerous for any elected official to return home, there to face a court of white Christian Americans who have chosen to die rather than accept a treasonous offer of national slavery by those whom they have elected to office with the full understanding that they would defend the Constitution and not throw it to the dogs as they have done. You officials were sent to Washington to represent white Christian Americans and *not* the riff-raff Jews, Negroes and other crosses as you have. It will be far better if you leave America as did Benedict Arnold." Posse Comitatus members have taken this admonition seriously, witness the increasing number of confrontations they have with assorted "traitors," especially federal and law enforcement agents, a special target being Internal Revenue Service agents (some Posse members refuse to pay taxes).

There is some overlap between Posse Comitatus and another fast-rising organization, the Christian Patriots Defense League. The League now has 25,000 members who subscribe to its theory that this country is on the road to ruin and that all believers must prepare for the inevitable collapse. The League is cautious about open expressions of anti-Semitism, but there are slips. One is its distaste for what it calls "racially impure" Americans; another is its attacks on "Zionism." More chilling is its obsession with "survivalism," the theory that stocking food, guns and other supplies is vital, because the inevitable great collapse will mean anarchy everywhere. This theory and its implications were best summed up not too long ago during the League's annual meeting in Illinois, when one speaker outlined the League's view of the future: "You should band together with a few other families, because you're going to need all the firepower you can get. If you have a nine- or ten-year-old kid, teach him how to shoot. . . . When things break down, there's going to be an initial surge of people from the cities. They'll kill you for a can of sardines." No one in the audience needed reminding of what the League means by "people from the cities." In case they do, the League's current platform calls for a "return to the Christian faith of our forefathers" and "rejection of all perversions of this faith."

Judged in strictly rhetorical forms, the League is cut out of the same cloth as the grandfather of extremist Christianity, the Christian Nationalist Crusade. Led for thirty-five years (until his death in 1976) by Gerald L. K. Smith, the Crusade has been among the more notorious anti-Semitic organizations in the United States. Smith's anti-Semitic career began in 1933 when he joined the Silver Shirts, the neo-fascist American anti-Semitic organization whose founder, William Dudley Pelley, was imprisoned for sedition in 1942 after he promoted Nazi propaganda. The Silver Shirts collapsed with that arrest, but Smith picked up its fallen banner and began the Crusade. He ran for United States president in 1948 on a platform that included deportation of all Jews, then began publishing *The*

Cross and the Flag, the Crusade's monthly magazine. For the next twenty-eight years the magazine (entirely written by Smith) published every conceivable type of anti-Semitism, marked by what he considered clever turns of phrase: "Jew York," "Christ-hating mobsters," "the Jew-N" (meaning United Nations), "the Anti-Defamation League, the OGPU of Jewry," and "Communism and Zionism, the twins of the anti-Christ."

Given that sort of hatred, and further given Smith's well-known credentials as a professional anti-Semite, it was therefore somewhat surprising to find that in 1969 the federal government awarded to the state of Arkansas a grant of $182,000 to build a road to Smith's pet project, a 67-foot-high statue of Christ near Eureka Springs, Arkansas. Publicity compelled the government to abandon this gross misuse of taxpayer's money, although Smith, in a letter to the people of Eureka Springs, blamed it on "the lethal enemies of Jesus Christ." Later, in a news conference, he went further, blaming the cancellation on a "conspiracy of organized Jews." Smith was even more infuriated when he learned that Jewish groups were protesting his idea to stage a Passion Play loaded with anti-Semitic hatred. Protesting Jewish groups were not only upset at the plan to stage the play, but also at the Humble Oil and Refining Company, whose vacation guidebook listed it among the "recommended" outdoor attractions for vacationers. The Anti-Defamation League complained to Humble Oil which responded it was unaware of Smith's record as an anti-Semite—but then added that the company didn't much care. The Anti-Defamation League made this thoughtless response public, which caused many irate Jewish customers of Humble Oil to publicly tear up their credit cards. The company got the point and issued an elaborate apology.

Smith went to his grave convinced that these episodes were proof of the insidious, all-pervasive power of American Jews, a conviction that is the hallmark of all similar extreme right-wing groups. These events sharpened Smith's anti-

Semitism in his last years, which seemed to be perfectly all right with his followers. Even after his death they continue to believe in the myth of the Jewish conspiracy, and however much such convictions might seem lunatic to others, the fact is that the Crusade still gets about $300,000 a year in contributions.

This conviction is a distinct feature of two other right-wing organizations, the Liberty Lobby and the John Birch Society—although they approach anti-Semitism in two markedly different ways.

In the case of the Liberty Lobby, its anti-Semitism is quite open, a dominant feature of this right-wing group ever since its founding in the 1950s by Willis A. Carto, a great admirer of Adolf Hitler. The Lobby sponsored a number of publications, many of them racist and anti-Semitic, although the Lobby's connection was carefully concealed. But beginning in the 1970s the Lobby dropped this caution and openly promoted anti-Semitism. That shift was signaled by the publication of a Liberty Lobby pamphlet called "America First," which among other things called Israel a "bastard state" that is the "product of the political machinations of one political group—the Zionists—made up largely of atheistic Jews." After claiming that Zionists control the United States Congress, the publication goes on to say that "Capitol Hill simply reeks with Zionist lobbyists." The pamphlet also claimed that "Hitler's hostility toward the Jews originated in the Zionist leaders having pushed the United States into World War I on the side of the Allies." As for subsequent events in world history, the pamphlet claimed that "almost all early Bolsheviks were Jewish," and "the Jews rejected their messiah, even had him crucified."

The Lobby has continued to propound an endless recitation of anti-Semitism, some of it in the pages of their weekly publication, *Spotlight*, which has a claimed readership of 200,000. A Lobby letter to members in 1973 was headlined, "Your Son Could be Drafted to Fight for ISRAEL," an eventuality the lobby blamed on "some highly professional propagandists (many of them holding dual citizenship in both the United States and Israel) who try to misrepresent and downgrade anyone who dares to speak up for America." Later that year Lobby officials went before the Senate Foreign Relations Committee to testify against the nomination of Henry Kissinger as Secretary of State. Nicholas C. Camerota, representative of the Youth Alliance, a Liberty Lobby front group, told the committee: "As a Jew, Kissinger cannot help but feel a personal stake in the fortunes of Israel." Why the committee would bother even allowing an organization like Liberty Lobby to testify is a mystery. (An equal mystery is why no senator bothered to rebuke Camerota for his nasty slur against Kissinger.)

Earlier, we saw the key role the Liberty Lobby has played in the publication of books denying the existence of the Holocaust, a circumstance that belies the Lobby's recent assertion that it is "not anti-Semitic, only anti-Zionist." It is also belied by recent issues of *Spotlight*, which among other things say that "Israeli agents" are infiltrating the United States government, one of whom, the newspaper alleges, is Richard Perle, a former aide to Senator Henry Jackson of Washington. (Perle is now Assistant Secretary of Defense for International Affairs.) Apparently the Lobby feels that Perle is a "Zionist" and an "Israeli agent," because of his role in helping to formulate Jackson's strong pro-Israel stand and his work on Jackson's legislation pressuring the Soviet Union to allow Russian Jews to emigrate. At the same time, Liberty Lobby is closely allied with the World Anti-Communist League, a Taiwan-financed operation that has become distinctly anti-Semitic. It recently admitted to membership MSI, the anti-Semitic Italian Fascist organization, and has at least two avowed Nazis in its organizational machinery.

Conspicuously absent from such groups as the World Anti-Communist League is a much more famous American right-wing group, the John Birch Society. The Birchers pulled out of the League when it began to demonstrate increasing signs of anti-Semitism, yet another demonstration of the Society's strong effort to avoid any taint of anti-Semitism.

This has been a strategy of the John Birch Society since its beginning in 1958, when founder Robert Welch made it clear he didn't want any anti-Semites in the organization. Before too much credit be assigned Welch for this laudatory stand, it is first necessary to examine the Society more closely. Welch worked hard to keep anti-Semites from leadership positions in his organization, and in 1969 he sharply rebuked prominent right-winger Dan Smoot for writing in *Review of the News*, the Society's major publication, about the "wealth, power and influence of world Jewry, especially in America." But while that was going on, the Society was also printing millions of copies of a shrill book called *None Dare Call It Treason*, currently a Birch staple (and something of a bible for the far right). The book's central thesis, which amounts to a claim that Communists have already taken over the American government, says that a small group of "insiders" controls America. This group, the book claims, are mostly "international bankers" (well-known code words for Jews); the sources for this assertion are cited as old czarist, professional anti-Semites. The book never mentions the word "Jew" in connection with this conspiracy, but lists all the names of these "insiders." Most of them are Jewish.

The reason why Welch has been careful to keep anti-Semitism (or at least overt forms of it) away from the Society is related to his political problems. Despite his attempt to found a broad-based political organization that would encompass most segments of the American right wing, Welch was immediately branded a kook because of his public assertions, including one that Eisenhower was a "conscious, dedicated agent of the Communist conspiracy." It took Welch quite some time to live that one down, and he didn't need the complicating factor of anti-Semitism. Further, at the beginning of this decade,

Welch worked hard to make the Society more respectable, and sought to join forces with the New Right, to whom Welch and his works were anathema. To overcome their doubts, which finally ended in 1975, Welch has had to soft-pedal some of the Society's more extreme beliefs (including the theory of the cabal of "insiders"), and to make certain the Society is not tainted with any form of overt racism, particularly anti-Semitism.

Events have proven Welch correct in his tactics, despite some grumbling from local Birch chapters. At the present time the Society has over 400,000 members and operates on an $8 million annual budget that helps support bookstores, a speakers bureau, and a summer youth camp for little Birchers. Two Birch Society members have been elected to Congress, and the organization is now an official part of the New Right. Indeed, the Society's role is pervasive in a number of prominent social issues, including the ones most dear to the right: anti-Equal Rights Amendment activism, school busing, abortion, gun control, and tax reform. (A noted tax reform group, Tax Reform Immediately, or TRIM, is in fact a Birch front group.)

And so, what do we have here? Simply, we have a growing American right-wing extremist movement, universally hostile to Jews in one form or another; some of the groups are small, others are growing rapidly, still others have enjoyed success for years. In terms of their anti-Semitism, some are outright storm troopers straight out of the nightmare of the Hitler era; others hate Jews, but have no thought of taking up guns to kill their enemies. One wonders (but not for too long) what they would do if the armed anti-Semites began killing Jews in the streets.

To talk of such a thing surely must be alarmist; really, is there even the remotest possibility of such a thing happening? At the moment, no, but there is this fact to contend with: the violent right is a growing force in this country—growing both in size and its propensity for violence. There is a prevailing assumption, however, that the American extreme right, judged in the context of an American population of 200 million-plus, is a tiny speck on the face of history.

And yet history also teaches us that in 1920 the extreme right in Weimar Germany—where for the most part, the Jews were prosperous members of society and dominated the professions and the arts—was considered insignificant. Its most ludicrous form lay in the activities of a group known derisively by many Germans as "the beer hall revolutionaries."

They meant the German National Socialist Workers Party. In the year 1920, it had a total of 64 members.

CHAPTER FIVE

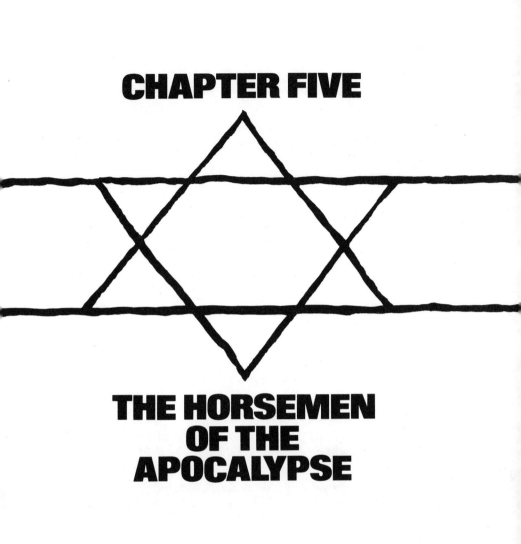

THE HORSEMEN
OF THE
APOCALYPSE

All we Jews have to do is to take a one-shot ad in
all the big papers saying that we hereby serve notice
that the next time we hear of any anti-Semitism,
we will all become Christians the next day.
Jews . . . would join . . . the Episcopal Church. . . .
The prospect of having 5,000,000 Jews joining
their church would send Episcopalians into a frenzy.
They would organize anti-defamation leagues, and police
anti-Semitism for us! Just think of it! We would have
all those Episcopalians working for us Jews!

Harry Golden

In the spring of 1940 an insurance agent appeared at the main desk of the New York Public Library and asked for help in researching "The Wandering Jew" one of the most persistent legends in Western civilization. The librarians were dutifully helpful, but noticed that the man was not researching a legend, but actually was researching himself. As he explained, he had become convinced that he was in fact The Wandering Jew—a conviction he underscored by the printing of calling cards that read "T. W. Jew."

The story, while quite true, seems harmless enough, but beneath its surface lurks one of the most dangerous of all stereotypes of anti-Semitism, a stereotype that leads us at once into the bedrock of that animus: Christian anti-Semitism.

The Wandering Jew legend, which first arose in the Middle Ages, asserts that just before the crucifixion of Christ, a Jew had scorned Jesus: "Go, go, thou tempter and deceiver." Christ is supposed to have replied, "I go, and you will await me until I come again," a curse which allegedly condemned the Jews to permanent exile for the crime of having rejected the Messiah.

Thus, according to the legend, the Jew who had rejected Jesus henceforth wandered the earth, never to die, never to find rest until the return of Jesus to this world.

This tale is, of course, a total fiction (for one thing, at the time of Jesus' crucifixion the Jews were already in exile), but it had the most profound effect on the medieval mind, and its effects lingered many centuries after that. The myth of The Wandering Jew was so prevalent in the fourteenth and fifteenth centuries that scholars debated at great length about how the man might be recognized. Around 1701, in fact, all England became agog over the supposed discovery of The Wandering Jew. He turned out to be a man who claimed to have been an officer of the Sanhedrin during the time of the crucifixion, and further claimed to actually have struck Jesus as he was being led from the judgment hall of Pontius Pilate. To buttress his claim, the man described the apostles in great detail (including the colors of their clothes), then said that during his existence in the centuries since, he had met both Tamerlane and Saladin and recounted minute details of the Crusades. Even the most skeptical among the large audiences who listened to his tales were impressed by his grasp of a number of foreign languages and his knowledge about many foreign countries. The man was briefly questioned by learned men from Oxford and Cambridge, but alas, he departed shortly thereafter for Sweden, where he disappeared.

The myth of The Wandering Jew represents the attempt to convey the image of all Jews as rootless, cursed objects of scorn, the "Christ-killers" divinely condemned to pay for their terrible crime. From the time of the thirteenth century, when the legend first appeared in written documents, The Wandering Jew has served as the spearhead of Christian anti-Semitism, its most traditional form.

Christian anti-Semitism occupies a unique place in history, for it is the only form of anti-Semitism which specifically accuses the Jews of the crime of deicide. For that reason, it must be differentiated from the Jew-hatred that has blotted history for so many centuries, from the time of the exodus from Egypt to the assaults by Assyrians, Philistines and Babylonians, to the Roman conquest, and to the pogroms of Europe. The difference is that these terrible assaults sprang from nationalist animosities; Christianity, on the other hand, has developed an anti-Semitism that springs from its very own roots. The central root is the Gospel itself, whose narratives of the trial of Jesus are most susceptible to anti-Semitic interpretations. While the four Gospels differ in details, they agree on what amounts to a prima facie case that the Jews were almost totally responsible for the death of Jesus Christ. Pilate is portrayed as a sort of figurehead who reluctantly washed his hands of the entire matter. (The Coptic and Ethiopian Christian churches still set aside June 25 as a holy feast day that honors Saint Pontius Pilate.)

Modern biblical scholarship raises doubts about the historical accuracy of the Gospel account of Christ's trial and execution, but the scriptural anti-Semitism remains. Even Vatican Council II, which declared that anti-Semitism was un-Christian, nevertheless did not make any attempt to revise the Gospel account of Jesus' trial, despite the verdict by a large number of modern Catholic scholars that it is scriptural anti-Semitism which is in fact the major cause of Christian anti-Semitism. In turn, this scriptural anti-Semitism can lead to a second, often more dangerous, expression of Christian anti-Semitism because the Jews refused to believe that the Messiah had come in the person of Jesus Christ.

It is this absolute and eternal error on the part of the Jews that forms the real dynamic of Christian anti-Semitism. Fundamentally the problem is that the two faiths, which share a tradition of covenant religion, cannot both be ultimately right. If, as devout Christians believe, Christianity is the true revelation of God, then obviously the Jews are living in the greatest possible error, in view of the fact that they have rejected this divine revelation. And alternatively, if the Jews are right in their conviction of a divinely-revealed religion, then just as obviously the Christians have committed the gravest error in making a man into God.

There is no escaping this very deep divide between the faiths. The mistake is often made in trying to ascertain how similar both religions are (one, after all, is the derivative of the other), rather than understanding how fundamentally different they are. Thus, the real road to understanding between the faiths lies in understanding the profound difference and recognizing the impossibility of ever resolving that difference.

On the whole, only in the United States has this sort of theological coexistence been achieved. The reason, of course, is the First Amendment which, contrary to popular belief, is not solely about "religious freedom," but is in fact an agreement between American society and its religions. Basically, the agreement says that no religious sect can be coerced by society via the power of the state (all religions, not otherwise defined, are guaranteed "free exercise"). In exchange, the religions implicitly give up their freedom to coerce society. Thus, Mormons are free to practice their religion, but had to give up polygamy.

The genius of the First Amendment is that it allows any religion or religious sect to regard itself as the sole, true revelation of God, and allows its adherents total freedom of speech in propounding its unique view, plus protection for those who freely accept its doctrines and disciplines. At the same time, the religions cannot claim the souls of those who reject their doctrines (including even atheists and agnostics, who also share in First Amendment protections). In the aggregate, the First Amendment guarantees that each religion can claim itself as the *only* true and revealed faith, but cannot in the least impose that claim on anybody else—whch amounts to a requirement that religions can advance their doctrines, at least publicly, only as tentative statements in the category of aesthetic opinions.

A major reason why American Jews have thrived in the United States in a manner unmatched in the history of Judaism anyplace else in the world, is precisely because of the First Amendment. As the history of Judaism shows, the Jews face the greatest danger when they live in a country with a state-supported (or official) religion; secularization is the milieu in which the Jews function best, since it offers the best protection against Christian anti-Semitism. Any environment in which the state draws a strong link between religion and public order increases the importance of religion (which in all cases will not be Judaism), and that will accentuate religious differences— the environment in which Christian anti-Semitism best flourishes.

But the First Amendment umbrella which has protected Jews for so long in this country is now under increasing strain. There is a steadily growing intrusion of religion into the political process, a development that spells the greatest danger to American Jews. The danger stems not only from the fact that the First Amendment is under some attack, but because the attackers represent some of the militant arms of Christianity. And the fact that many Jews do not recognize the danger makes the situation even more ominous.

According to popular sociology, this wasn't supposed to happen. In the past two decades especially, there has been a pronounced diminution of interreligious tension in this country. Catholic and main-line Protestant denominations especially, have done much work toward improving Jewish-Christian relations, to a large extent the result of the liberalizing process among the leadership of the leading Christian denominations. But the popular conception of this great thaw failed to detect that while the leadership was saying one thing, a significant portion of their adherents were saying something quite different. And what they have been saying is that their liberal leadership does not speak for them at all; they're moving in a whole different direction.

The most pronounced trend has been the sudden rise of the evangelical movement, a modern version of the longstanding streak in American Protestantism, which in the nineteenth century crusaded against such evils as slavery, urban vice and alcohol. Prohibition marked the high point in that trend, and widespread public dissatisfaction over the failure of the experiment in religious regulation of public morals drove the evangelical movement from the American mainstream. It remained very much a minor consideration until the late 1960s, when evangelism seemed to explode from the backwaters and became one of the most significant political factors in the United States.

Evangelicals are split into two major types. One, the so-called "orthodox," believes in the literal word of the Bible, and further believes that Jesus is divine and represents the only hope for "personal salvation." The second, known as "conversionalists," believe they have had a powerful religious experience during which they actually spoke with Jesus in some form and asked him to be their personal savior. This experience is often called "born again," most prominently popularized by the experience of former President Jimmy Carter who, like many "born again" Christians, is not fundamentalist. However, all evangelicals share a belief in a commitment to "reach out with a message of salvation," which means an effort to convert others all over the world.

The growth of evangelism in just the past decade has been nothing short of extraordinary. A 1979 poll, conducted by the Gallup organization, found that at least 20 percent of all Americans aged eighteen or older—or about 31 million Americans—consider themselves evangelicals. And 40 percent of those polled believed the Bible to be free of error. (About 10 percent of those who described themselves as evangelical belonged to the Roman Catholic faith, where evangelism is usually known as "charismatic," and often takes the form of opposition to certain liturgical reforms in the Catholic mass.)

Clearly, the widespread boom in evangelism shatters the old stereotype of evangelicals as primarily backwoods Southerners. More importantly, the boom underscores what Protestant leaders have sensed for some time: American Protestants are turning away from the mainstream denominations. In the past ten years, according to one study, United Methodist Church membership declined by 11.4 percent, a falling away exceeded by other denominations: United Presbyterian Church, 23 percent, Episcopal Church, 16.9 percent; and Christian Churches, 22.6 percent.

Why the decline? Primarily, the mainline denominations have overlooked a lesson the fundamentalist churches and the theological conservatives have never forgotten—for most American Protestants, their search is for *meaning* in the religion, not social or ecumenical activism. However much leaders of the major faiths might applaud efforts to ease interreligious tension—such as Protestant clergymen participating in Passover seders with Jewish rabbis—the fact of the matter is that for a significant percentage of Protestants those kinds of activities are not only meaningless, but probably insidious. They are seeking answers, not philosophical or theological debates. And it is conservative Christianity, including the evangelical movement, that provides those answers. For some years, many Protestants have been disturbed by their leadership's propensity for social activism and what is regarded as a turning away from basic spiritual values of the Protestant movement, notably literal interpretation of the Bible and a failure to uphold the basic issues (moral and theological) of their religion. One can imagine the reaction of a good number of Protestants as they watched a Barbara Walters interview with the first woman ordained as an Episcopal priest. In answer to a question about whether she was of strong religious faith, the new priest replied, "No Barbara... but I do believe in caring, and that's what religion is all about, isn't it?"

This exposition on changes in the religious establishment might seem out of place in a study on anti-Semitism, but the analysis has been necessary for an understanding of an important lesson of the evangelical tide sweeping over American Protestanism. Its threat to American Jews should not be underestimated.

That threat has at least two dimensions. One is the implication of the evangelical belief in the literalness of the Bible, a belief that has obvious impact on Jews; if the New Testament is to be taken literally, then in fact the Jews are guilty of deicide. This literalness threatens to wipe out many years of effort by the leaders of some Christian denominations to at least mitigate that old libel. Second, and more serious, is the muscularity of contemporary evangelism, and the role evangelicals seek to play in the political process. The problem is an attempt by the evangelical movement to link its moralistic crusade with political ideology, an ominous assault on the First Amendment's guarantees separating church and state. Christian Voice, one of the largest evangelical movements, makes this disturbing assertion in its official statement of purpose:

> We believe that America, the last stronghold of faith on this planet, has come under increasing attack from satanist forces in recent years... that the standards of Christian morality... are now under the onslaught... launched by the "rulers of darkness of this world" and insidiously sustained under the ever more liberal ethic.

There is a pronounced fanaticism in that statement, not to mention the reference to "rulers of darkness of this world," which amounts to a full-fledged conspiracy theory. The significance lies in a reversal of the American political ideal: a political opponent can be stupid or misguided, but the marketplace of ideas will finally decide just how stupid or misguided he or she has been. But in the evangelistic view, differing political opinions arise not from varying views of a particular problem, but because a political opponent is wicked. The common thread that runs through all evangelistic rhetoric is this view of opponents as morally wicked—deliberately so, in fact. It is only a short step from that view to the conviction that these morally wicked people are part of an evil cabal of evil-minded people who conspire secretly to thwart popular will.

That would represent an almost classic exposition of the "conspiracy" most anti-Semites see. Nevertheless, overt anti-Semitism for the most part is a stranger to the evangelical movement, even though much of its force is directed toward such goals as winning tax exemptions for private Christian schools and imposing voluntary school prayer (Christian prayer, of course), plus other "family" or "morality" issues, most particularly an offensive against homosexuals. Further, the evangelicals often make a point of their support of Israel as part of their foreign policy positions, and that, combined with a general absence of hate-mongering, has lulled many American Jews into a benign view of the evangelical movement, despite their uneasiness over the movement's theological thrust. They could not be making a greater mistake. How large that mistake has been can be seen by taking a close look at what is probably the most important and publicized evangelical movement, the Moral Majority.

Moral Majority was born during the first great manifestation of the New Right in 1976, when Richard Viguerie, the fund-raiser for conservative groups (his ability to raise money through the use of sophisticated, computerized mailing lists has become legendary), predicted during an interview, "The next major area of growth for conservative ideology and philosophy is among the evangelicals." Viguerie correctly foresaw that the then nascent evangelical movement could be harnessed into conservative political action. His prediction was first proved two years later, when one conservative group used the mailing list of the Old Time Gospel Hour—a growing conservative Baptist organization in Virginia headed by Reverend Jerry Falwell—to mobilize a massive letter-writing campaign that opposed Internal Revenue Service rules denying tax-exemptions to private Christian schools that were not integrated. The drive was immensely successful, and it alerted conservative groups to the great political potential that resided within conservative and evangelical Christian organizations. In August 1979, Falwell formed Moral Majority, which immediately set out to function as a political lobbying group to "do something about the moral decline of our country."

Moral Majority played a role in the 1980 elections—the exact extent of its impact is a matter of some debate—campaigning against what it had concluded were the main reasons for the "moral decline of America" including: abortion; "creeping socialism, which is a first cousin to Communism"; giveaway programs and welfarism; attacks on family, schools and national defense; the danger of capitulation to the Soviet Union; humanism; moral permissiveness and lack of leadership. These problems, Falwell said, would become critical during what he called the "decade of destiny" (the 1980s), during which time the monogamous family "may become extinct."

There is some difficulty trying to sort out all the Moral Majority targets and to know the meaning of such phrases as "humanism" (sometimes called "secular humanism," apparently to distinguish it from nonsecular humanism). They appear to be some sort of code words, since they draw heavy applause whenever uttered by Falwell or other leading lights of the Moral Majority. Whatever their meaning, they seem to hold no dread for the Jewish community, some segments of which regard Falwell as an ally. Falwell is on record as testifying to his great love of Jews, and there is one photograph of Falwell, on bended knees, planting a tree in the Falwell Forest in Israel. He was honored by the Jewish National Fund in 1980, and last year received a medal from Israeli Prime Minister Menachem Begin for the preacher's support of Israel. But there is more here than meets the eye.

In 1980 Falwell was among the luminaries of the New Right who gathered in Dallas, a meeting distinguished by the appearance of candidate Ronald Reagan, who captured the group's allegiance with a brilliant speech that included the phrase, "I know you can't endorse me... but I endorse you." This news, however, was obscured by a more sensational development. One of the attendees at the meeting was a relatively obscure Oklahoma Baptist minister named Bailey Smith, the newly-elected president of the Southern Baptist Convention, that denomination's most important organization. Smith gave a little religious speech to the meeting, at one point noting, "God Almighty does not hear the prayer of a Jew." We shall hear more of Bailey later in this chapter, but for the moment it is important to focus on the activities of Falwell in this episode. Asked about Bailey's statement, Falwell sought to make light of it (he asserted that newspaper stories about the remark were "of political origin"). When that didn't work and Falwell was asked his own views, he replied, "I believe that God answers the prayer of any redeemed Jew or Gentile and I do not believe that God answers the prayer of any unredeemed Gentile or Jew."

The Falwell statement only seemed to make things worse, and the matter was soon a full-blown controversy. Reagan's campaign strategists became alarmed, and Reagan himself administered a subtle slap to the wrists of both Bailey and Falwell by noting, "Both the Christian and Judaic religions are based on the same God, the God of Moses." Falwell got the hint, and under pressure by Reagan aides to dampen the controversy, he carried out a highly publicized meeting with Rabbi Marc Tannenbaum, Director of Interreligious Affairs for the American Jewish Committee. Tannenbaum took pains to educate Falwell on some basic theology, and Falwell emerged from the meeting with an agreement on a statement that sought to reassure Jews that neither Falwell nor the evangelical movement was in the least anti-Semitic. The statement said, "God hears the cry of any sincere person who calls on Him."

This was meant to calm the restiveness within the American Jewish community (no small matter in a presidential election year), but there were many who wondered how Falwell could have reversed himself so easily on so vital a theological matter. The suspicion grew that Falwell's statement with Tannenbaum was a matter of expediency, not conviction, a suspicion that hardened when Falwell appeared on the "Meet the Press" television program. The show featured this exchange:

> *MARVIN KALB: You have spoken of the Judeo-Christian tradition in this country. I want to quote you on something that's been in the press. "I believe God does not hear the prayers of unredeemed Gentiles or Jews." Did you say that?*

> *FALWELL: All right. Yes, I've made that statement. I believe . . .*

> *KALB: How can you say that and talk about fidelity to the Judeo-Christian . . .*

> *FALWELL: Wait a minute now. I believe that God hears the prayers of all persons, black, white, red, yellow, Jew, Gentile. God hears everything. I believe that the Jewish—Judaism, for example . . . does not believe that our Messiah has yet come.*

Later, in the same broadcast, another panelist asked Falwell about his previous answer: "Does he answer the prayers of Jews? Does he answer them in the same way that he answers Christians' prayers?" Falwell replied:

> *All right. The New Testament, in the Tenth Book of Acts, a Jew, a non-Christian Jew, Cornelius, prayed and God specifically answered his prayer in the New Testament era. God . . . knows the sincerity of our heart . . . There are no doubt evangelicals who believe and would say, that God does not hear the*

prayer of any Jew, period so on. Most of them would
not be anti-Semitic.

Falwell's answer betrays a good deal of discomfort with the
question, and no wonder: as Falwell was perfectly aware, what
he was saying was arrant nonsense. In fact, evangelicals (himself chiefly among them) devoutly believe that Jews have
nothing to do with God, and are past redemption for their
rejection of Christ as Messiah. Fortunately for Falwell, none of
the questioners on the television program had noticed that
their target, only shortly before his appearance, had written in
his own publication, *Listen, America!* that Jews "are spiritu-
ally blind and desperately in need of their Messiah and Savior."

Falwell was guilty of talking out of both sides of his
mouth, and the evangelical movement soon began to take him
to task for his denial (at least in public forums) of what they
knew was established fact: evangelicals do not like Jews. James
Robison, a Texas evangelist who is regarded as something of a
senior statesman for the evangelical movement, tried to set
things right by reminding Falwell of how evangelists really
stood on the question of the Jews. "Every born-again Christian," Robison said in an article under his name in *Life's
Answer*, the Robison ministry's main publication, "should
know that God hears only the prayers of those who seek Him
and His salvation." Robison defended Smith's original statement about God not listening to Jewish prayers, noting that
those who disagree with Smith "seem to disagree also with the
Lord Jesus Christ."

Falwell's claim about Jews finally figured in a campaign
commercial sponsored by the Carter-Mondale Reelection
Committee, on the air only a short while before being withdrawn. (It was felt it might be dangerous to attack Falwell so
openly.) The withdrawal of the commercial seemed to calm
things down a bit, although Jewish community leaders were
still uneasy about Falwell—who then proceeded to give them

cause for even more concern. At an "I Love America Rally" in the Virginia state capitol in Richmond, Falwell said, "I know a few of you here today don't like Jews. And I know why. He can make more money accidentally than you can on purpose." Jews criticized this unthinking slur, which Falwell first tried to pass off as mere "buffoonery," then restated his strong support for Israel as proof of his lack of anti-Semitic bias.

It is Falwell's strong support for Israel that led Israeli officials to awarding him a medal, an incident mentioned earlier. The Israelis demonstrated a monumental expediency in their selection of Falwell for this award, not only because of Falwell's fundamentalist anti-Jewish bias, but also because the Israelis somehow ignored the fact that another recipient of a medal, Senator Frank Church, had only recently been defeated in his bid for reelection—in no small measure because Falwell's Moral Majority forces in Idaho had unleashed a torrent of abuse on the senator, including the charge that he had been using "outside Jewish money" in his campaign. Church refused to appear at the awards ceremony with Falwell, a fact which seemed to make no difference to the Israelis. (As one Israeli embassy official said privately, "We need every friend we can get.")

Possibly. But awarding a medal to Falwell has caused some confusion among the American Jewish community, many of whose members refuse to believe that Falwell could be anti-Semitic if Israel gave him a medal. The more perceptive among them may have thought that Israel had coined, in addition to a medal, some sort of new definition of "friend." For example, overlooked was a 1979 sermon by Falwell, in which he said that during the Old Testament era, God "came unto his own, the Jews. His own received him not. The Jews rejected him." Also overlooked was the ad Falwell's Moral Majority placed in newspapers throughout the country in 1980, asking people to sign a "Christian Bill of Rights." In the ad, Falwell said that shortly after the election, "I will present a formal Christian Bill of Rights . . . to the next President . . . and ask him to commit himself to uphold these God-fearing principles."

Falwell's followers have made their ultimate goal even clearer; one opinion article written for *The New York Times* by a Moral Majority activist said, "The majority of Americans are Christians.... Why should not a nation's laws, policies, and even public ceremonies reflect the values, beliefs, and principles of the majority of its people?" And as for his often repeated claim that he "loves the Jews," the Reverend Dan C. Fore, chapter president of the Moral Majority organization in New York, made it clear what Falwell and the other leaders of Moral Majority mean. "I love the Jewish people deeply," Fore said in one interview. "God has given them talents He has not given others. They are His chosen people. Jews have a God-given ability to make money, almost a supernatural ability to make money.... They control the media, they control this city [New York]."

With friends like these, the Jews hardly need enemies, yet many Jews remain confused about Falwell and the Moral Majority. The slogans of Moral Majority—home, family, religion, morality—are appealing to Jews, as they are appealing to just about every other religious or ethnic group in America, since Jews are as concerned as anyone else about what can be regarded as a disruption of traditional family values in this country. Further, there is the Moral Majority's firm support of Israel. Thus, Jews are presented with a terrible irony: could any organization advocating support of traditional American values, and Israel to boot, possibly be anti-Semitic? Yes; the fact is that Falwell's support for Israel has little to do with the Jews. In their theology, Fundamentalists regard Israel as a necessary precondition for the return of Christ, so Israel must remain a viable state pending the Second Coming. And as for Moral Majority's views on morality, its statements and writings make it clear that this vanguard of the evangelical movement regards Jews as infidels, with no role to play in a "Christian America."

Falwell and the Moral Majority are outgrowths of the strong fundamentalist trend in Christianity, and it is in fundamentalism that the strongest growth of that religion is occurring. While the main-line denominations are suffering a marked decline in enrollments, fundamentalist (or conservative) denominations are enjoying unparalleled growth. Nothing better illustrates that trend than the activities of the Reverend Bailey Smith, the Baptist clergyman mentioned earlier.

Eight years ago Smith, a fundamentalist's fundamentalist, took over the Southern Baptist Church in Del City, a suburb of Oklahoma City, Oklahoma. Preaching a strong fundamentalist message—literal interpretation of the Bible and "traditional" roles of men and women—Smith nearly doubled the size of his congregation, at one point holding a mass baptism of nearly 2,000 new converts. That sort of success ultimately brought Smith to the presidency of the Southern Baptist Convention, one of America's leading religious organizations, that represents over 13 million Baptists. Smith's presidency has been marked by his attempt to purge the denomination of leaders and seminary teachers who do not conform with his strict code of biblical infallibility and rigid moral principles.

Ordinarily that would be a matter of concern only to Southern Baptists, but Smith, among the most prominent figures in the fundamentalist movement, has also been flirting with the New Right movement. It was during this flirtation that Smith made his infamous remark about God not hearing the prayers of Jews. Smith later expressed "regret" about making the statement, but never repudiated it. (Indeed, only shortly afterward he said, "A person without Jesus Christ is eternally lost.") Smith claimed that he was not anti-Semitic, an assertion at variance with a sermon he delivered only two weeks after his "regret" at having expressed publicly his conviction that Jews cannot possibly communicate with God. The sermon, which was broadcast over a local Oklahoma radio station, said in part:

*There are some people with whom God works more
intimately than others. Why, you say? I don't know.
Why did he choose the Jews? I don't know why he
chose the Jews. I think they got funny-looking noses,
myself. I don't know why he chose the Jews. That's
God's business. Amen.*

This sermon caused some deep disquiet among the Jewish
communities in the Southwest, but Smith said he did not
understand what all the fuss was about. "I was teasing as I
talked to the people of my church," Smith explained. "It was
not a public meeting. Can't people tease any more at all?"

There are any number of aspects to this event which are
extraordinary, not the least of which is the fact that, while
Smith was making this sermon, he was part of an effort by the
Baptist establishment to "reach out" to Jews and attempt to
heal the widening split between Jews and Baptists. To that end,
the Anti-Defamation League announced the formation of a
committee to improve relations between the two religions. One
of the committee's two chairmen was Smith, who subsequently
was reported to have participated in a Passover Seder at the
home of a prominent Dallas Jewish leader. Additionally, a
number of Protestant and Jewish groups have been joining in
efforts to "improve their relationship," which amounts to the
delicate task of determining whether the evangelicals really
want to return to the days of a militant Christianity, when Jews
were the targets of attempts at forced conversion. (This is
certainly an obvious implication of such things as "Christian
America.")

No one can fail to hope that these outreaches are finally
successful, although it is difficult to imagine what can be
accomplished by such dialogues. The fundamental fact remains that the evangelicals are firmly committed to their goal
of a "Christian America," and they are equally committed to
proselytizing and conversion of all non-Christians. To be sure,

the evangelicals like to say that all conversions must be voluntary, but one wonders about their definition of the word "voluntary." The evangelicals also like to claim that they are as concerned as the Jews about religious freedom, but again, there is cause for wonder about how that assertion can be squared with the evangelicals' pursuit of such goals as prayer in public schools, and demands that political leaders swear to a "Christian Bill of Rights."

The alleged willingness of evangelicals to create good relations with Jews might be more persuasive if the evangelicals took some concrete action to reassure an American Jewish community that is increasingly nervous about their views and activities. One good place to start might be elimination of an especially odious by-product of the Christian fundamentalist movement, the "Christian business directories." These directories are the brainchildren of a franchise group based in California called The Christian Yellow Pages. The group produces Christian business directories in six states (with plans for expanding the operation to twenty-four states this year). Each directory exhorts users to "give your business to those who are of 'like faith,'" and lists Christian businessmen in the area. The directories, set up in the familiar format of the phone company's Yellow Pages directory, are distributed free through churches and religious bookstores. Those advertising in the directories must sign a statement avowing that they are "born-again Christians."

The directories have outraged Jewish groups wherever they've appeared (and Catholic groups as well, since the directories also regard Catholics as non-Christian), leading to a number of lawsuits charging discrimination and illegal boycotts. The state of mind of those who produce these directories can be divined by the remarks of one Texas publisher involved in their publication who, when asked about the lawsuits by Jewish groups, asserted, "This is the pot calling the kettle black—the Jews have been doing business with one another for thousands of years." Needless to say, no evangelical group has joined these lawsuits or exerted the slightest effort to get them stopped.

The important point is that the directories (and many of the other signs of the evangelical boom) are only symptoms of the larger trend at work. Fundamentally, that trend is religious dogmatism, and it was a trend that was there for all to see even before the evangelical explosion during the past decade. The first real clue came during the "Jesus freak" revolution among many young people during the 1960s.

Much of the steam has gone out of the Jesus movement, since it has to a large extent been co-opted by the evangelical movement. But at its height, the Jesus movement displayed a near-frightening fascism, exhibited in the story of a Missouri professor of religion who attempted to reach some sort of a meeting of the minds on the issue of the varying degrees of Chrisitian faith. The conference was disrupted by a sit-in of "Jesus First" adherents, who refused to hear any views opposing their own, which amounted to a conviction that the New Testament account of Jesus' life was literal truth, and that Jesus in fact was a God. As one of the Jesus freaks explained: "I thank God that I don't need any theologian or Bible commentary to tell me about you, Lord. I know that you have come to me and talked to me through your son, Jesus."

There is not much to be said in the face of such fanaticism. At its height, the Jesus movement claimed several thousand adherents, but precise figures are difficult to establish because the movement was too diverse. For the same reason, the Jesus movement never became a powerful force on the American scene, since it never developed a comprehensive creed or systematic theology, as have the modern fundamentalist and evangelical movements. Still, the Jesus movement had important anti-Semitic implications, which centered on an uncritical use of scriptural passages—in their view, the Jews were responsible for the death of the Messiah. And it was the Jews who had prevented what all of them fervently believed: there was a Kingdom of God that was possible of immediate attainment, and only the Jews had prevented that by killing Christ.

The illusory dream of immediate attainment of a Kingdom of God on earth has been, and continues to be, the central driving force of a wide range of religious cults in this country. Since a fair number of them center on Jews as conversion targets, they are worth some examination.

According to one study, there are just over 500 religious cults in the United States, about half of them concentrated in the states of California, New York and Illinois—the three states where more than half of the American Jewish population lives. This is no mere coincidence, since modern religious cults often concentrate on enrolling Jews. Many of the cults take the position that Jews especially "live in shadow," and "true communion with God" can only be achieved when the planet's most notorious apostates—the Jews—are converted.

The most controversial of the cults is the Iskon (Hari Krishna) sect founded in 1965 by a swami in New York. The group now has about 10,000 members in the United States, with about 15 to 20 percent of its membership Jewish (an estimated 35 percent of its national leadership is Jewish). Why would Jews join such a group? The subject has been studied nearly to death, but there are still no firm answers. Generally, the conclusions are that the cults offer young people positive thinking in an age of uncertainty; the young people are offered, often via behavior-controlling techniques, a charismatic or messianic leader, and what amounts to an extended family. According to most studies, the average Jewish convert to cults is eighteen to twenty-two years old, middle or upper-middle class, with some college education and a nominally religious upbringing. This may be true, but the problem is that it does not account for the most recent development in the cults: recruitment of elderly Jews, primarily in retirement communities and nursing homes in Florida and California. One fundamentalist movement, for example, known as Church Universal and Triumphant, has nearly a 20 percent Jewish membership. Some of the Jewish members, according the one study, donate all their cash, jewelry and property to the cult; less wealthy members surrender their Social Security benefits or pension checks.

Whatever the sociological truth, the fact is that the cults are increasingly successful in attracting Jews, to the point where current estimates say that although American Jews make up about 3 percent of the American population, they represent nearly 50 percent of cult membership. That figure may be a little high, but there is no doubt that despite the pronounced anti-Semitism of the religious cults, they are nevertheless succeeding in recruiting Jews. (In the New York area alone, there are over 100 cults whose primary goal is to recruit Jews; some of them concentrate on the growing population of émigré Russian Jews.)

The most controversial of the groups aimed exclusively at recruiting Jews is Jews for Jesus, founded in 1972 in San Francisco. By last year, the group had an annual budget of $2,500,000 and a full-time professional staff of sixty-five people. It is difficult to arrive at a definitive figure on the group's membership, but most estimates place it somewhere around 1,000.

Mainstream Protestant groups have become increasingly uncomfortable with both the evangelical and cult movements, and have taken some pains to condemn them for causing divisiveness in American life, a divisiveness that presumably includes implications of anti-Semitism. That is cause for some applause, but it is also a fact that the prime representative of American Protestantism, the National Council of Churches, has demonstrated something less than concern for interreligious relations and the feelings of the American Jewish community. In fact, the Council has increasingly shown an indifference to American Jews that occasionally has strayed into outright anti-Semitism.

For more than two decades after the end of World War II, the Council—primarily liberal in persuasion—enjoyed warm relations with the American Jewish community and both groups devised a number of interfaith programs. But in 1967, when Jewish groups turned to the churches for expressions of support for Israel, they were shocked to find no support forthcoming. Instead, shortly after the war the Council issued a policy statement that condemned Israel, noting that the Council could not "condone by silence territorial expansion by armed force."

That was the first indication that the close relationship the Council had with the Jewish community was undergoing some strain, primarily over the question of Israel. A Council statement on the matter was generally balanced in 1969, but by 1974 the Council began to show a pronounced anti-Israel bias. In that year, the Council urged open contacts between the United States government and the Palestine Liberation Organization, and in 1978 the Council offended many Jews with an especially one-sided statement about the Middle East. Immediate cause of the statement was the Israeli retaliatory raid on PLO guerrilla bases, carried out after a team of guerrillas murdered thirty-six Israeli civilians and an American photographer. "We as Christians affirm the sanctity of human life," the Council declared, after which its governing board went on to approve a resolution calling upon the United States to end shipments of any anti-personnel bombs to Israel. The Israelis, the board's statement said, had used such bombs to "wantonly" kill what the statement called "thousands of men, women, and children." There was no mention of the people murdered by the PLO guerrillas. And even worse was to come.

The Council criticized the Camp David accords on the grounds that they did not give proper emphasis to the "Palestinian people" in order that they could become "full partners in the peace process." By which the Council meant the PLO, an omission that led the Council in 1980 to the deduction that the accords were "seriously flawed." After American Ambassador to the United Nations Andrew Young was fired, when he denied carrying out secret contacts with the PLO, the Council described Young—who had made a number of remarks critical of American Jews—as "a fearless prophet and preacher of liberating news," and also a "world ecumenical statesman." By November 1980, relations between the Council and the Jewish community had broken down completely, and Jewish groups boycotted a series of Council-sponsored hearings that month which were supposed to arrive at a policy statement on Israel and the Middle East.

It is just as well that the Jewish community did boycott, for the Council proceeded to establish a new low. It found that it was "morally imperative" for the PLO to be given a separate state, a conclusion reached with little difficulty. But then the Council arrived at the question of what to do about Israel, and it was there that the Council demonstrated a disturbing bias. The governing board's 250 members debated the matter at some length, arguing most about whether the Council should approve a resolution advocating the continued existence of Israel. Such a debate seems incredible in 1980, and yet the debate ensued. And even more incredibly, the governing board finally approved a resolution calling for the continued existence of Israel—by only nine votes. To Henry Siegman, executive director of the American Jewish Congress who was an observer at the meeting when all this was debated, that vote represented to him the most upsetting aspect of the entire affair.

But there was even more in the governing board's final policy statement to be agitated about. It took the position that the United States was the main villain, concluding that the deepening dependence on oil by this country and other nations had made Middle East countries more susceptible to great power "intervention and exploitation." The United States was further blamed for selling arms to the oil-producing states, an act interpreted by the Council as part of its overall bad record, including what is puzzlingly referred to as "violence and deprivation of civil rights" against Muslims and Jews living in this country. This is not otherwise explained, although the Council is much clearer on what it means by "giving voice to the voiceless and power to the powerless"—the PLO. It is the PLO that is the real star of the Council's final resolutions on the Middle East, representing, in the Council's view, the sole repository for the hopes and aspirations of the Palestinian people.

All this should be judged in the context of another Council action that many Jewish groups found disturbing—its refusal (reversed only after strong pressure by Jewish militant groups) to suspend one of its members, Archbishop Valerian Trifa, during disposition of charges by the United States government that he was a Nazi war criminal. Trifa, now head of the Romanian Episcopate in this country (an Orthodox Christian denomination), was accused by the government of leading anti-Jewish riots in Bucharest, Romania, during World War II, during which Jews were hacked to death in the streets and their bodies hung up on meathooks. It took nearly a year of pressure by some Jewish groups for the Council to even consider the matter. Council officials did not seem to understand that Jews were offended by the fact that an accused Nazi war criminal was sitting on a council that was, at least partially, supposed to be fostering greater interreligious ties.

Since then, things have not gotten any better. Last year, following the Israeli air strike on the Iraqi nuclear reactor, the Reverend William Howard, president of the Council, not only condemned the raid but also advocated a complete cutoff of all American military supplies to Israel. In this connection, it should be noted that while the Council was upset about the raid on Iraq, it has never said anything about the 1975 United Nations vote equating Zionism with racism—although there have been any number of Council resolutions supporting the inmates of Attica, the rebels in Angola, and the new government of Vietnam.

Howard was simply following the lead set as far back as 1972 by one of the doyens of the American Protestant establishment, The Very Reverend Francis B. Sayre Jr., dean of the National Cathedral in Washington, D.C. Perhaps the most prominent Protestant clergyman in America at the time, Sayre, a grandson of Woodrow Wilson, had always enjoyed close relations with the Jewish community. (One of his closest friends was Rabbi Joshua O. Haberman, of the Washington Hebrew Congregation.)

There was, therefore, that much more shock when Sayre began his sermon on the subject of Jerusalem during the solemn moment of Palm Sunday in 1972 by saying, "Now the Jews have it all. But even as they praise their God for the smile of fortune, they begin almost simultaneously to put Him to death.... As if Jerusalem could ever be altogether theirs—or anyone's! But now oppressed become oppressors..." Several months later, Sayre presided at a memoral memorial service in the cathedral for the victims of the massacre at the Munich Olympics. Sayre announced that not only were the congregants mourning the Israelis slain in Munich, but also "those villagers in Lebanon and Syria whose lives have been extinguished by the Israeli Air Force..."

Rabbi Haberman subsequently described himself as "pained" by these events, and well he might be, for Sayre's mindless pro-Arabism had undone many years of patient effort to improve relations between Christians and Jews. Rabbi Haberman also might have been pained by some other disturbing rumbles from the Christian community. One was the attempt by the Quakers to produce a report on the Middle East. The report concluded that the 1967 war was the equal fault of both Israel and the Arabs, and went on to claim that Israel was created by Western countries who felt "guilty" about anti-Semitism, and "imposed" Israel on the Arabs. (This is, of course, quite wrong; the fact is that most Western states were opposed to the creation of Israel.) It turned out that the Quaker report actually had gone through twelve drafts before the final version was produced; one early draft had read in part: "We appeal to the leaders of the powerful Jewish community... to reassess the character of their support and the nature of their role in American politics." The draft went on to warn of an "anti-Semitic backlash" if American Jews did not trim their support for Israel.

The Quaker report, like the National Council of Churches and the sermon of the Reverend Sayre, represents a turning away from the American Jewish community by the Protestant establishment in what they perceive is the name of a higher good: the cause of "downtrodden" peoples everywhere. In this category they include the Palestine Liberation Organization, leading to accusations of a pronounced leftward drift in the leadership of a considerable number of mainline religious organizations. It might be comforting to note that this "leftward drift" is also one of the main causes of the drift of adherents away from these organizations—except that, as we noted earlier, the adherents are joining groups whose anti-Semitism is even more pronounced.

The mainstream denominations vigorously deny they are in the least anti-Semitic because of their statements about Israel. In that conviction they are, at the very least, the victims of a terrible self-delusion—that they can somehow separate what may be their genuine concern for the survivability of the American Jewish community from their animus toward the Jewish state, and that somehow they can on one hand express sympathy for the victims of Nazi terror, while on the other express indifference to the Israeli victims of PLO terror. This self-delusion undercuts such laudable actions as the more than forty official statements by Protestant and Catholic organizations in the past three decades condemning anti-Semitism as un-Christian.

Of these statements, the most significant one was the *Nostra Aetate no. 4* produced by the Second Vatican Council, which is a ringing denunciation of all forms of anti-Semitism. Combined with the Catholic Church's strong effort to exorcise the roots of the Christian teaching of contempt which helped pave the way for the secularist ideology of anti-Semitism, the

American Catholic establishment has probably done more than any other Christian organization to try and stamp out Christian anti-Semitism. And yet, as with the Protestant mainline organizations, there is a problem here. While the Catholic Church is commendably diligent in combating anti-Semitism, its left-wing elements have been busy spreading some anti-Zionist poison (which they insist is not anti-Semitic).

The most prominent example is Daniel Berrigan, the Jesuit hero of the Catholic left. Berrigan's causes are too numerous to list here, but one of them—his foray into Middle East politics—betrayed a mindless bias of some interest to this study. Berrigan, noted for his fierce opposition to the Vietnam War, made his first important speech on the Middle East late in 1973, when in an address to the Association of Arab University Graduates in Washington, D.C., he accused Israel of "domestic repression, deception, cruelty, militarism..." He then turned his attention to American Jews, noting that many of them are "Zionists in our midst," and that there was a distinction to be made between the "leaders of the Jewish people" and "the great majority of the Jewish people." As for the American Jewish community leadership, Berrigan accused them not only of being fervent supporters of President Nixon (and therefore presumably responsible for the crimes of that administration), but also indifferent to the fate of Vietnam. "To put the matter brutally," Berrigan said, "many American Jewish leaders were capable of ignoring the Asian holocaust in favor of economic and military aid to Israel."

This speech—repeated in various forms and forums by Berrigan since then—offers a rich field for analysis. It has the classic staples of anti-Semitism, including dangerous enemies who have burrowed their way into power ("Zionists in our midst"), secular anti-Jewishness (contrasting leaders and "the great majority of the Jewish people"), and scapegoatism ("ignoring the Asian holocaust"). It is also grossly inaccurate: nearly 66 percent of American Jews voted *against* Nixon in 1972. Although in his speech Berrigan also criticized Arab nations, he reserved most of his criticism for Israel. Berrigan explained this by later saying that his own background is more closely related to Israel than to the Arabs, and therefore his criticism was his way of "paying our old debt...a debt of outraged love."

It is impossible to square that statement with Berrigan's speech and the animus it reveals, not only about Israel, but also about American Jews. Possibly, Berrigan—and the Catholic left—actually believes it, which would then raise the question of the limits of their ignorance, for no intelligent clergyman (which Berrigan demonstrably is) could fail to know of the close relationship of the concept of Zion with American Jews; one can only imagine Berrigan's reaction if Jews were to attack the Pope and the concept of the Vatican, while maintaining they were not anti-Catholic, merely "anti-Vatican."

The Berrigan speech incident has been selected for some exposition here not as an isolated example, but as representative of the sort of mind-set that seems to afflict the Catholic left in particular. For example, last year 150 representatives of left Christianity, most of them from the Catholic left, met in Illinois to decide on how to approach their major project, the Palestine Human Rights Campaign. The campaign, according to its sponsors, is to generate anti-Israel and pro-PLO sentiment among American Christian denominations. One suggestion during the three-day conference was that the groups sponsor field-workers in Israel "to spy on the Israelis," a proposal accepted without dissent. Curiously, the conference also decided that evangelicals represent Israel's most potent ally in the United States—an idea that would surprise Israelis and American Jews. In any event, the conference wound up preparing a final declaration, which pledged "action to achieve an end to all military aid to Israel and to all humanitarian aid except insofar as an equal amount of such aid is given to the Palestinian people." The declaration went on to say that the group would "let the government of Israel know that U.S. Christians support Palestinian aspirations..."

There is much terrible irony in this account of the curious byways of modern anti-Semitism among the Christian community—the Catholic left making common cause with its traditional enemies on the Protestant right; Protestant establishments losing adherents to groups whose anti-Semitism is only a different form of the anti-Semitism of their establishment enemies; evangelical groups propounding a literal interpretation of the Bible, and somehow missing what the holy book says about the Jews.

Nothing that has happened within Christianity and how it now regards the Jews has fallen out of the sky; it is another step in the long continuum stretching back nearly 2,000 years to certain events in Galilee. It is fair to wonder what Christ himself, the Galilean Jew, might think were he to return to earth today and survey the wreckage of what has been done in His name. It is an eventuality that holds no fear for such people as Jerry Falwell, who not too long ago reassured his adherents as to what would happen if Christ did return: "Jesus was not a pacifist. He was not a sissy."

CHAPTER SIX

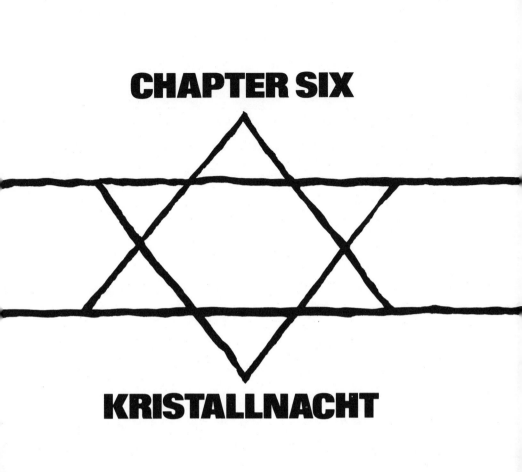

KRISTALLNACHT

*Anti-Semitism is not to be overcome by
getting people to forget us, but to know us.*

Meyer Levin

Knowledge is ruin to my young men.

Adolf Hitler

Shortly after sundown one evening last September, the members of the Jewish Center of Lake Grove, a middle class community in the New York suburb of Long Island, gathered at their temple to begin the somber holy services for Rosh Hashanah. Their gathering was even more solemn than the occasion usually demanded, for as they entered the building they had spent nearly $1 million to build, they were confronted with sights none of them could have imagined would ever happen in America.

The top windows of the temple were all boarded up, having been smashed out during an attack by vandals. There was a faint smell of smoke in the air, the vestige of a fire, set by vandals, that had burned the upstairs sanctuary; the fire had also destroyed one of the center's three Torahs. The place was still littered with the scars of that attack by the vandals. The members sadly held their services in the temple's school.

Meanwhile, only a few miles away, the newly-reopened Hebrew Academy of Suffolk County was being guarded around-the-clock by police patrols. The Academy, which the previous year had been closed after vandals broke in and flooded the building, now had a smashed window—the result of a new attack just before Rosh Hashanah. And students had been taunted and were the targets of rock-throwing attacks as they walked down the streets wearing their yarmulkes.

Further west, toward New York City, dozens of members of the Jewish War Veterans were spending their nights riding around in unarmed patrols, looking for swastikas painted on synagogues or other signs of desecration; still other Jews were complaining about anti-Semitic phone calls and anonymous hate letters.

For many of these American Jews, products of the World War II or post-World War II "golden age" of American Jewry, these incidents are puzzling and unsettling intrusions into their middle-class existences. They are second and third generation graduates of the New York City Jewish ghettos, proud of their heritage (but not especially devout), living in what for years has been relatively placid harmony with their neighbors of other religions; for these Jews, anti-Semitism—especially violent anti-Semitism that desecrates their homes, schools and synagogues—has been an abstraction. But for other Jews, older and with longer memories, what has been happening on Long Island and other Jewish communities throughout the country is a much more frightening experience. For them, the sound of breaking glass as windows are smashed in synagogues is a horrible echo of a time nearly forty-three years before, when the sound of broken glass in another country heralded the first violent step in a program of extermination.

Even for Jews who did not live through it, the German word "Kristallnacht" (crystal night) is instantly recognizable: it symbolically describes the night of November 9-10, 1938, when Nazi mobs rampaged throughout Germany, destroying Jewish stores and wrecking synagogues. Kristallnacht as a term stemmed from the broken glass caused by the mobs smashing the windows of virtually every synagogue in Germany.

Actually, far more terrible things happened that night: more than 20,000 Jews were arrested, and at least 36 Jews were murdered. While police looked on benignly, the mobs beat up Jews in the streets and forced others into humiliating acts, such as washing streets with toothbrushes. The police looked on without interference because the mobs were in fact carefully organized by Hitler's secret police to carry out these "spontaneous" demonstrations against Jewish property. According to Nazi propaganda, the mobs were enraged over "Jewish crimes," in particular the shooting of Ernst vom Rath, secretary to the German embassy in Paris, by a young Jew. This "crime" turned out to have been committed by Herschel Grynszpan, a nineteen-year-old Jewish refugee from Germany, as a protest against the Nazi treatment of Polish Jews in Germany. Grynszpan's father was among several thousand "stateless" Jews in Germany who had been deported in railroad cattle cars to Poland, where Polish authorities refused to accept them. The elder Grynszpan died, and his infuriated son went to the German embassy, intending to kill Johannes von Welczek, the German ambassador, who was a notorious Nazi. But in a terrible historical irony, Grynszpan could not find the ambassador so he shot the first German he could find— who turned out to be vom Rath, actually a bitter anti-Nazi. Two days later vom Rath died of his wounds, and the Nazis ordered Kristallnacht.

It may seem extremist to compare recent events with Kristallnacht, for the differences are stark. In 1938, the mobs who desecrated synagogues were under official direction and protection, and they carried out their assaults in an atmosphere of officially approved lawlessness; today, assaults on synagogues result in renewed police action and official disapproval. In 1938, no one lifted a finger to help the Jews of Germany; today, Catholic and Protestant organizations have come forward to vigorously protest such desecrations and to offer their full aid to American Jews.

And yet it is well to remember that the Berlin Jewish community (the major target of the Nazis during that night in 1938) was at the time the golden pinnacle of European Jewry. Berlin's population of nearly 200,000 Jews regarded themselves as fully assimilated with the Germans, and their role in the arts, sciences and other professions made them world famous. They considered themselves so unassailable, in fact, that not even Hitler and the Nuremberg Laws (which promulgated a whole series of restrictions on Jews in Germany) could shake the Berlin Jewish community in its conviction that this, too, would pass. It did not, and a year later, when many German Jews had fled to France, the famed theologian Martin Buber, among the more famous of the exiles, wrote:

> *I testify: it was the most extraordinary and meaningful circumstance. For the symbiosis of German and Jewish existence, as I experienced it in the four decades that I spent in Germany, was the first and the only one since the Spanish Era to receive the highest confirmation that history can bestow, confirmation through creativity ... but this symbiosis is at an end and is not likely to return.*

Buber was quite right; this golden time, which lulled so many German Jews into the tragic belief that nothing Hitler could do would ever change what the Jews of Germany had achieved in that country, came to an end in a way none of them dared to foresee. Today on the Steinplatz, just north of the Kurfurstendamm in West Berlin, there stands a memorial to the victims of nazism, the stones for which were built with the ruins of what used to be Berlin's magnificent main synagogue; the synagogue windows, all beautiful stained-glass masterpieces, had been smashed on Kristallnacht and the building itself burned to the ground by the mobs. Only two other pieces of that building remain: a mosque-like doorway and one pillar from the des-

troyed temple, which are now imbedded in a stark new building
that is the headquarters for the Berlin Jewish Community Center. It serves 2,000 remaining Jews, most of them
elderly.

The mobs that destroyed the synagogues of Berlin were,
for the most part, the ignorant flotsam of the streets, along with
the young Nazi brownshirts. They rampaged all over Germany
on the promise of a night of adventure and much loot. The men
who directed them—Hitler, Goebbels and others—stayed
carefully out of sight, so as to be in a position to deny any
complicity during what they were certain would be worldwide
condemnation. And it is here that the real echo in current
events begins, for ignorance, used as an instrument of official
state policy, was the real weapon the Nazis wielded during
Kristallnacht. Today there is no official state policy to dese-
crate synagogues but, as we shall see, ignorance lies at the root
of the current problem.

The dimensions of the problem can be summed up in
statistics: in 1978, there began a wave of attacks on Jewish
temples and homes. In 1980 there were 377 such incidents
reported nationwide; just over 400 were reported last year. In
the past two years there has been a 50 percent increase in such
reported incidents. No one has been killed yet, but these ram-
pages include ten cases of arson, four firebombings, and many
death threats; as well as window-smashing (the most common
form of these incidents) and the spray-painting of swastikas
and anti-Semitic slogans on synagogues and homes of Jews.
The incidents include:

• A young Jewish couple in Rhode Island harassed by anti-
Semitic threats, including swastika-adorned letters left in their
mailbox.

• More than $180,000 worth of damage to the synagogue in
Temple City, California, including arson and the smashing of
the temple's stained glass windows.

- Three separate incidents of vandalism committed against the Simon Wiesenthal Center for Holocaust Studies in Los Angeles.

- Anti-Semitic graffiti sprayed on buildings of the campus of the University of Florida. When the wife of the university president spoke out publicly against the incident, she was harassed by anonymous phone callers threatening to kill her.

Only a tiny percentage of these acts are committed by extremist groups; overwhelmingly, the culprits are youngsters (some as young as twelve years old). Despite renewed emphasis by police to investigate these crimes—in some cases, including the formation of special units—the fact remains that of the 377 incidents reported in 1980, ultimately only about 20 arrests resulted in those cases. Even when arrests are made, at best the charges are misdemeanors, and young offenders rarely get any sort of jail sentence. Jewish groups, alarmed over the rising tide of desecration, have lobbied for stiffer laws governing vandalism against religious buildings, held seminars on bigotry and rallies against anti-Semitism.

If the Jewish response seems somewhat diffuse, that's because it is. Plainly, the leaders of the Jewish community are at once appalled and confused about the desecrations; it makes no sense in areas where interreligious relations are good for young people to smash windows or paint anti-Semitic slogans on the walls of synagogues. How could such things happen in this time? How could youngsters, raised in homes where anti-Semitism is a virtual stranger, commit such acts of hate?

To some Jewish groups, notably the Jewish Defense League, the situation is quite simple: out there someplace lurks a violent army ready to demolish synagogues. Thus, Jews must arm and shoot down the marauders. To that end, the League has announced a 10-week course on "warfare tactics" at training camps in New York, California and Michigan, where young Jews are given firearms training. What they will do with such training is open to some question. In the New York City borough of Queens, plagued by vandalism against Jewish temples and schools, the League announced that its members would begin armed patrols—an idea dropped after pressure by police. At the same time, the idea came under strong attack by main-line Jewish groups, who see such tactics as inflammatory.

They're probably right, but that still leaves the problem of what to do, aside from around-the-clock patrols and other such security measures. Actually there isn't that much to be done by Jews, especially as a preventative, for the problem of vandalism against Jewish temples and homes goes far deeper than that. Indeed, it has very little to do with the Jews themselves; it has much more to do with a fundamental failing in the American system—a failing that will require much work and years of effort to correct. There is a terrible irony here: while the efforts of such desecrations certainly represent one of the more odious kinds of anti-Semitism, the reason why the desecrations are being carried out has almost nothing to do with anti-Semitism. This may seem like a paradox, but to understand how it works, a close look at the suburban communities of New York's Long Island is in order.

More than 100,000 Jews live on Long Island, and if ever there was a prototypical modern Jewish community, suburban division, Long Island is it. The Jews of Long Island are predominantly middle class or upper middle class. About half are clustered in quasi-enclaves nearest to New York City where the first Jews to migrate from the city settled, forever unofficially marking them as Jewish neighborhoods. (That is beginning to change as the newest generation of Jews tends not to want to live in areas known as primarily Jewish.) Other Jews are scattered all over the vast, sprawling 100-mile-long island suburb. In the past several decades, particularly, they have enjoyed prosperity as well as a thriving religious community—with activities from cradle to grave—and very good interreligious relations, especially with the Roman Catholic Church, Long Island's dominant religous affiliation. Overall, it is the sort of thriving Jewish community that survivors of European *shtetls* and ghettos find nothing short of extraordinary.

The Long Island Jewish community has been singled out for some examination, for while its situation would seem to be nearly ideal (it remains to a large extent undisturbed by the classic manifestations of anti-Semitism), there is nevertheless an unsettling statistic: nearly 20 percent of all acts of vandalism against Jewish facilities occurs on Long Island. And although an imaginative police effort in one of Long Island's two counties has begun to cause that rate to decline, there are still enough incidents occurring to be concerned, especially as to *why* they are occurring.

The incidents are generally similar to those that have happened elsewhere in the country. In one such incident, an eighteen-year-old youth painted a swastika and the word "Jew" on the home of a Jewish couple, an act which apparently stemmed from the fact that the husband had once yelled at the youth for driving too fast down the local street on a motorcycle. (In this case, a judge took the rare step of sentencing the youth to six months in jail, after learning that he had committed the same act against the same couple only a year previously.)

A more common type of anti-Semitic vandalism is the spraying of Nazi symbols on a synagogue. In one case, four youths ranging in age from fifteen to seventeen sprayed swastikas and anti-Jewish obscenities on the front entrance to a large temple; in another, several youths the same age spray-painted anti-Semitic slogans on buildings and signs at a large summer camp run by the YMHA. The director of camp operations thoughtlessly described the incident as a "terrific experience for the kids [at the camp], because now they know what anti-Semitism is and how to deal with it"—although he left unexplained how six-year-old day campers were supposed to "deal" with slogans telling them that they deserved to be shoved into gas chambers.

One of the more disturbing aspects of this wave of anti-Semitic vandalism is the age of those involved. For example, two youths who burglarized a Jewish home and spray-painted the word "Jew" inside were both fourteen years old. And the boy who smashed the windows and a glass door of a synagogue (and scrawled obscenities on one wall) also turned out to be fourteen. One of three boys who terrorized a rabbi and his wife for over a month with anti-Semitic vandalism and harassment turned out to be only thirteen years old (more shockingly, he was also Jewish, just about to make his Bar Mitzvah); the other two boys were fourteen years old.

These occurrences engendered some concern, particularly in the Jewish community, but the most sensational incident occurred last year and had nothing to do with vandalism. This incident concerned the publication of a grossly anti-Semitic notice, on the front page of a student newspaper for a high school whose enrollment is about 20 percent Jewish. Appearing in a special Valentine's Day issue of the newspaper—normally cluttered with messages encircled in hearts—was a heart-shaped valentine that contained this message: "To the princesses, it's been a gas knowing *yews*. Meet us in the *showers*." It was signed with the initials of four seniors at the high school.

The town of Lynbrook, where the school newspaper circulated, contains a large Jewish community, a number of whose members are survivors of the Holocaust. They were outraged when they caught sight of that newspaper, and their outrage was not the least assuaged when one of the mothers of the students involved in the ad said, in response to criticism: "My son has suffered mentally in this. If those girls keep flaunting their wealth, what can you expect?" This remark was nearly as insensitive as the one made by one of the school district officials, who said that he did not understand why other newspapers wanted to write about the incident: "There is nothing to be gained by having a sensational article about anti-Semitism in Lynbrook." The 300 Jews who packed a school board meeting, demanding to know how such a thing could have happened, might disagree. To a certain extent, they have been mollified by the school district's hiring of "human relations consultants" who are supposed to "sensitize" faculty and students to the "problem of human relations" (although there is some question as to what this educational gobbledygook means). They have also been at least partially calmed by a public apology from the students who wrote the ad.

Still, the question remains: how could such things happen? Police experts have arrived at what they consider the profile of typical youngsters who carry out anti-Semitic vandalism. They are almost always male, between the ages of fourteen and seventeen; and they are usually frustrated non-achievers whose parents are lower-middle class, economically. In the police view, the main cause of anti-Semitic vandalism stems from the parents of these youngsters (although as we shall see, this may be an oversimplification). At least 95 percent of the crimes occur in the same neighborhood where the youngsters live, and such crimes are always premeditated—as the police noted, youngsters don't normally walk along the street carrying spray paint. Anti-Semitic violence tends to follow no set pattern; there will be occasional flurries in one particular neighborhood, usually because one youngster commits an act and then tells others, who will then commit their own acts for "kicks." The most common crimes involve swastika-painting, followed by harassment, assault (about 8 percent of all cases involve anti-Semitic violence), and arson (now averaging about four cases a year in the New York area alone).

In the police view, media influence accounts for a large portion of such crimes; newspapers and television stations are now asked to publicize anti-Semitic violence only after an arrest is made, on the theory that publicity tends to multiply the originally reported incident. Police are also convinced that unless judges start handing out stiff sentences for those convicted of anti-Semitic violence, there will be no real deterrent to the crime. (Several states have either passed or are about to pass laws calling for stiffer penalties for what is usually known legally as "ethnic harassment." In most states, such a crime is normally a violation, which carries a seldom-imposed fifteen-day jail sentence.) Police experts have had trouble convincing some judges and lawmakers that laws covering ethnic harassment need stiffening—and they have also had trouble convincing police on the street that such crimes are not simple mischief, as most police officers seem to believe, but represent an outright hatred that is highly shocking, in particular to Jews. To that end, police experts have been holding a number of seminars and training sessions, and as one expert remarked at a recent session, "When a Jewish child comes home and finds a swastika on his house . . . the crime is terrorism."

This represents, in summary, the police view of the problem. While it is valuable—since it comes from the people most responsible for stopping this "ethnic harassment"—it nevertheless suffers from the typical narrowness of a police outlook on a complex problem. Their view certainly does not explain exactly why such violence happens. For that answer we must dig deeper, into the family of a sixteen-year-old boy who was arrested for the desecration of a synagogue. His case was not extraordinary, but what his family did afterward was—they allowed in-depth newspaper interviews of themselves and their son, as an act of atonement for the shame and acute embarrassment they felt their son had brought upon the family.

The boy, whose name is not important in this context, is the oldest son of a working-class family in one of the largest suburbs on Long Island. On Halloween 1980, the boy and three friends were among a group of ten teenagers out looking for mischief. They threw eggs at some cars, soaped a few windows, and squirted shaving cream on the front doors of several homes. By 9:30 P.M. the group had thinned out and the boy and his friends found themselves in front of the community's main synagogue. One of his friends began talking about being an Aryan and hating Jews. According to the boy's account, they then raced up the steps of the synagogue and began spraying the glass doors with swastikas; one of his friends sprayed the word "Jude" which, he explained, meant "Jew" in German. Then the boys ran, only to be caught by one of the synagogue's congregants who was driving by. Meanwhile, Jewish worshippers in the temple got their first look at what had been sprayed on the temple doors. Their reaction can only be imagined, since among the temple's members are a number of survivors of the Holocaust.

The boy's parents borrowed money to hire an attorney for the case, but insisted that their son admit the crime. He ultimately was sentenced to a $150 fine and 100 hours of service to the local Roman Catholic Church. The mother, a devout Catholic, publicly apologized for what her son had done, and the father went to his Jewish boss and told him what had happened. In further public atonement, the family granted an extraordinary series of interviews, during which they discussed what had happened—and why. And it was during these interviews that some of the real causes for anti-Semitic vandalism emerged, reasons that are critical to this study. Here are several of the more important quotes:

THE BOY: "I just thought it was a different religion from Christianity, that's all."

THE BOY: "I have nothing against the Jewish people. I have Jewish friends. I was dating a Jewish girl."

THE MOTHER: "I'm saying there is no anti-Semitism in this house. And I know, because I'm the mother in this home."

THE FATHER: "I work for a Jewish concern. I went to my boss and I said, 'I don't want you to hear about this from around.' And I told him. He said, 'What is your son? Is he mental?' I said, 'No, he's not mental. As far as I know, it was just a prank."

THE MOTHER: "The Holocaust isn't fresh for them. It's history. And it isn't taught. They just don't understand."

THE BOY: "So I asked this kid, what does this 'Jude' mean?"

THE BOY: "I knew what a swastika was, but I really didn't know what it meant."

THE MOTHER: "To tell you the truth, I watched a TV program [on the Holocaust] last Sunday, and that's the first time I realized what they had suffered through."

These quotations amount to a simple conclusion: there is an inexcusably appalling ignorance about Jews—including their history, concerns and the Holocaust—among large portions of the non-Jewish population. And it is an ignorance that is particularly marked among the younger generation. Who can imagine a high school student like the boy in the preceding account not knowing the meaning of a swastika, or thinking that Judaism was "just . . . a different religion," or having no real idea of what the Holocaust was all about? The boy's ignorance is actually not very much different from the ignorance that seems to afflict a distressingly large percentage of high school students today. It is in this ignorance that the real causes for anti-Semitic vandalism lie.

There are any number of studies on what American high school students know about the world, and the results have been almost uniformly depressing. One recent survey by the National Assessment of Educational Progress revealed that 47 percent of this country's seventeen-year-old students did not know that each state has two senators. The picture is not much brighter in higher education. One study at Columbia University where, presumably, students ought to know something, revealed that one entire class of twenty-five students had no idea of the Oedipus complex—or, for that matter, who Oedipus was.

Scores on the assorted aptitude tests—especially the Scholastic Aptitude Test—have been falling for years. In 1966, high school seniors got an average of 467 points on the verbal section of the test; a decade later that figure, not exactly a stunning achievement to begin with, had fallen to 429 points. One need look no further than the textbooks, which are for the most part colorful but simplified documents, seemingly designed to grab the attention of minds raised on television and movies. It is no wonder that one survey found that more than half of the seventeen-year-old high school students in this country and over three-fourths of the thirteen year olds had not the slightest conception of what the Fifth Amendment to the United States Constitution was all about. Worse, at least half the students in both age groups believe that the President appoints members of Congress, and half the thirteen year olds believe fervently that the law forbids anyone from starting a new political party.

It does not require much imagination to realize that if students throughout America are so abysmally ignorant about their own basic laws—supposedly a major pedagogical target—their knowledge about such things as Jews and the Holocaust cannot be any greater. And indeed it is not. One of the consistent threads that runs through all the cases of anti-Semitic vandalism, on which any study has been brought to bear, is the universal *ignorance* non-Jewish young people seem to have about Jews. Almost unanimously, none of them seem to have the slightest idea of how Jews react when somebody paints a swastika on their walls, or how deeply offended they are when they become the targets of anti-Semitic epithets, or how they feel when they are reminded of the gas chambers and the concentration camps of the Holocaust.

For adults who have not looked at history textbooks in some years, the modern editions may come as something of a shock. To begin with, the texts are no longer really written, in the sense of an historian sitting down and writing, say, a general history of the United States. Instead, textbooks are "developed," meaning an often-large committee process that decides such modern educational clichés as "values" and "skills," a process which may produce homogenized, nearly-unreadable pap. The homogenization stems not only from the intrusion of educational bureaucrats, but also from pressure by a wide range of groups—the Jews among them—demanding that they be more accurately or more fully represented in the textbooks.

Serious revision of American school textbooks actually began in the late 1940s, when so-called liberal books were attacked by right-wing groups, who demanded a more "positive" view of America. Textbook publishers, highly susceptible to outside pressure (citizen-staffed local school boards make decisions on textbook purchases), dutifully rewrote history textbooks into imitations of Chamber of Commerce tracts. That wasn't enough for the more militant right-wing groups, among them the John Birch Society, which insisted that the North Korean "brainwashing" of American soldiers in Korea was due solely to a lack of "Americanism" in history textbooks. (Things got so bad that some textbook publishers agreed, under pressure by right-wing groups, to delete the story of Robin Hood; it was charged that Robin Hood was in fact a Communist, and his story was part of an insidious Communist master plan to subvert the minds of American youth.)

In the 1960s the compass suddenly swung wildly in the opposite direction, with a wide range of minority groups concluding that the textbooks either overlooked or distorted their

history. (One commonly used textbook even had a favorable
view of slavery.) So a whole new round of revisionism came to
pass, this one decreeing that the dominant impression of school
history textbooks—America had always been a white, middle-
class society—was quite wrong, and that a new view of this
country as multiracial and culturally diversified was in order.
Jewish groups, especially the Anti-Defamation League, were
deeply involved in this critique, the League producing an
extensive study in 1960 which concluded that current junior
and senior high school textbooks failed to "present a reason-
ably complete and undistorted picture of America's minority
groups." The League study, which examined forty-five school
texts in use by school districts in fifty areas of the United
States—fifteen American history texts, fifteen world history
texts, and fifteen texts on government processes and social
problems—found that they generally presented a white, Anglo-
Saxon view of American history. The study found these major
deficiencies in the textbooks:

1. A neglect of black history in Africa from 1876
onward.
2. Superficial accounts of the crucifixion of Christ,
some of them specifically linking Jews to Christ's
death.
3. A neglect of Chinese and Japanese-Americans.
4. A neglect of Hispanic-Americans.
5. Inaccurate portrayals of American Indians.

About nine years later, the American Jewish Committee carried out its own study, this one concentrating on how Jews
were portrayed in school textbooks. This study, which examined forty-five textbooks in wide use throughout the country—
nineteen of them dealt with American history and the remainder with world history—found that almost all of the books
contained errors, misconceptions, and prejudicial material

about Jews. In the case of the American history textbooks, the study found that all of them were marked by a conspicuous absence of references to anti-Semitism, bigotry, ethnic and minority groups, discrimination and prejudice. The world history textbooks had even more serious faults, ignoring Jewish history since the time of the Bible, omitting any mention of contributions by Jews to America, and virtually ignoring the Holocaust and the creation of the state of Israel.

Those formulating the study were clearly upset at what they found in the history textbooks. In *A History of the United States* (American Book Company, 1960), for example, they found: "There is no listing for the Jews in the index, no mention of the presence of Jews among the early settlers in the United States . . . no mention of any Jewish contribution." Another book, *The American Story* (D. C. Heath and Company, 1959), "makes no mention of the large Jewish migration to this country and its contribution, and also makes no mention of the Holocaust."

In a widely used world history textbook, *A Global History of Man* (Allyn and Bacon, 1962), it was found that "The text devotes half a sentence to the fact that six million Jews were murdered during World War II. This is referred to as one of the costs of the war." Another widely used world history textbook, *The World Story* (D. C. Heath and Company, 1963), concluded its brief narrative on the history of the early Hebrews by saying: "Their [the prophets'] teachings, together with the earlier records of the Hebrews, were later put together to form the Old Testament of the Christian Bible." (Which, of course, is quite wrong, aside from being irrelevant.)

The Anti-Defamation League study mentioned earlier also found a number of bothersome references to Jews in the textbooks, including several that flatly blamed the Jews for the crucifixion of Christ and others that seriously distort the history of Jews during the Middle Ages. Consider this breezy excerpt from one textbook:

Jews, however, saw nothing wrong in doing so
[lending money for interest] and thus they became the
first great money-lenders of Europe. This was one
reason why they were unpopular and were often per-
secuted in Christian communities. Kings sometimes
tried to protect Jews against violence, partly, no
doubt, because they might sometime be a source of
obtaining money for a king who was hard up. Often,
however, Kings felt obliged to join their people in
persecuting the Jews.

The League study took note of a 1949 analysis by the American
Council on Education, which sharply criticized how minorities
were treated in history textbooks, taking some comfort in the
fact that the texts no longer referred to Jews as a "race." But
there was less comfort to be detected when the League got
around to taking a close look at how Jews were being depicted
in textbooks eleven years after the Council analysis. Actually,
there was not much to look at: for all intents and purposes, the
Jews were invisible as far as the textbooks were concerned. Out
of sixteen American history textbooks that were examined, the
study found that only one even bothered to discuss the Jews of
contemporary America; another textbook never even mentions Jews, despite a short section about Nazi concentration
camps. And in sixteen social problems textbooks, eleven say
nothing about Nazi mistreatment of Jews; of the other five, one
simply states: "A generation now living knows that thousands
of people were killed in gas chambers because they were a
minority group in Germany."

Since the American Jewish Committee study on the same
subject took place about ten years later, it might be reasonable
to expect some improvement, especially considering the agita-
tion by minority groups for a more balanced presentation in
school textbooks. True, some minorities—particularly the
blacks and Hispanic-Americans—did notice a marked improve-

ment, but the Jews were still largely invisible or distorted. As the Committee noted in some pain during its 1969 study: "While a number of groups in the general community have intensified their demands for a more balanced portrayal of the life, culture, and history of ethnic minorities in American society, any number of instances of inaccuracy, inadequacy, and imbalance in the portrayal of Jewish history and ideas have been allowed to go unchecked in numerous history and social studies textbooks..."

The American Jewish Committee's concern led to the publication of a detailed set of "publisher guidelines" to end the distortions and omissions, which amounted to a guide for the authors of textbooks. It listed fifty-seven books, written by both Jewish and non-Jewish authors, covering all phases of world and American Jewish history; the hint, presumably, being that there were plenty of tools to work with if the authors wanted to present a truly balanced picture of American minority groups, especially the Jews.

The only possible conclusion is that neither they nor the textbook publishers saw any such necessity, for during the great textbook revolution of the 1970s, when some sort of mass conciousness-raising took place on the role of American minorities and their portrayal in textbooks, the Jews again seemed invisible. By 1974, some of the new textbooks being produced bore as much resemblance to their predecessors as the space shuttle does to the Wright brothers' first airplane. One such work, a triumph of graphic design—a significant consideration in this television age—devoted large chunks of space to the history of the civil rights movement, life in urban ghettos (including reproduction of part of the sheet music of the rock and roll song "Downtown") and the treatment of Japanese-Americans. Other books suddenly discovered women, devoting large sections to women garment workers, women pacifists and even women politicians. (Franklin Roosevelt's Secretary of Labor Frances Perkins is pictured shaking hands with steelworkers.) Other textbooks produced during the same period featured equally startling revisionism, especially in their portrayals of Hispanic-Americans, Puerto Ricans, Indians and blacks.

And where were the Jews? They were in the new textbooks, but in forms hardly different from the way they had always been portrayed, which is to say hardly at all. Many world history textbooks continued the puzzling practice of introducing the Jews during the crucifixion, then moving them off the stage of history until World War II. Complaints by Jewish groups to publishers about the portrayal (or non-portrayal) of Jews have met with spotty results; some are receptive to suggestions for changes, too many are not. (The Anti-Defamation League estimates that it receives an average of one complaint each week concerning the portrayal of Jews in school textbooks).

Jewish groups have been especially unsuccessful in their attempts to get more information about the Holocaust into textbooks. The Holocaust, in particular, is a matter of critical importance to these groups, since it is not only an important part of Jewish heritage, but also because for some years Jews have regarded teaching of the Holocaust an important resource in combating anti-Semitism. The theory is that the more people know about the Holocaust, the less likely they will be to be anti-Semitic, since the Holocaust represents the inevitable result of anti-Semitism left unchecked. There is a good deal of merit to this theory; but again, like so much else connected with Jews, the Holocaust seems invisible in our school's history textbooks.

By 1979, despite the popularity of "The Holocaust" television series, that subject remained very nearly unmentioned in textbooks. Jewish groups became increasingly upset about this omission, and the Anti-Defamation League carried out an extensive study of how the Holocaust was being portrayed to millions of American schoolchildren. In sum, the study found that it was hardly being portrayed at all, and those textbooks that did write about the subject handled it inadequately.

The 1979 study bears some examination, for it not only concerns material still in use in classrooms today, but also because it goes to the very heart of why anti-Semitic vandalism is a crime mostly committed by students. The study examined in detail forty-three textbooks, representing virtually all the major textbook publishers in this country. Out of the forty-three books, only five devoted as much as forty lines to the Holocaust. In the words of University of Arizona Professor Glenn S. Pate, who carried out the study:

> *Most books give a few facts of what happened without any serious attempt to explain why the events occurred. In general, they mention that Hitler hated the Jews and blamed them for the loss of World War I and the economic depression. Not one book makes any reference to historical anti-Semitism in Europe, and only one author indicates that the Nazis intended to kill more Jews than they actually did. . . . Even the five texts offering the most extensive coverage were found wanting.*

A close reading of Pate's study is a sobering experience, for it reveals beyond question that American junior and senior high school students are being taught virtually nothing about the Holocaust. As Pate notes, "Talk with high school or college students in an effort to plumb their understanding of the Holocaust. Their ignorance is appalling."

True—and it should be noted that it is not their fault. The plain fact is that on this crucial aspect of education of our modern youth, the schools have failed, and failed miserably, largely because the textbooks with which the teachers work are plainly inadequate on the subject. Not all teachers rely heavily on textbooks for teaching history and/or social studies, but most do, so it is the textbooks where concern must be focused. And to understand how deficient those textbooks are, take a close look at the forty-seven books examined in the Pate study.

Of those forty-seven books, twenty-seven do not give even a separate paragraph to the Holocaust. Among the books that devote even minimal attention to the Holocaust is one of the more popular high school history textbooks, *Freedom's Trail* (Houghton Miffflin Co., 1979). Here is the total coverage in that book on the subject:

> *All people in Nazi Germany had to follow the orders of Hitler's government. Those who spoke out against the dictatorship were thrown into jail. Some were forced to leave the country. Others were even killed. German Jews were blamed for all the country's troubles. At first, Jews were denied any rights under the law. Then their property was taken away. Finally the German Jews were forced into concentration camps. The same thing happened to Jews in other European countries that Hitler attacked and conquered. Eventually, six million Jews (and many other Europeans) went to their deaths in those camps. About 250,000 Jews managed to escape from Europe. Many came to the United States. They included artists, writers and scientists.*

There is hardly a single redeeming feature to praise in this excerpt, and it should be emphasized that it represents considerably more coverage than found in at least half the major school textbooks now in use. It is difficult to understand what comprehension any student—especially an average student— could derive from the excerpt quoted above; there is a total dearth of any explanation about Hitler's obsession with creating a "master race," or his efforts to build a "new social order." The argument might be made that this lack could be compensated by the teachers—but teachers have their own problems in this area. Aside from a lack of interest on the part of their superiors, there is also a pronounced lack of good curricula on the subject, a reflection of the fact that for some years the Holocaust was a taboo subject at educational conferences. (One argument some educators make privately is that teaching the Holocaust is fraught with dangers, notably, teaching it without traumatizing students. Less discussed is the feeling of many educators that the Holocaust is a "Jewish" subject, and therefore out of the educational mainstream.)

This squeamishness is reflected in textbooks, only two of which (among the previously-cited list of forty-seven most-used) describe the concentration and extermination camps. Indeed, thirty-nine textbooks do not name a single concentration camp, and only four even mention Auschwitz. Not one textbook mentions the Warsaw Ghetto, and thirty-two of the forty-seven books have no reference to the Nuremberg war crimes trials. Judging by the textbooks' presentations, any student might logically conclude that the Nazis' drive against the Jews just sort of happened suddenly, then was quickly over. More broadly, it is impossible to imagine that any student could possibly reach an understanding of the Holocaust by reading only the school textbooks.

Aside from the anti-Semitic vandalism committed by young people, there is one other interesting indication of the paucity of students' knowledge of the Holocaust. In April 1978, following presentation of "The Holocaust" series on television, the American Jewish Committee commissioned a viewer reaction poll on the programs, in an attempt to determine their impact on a broad spectrum of Americans representing diverse age groups and attitudes. While the poll had all the normal problems such sociological investigations represent, it nevertheless had a number of interesting results of some relevance to this study. One was a question to viewers on how well informed they regarded themselves on Hitler's treatment of the Jews before they watched the program. In the eighteen to twenty-nine age group, the poll reported that fully 79 percent of the respondents considered themselves either "poorly informed" or only "fairly well informed." And on another question, this one asking if respondents thought that the Nazis treated other people the same way they treated Jews, 65 percent of the respondents aged eighteen to twenty-nine believed, or weren't sure, that the treatment was the same.

The figures are obviously not definitive, but they do indicate a shocking lack of knowledge about the Holocaust. Why has it happened? There are no easy explanations. It is not a conspiracy, nor can it be argued that the subject is too depressing for young minds to handle (textbooks are full of depressing things, including American slavery). And by the same token, it cannot be argued that textbooks seek to avoid the dark side of history. For many years, American history textbooks presented only a sanguine view of American history, but now they include such shames as the internment of Japanese-Americans, slavery, and the deliberate destruction of the American Indians. No, the reason is much broader than that: an inability by the people in the American education establishment to understand that the Holocaust has any relevance to history at all, much less American history. They are guilty not only of a terrible blindness, but a sheer inability to understand current events—terrible acts of inhumanity, racial genocide, prejudice, discrimination—which are there for them to see every day in the newspapers and on television. How they expect their students to understand today without the lessons of the past is a mystery.

This is, to be sure, a pessimistic account, and in the interest of fairness it should be noted that there is at least one bright spot. That concerns a unique effort by an interreligious group of Catholic and Jewish leaders to remove anti-Semitic prejudice from Catholic teaching materials. This largely-unheralded effort has centered on major studies involving the

American Jewish Committee and three prominent Catholic universities—Pro Deo University in Rome, Louvain University in Belgium, and St. Louis University in this country. Generally, the Catholic-Jewish research teams have concluded that:

1. Christian churches are still reluctant to face the implications of Hitler's murder of six million Jews.
2. There is widespread indifference toward the continued existence of Israel.
3. Too many Christians still regard Jews as "soulless."
4. The stereotype of Jews as obsessed with money persists.
5. In Europe, many Catholics still believe in such things as Jewish ritual murders and similar blood libels.

A good deal of these problems are still reflected in Catholic school textbooks, and even though both Catholic and Jewish groups say there has been noted improvement in the perception of Jews in Catholic textbooks—and to a much more limited extent in Protestant texts, as well—there is still a problem with how those texts handle the Holocaust. Some progress is being made, mainly because there continues to be a renewed effort by the American Catholic hierarchy to remove sources of tension between the Catholic and Jewish communities. The Catholics have a Secretariat for Christian-Jewish Relations, and a decade ago the Roman Catholic bishops in this country published *Guidelines for Catholic-Jewish Relations,* part of the major effort inspired by reforms of the Second Vatican Council.

Under Catholic guidelines, each diocese must have a local committee on Christian-Jewish relations, although the effectiveness of these committees varies widely, depending on the individual strength of each committee and its chairman. No similar organization exists within the Protestant hierarchy, partially a reflection of the fact that Protestantism is less structured than the Catholic Church, and also because the matter of relations with the Jewish community receives somewhat lower priority. (But while the Catholics in the United States have done much to eliminate tensions with the Jewish community, there is still much work to be done overseas, where Spanish Catholics continue to venerate the memory of Domingo del Val, a choirboy allegedly crucified in the thirteenth century by Jews angry over his hymn-singing; or Austria, where a gruesome set of statues, commemorating the alleged murder by Jews of a small boy, were finally removed.)

Thus far, we have been examining school textbooks in an attempt to discover why young people are so appallingly ignorant about the Jews and the Holocaust. Implicitly, our examination stopped short of college and university textbooks, and while the idea that ignorance stops at the university gates might be tempting to believe, the sad fact is that anyone who moves beyond a high school education has no guarantee that higher education cares any more about Jews and the Holocaust than does an average American high school. This statement would seem, on the face of it, to be quite wrong. There are courses on the Holocaust in a number of colleges and universities, and certainly the more specialized courses on history, given in greater depth, should adequately treat the subject. But that is not quite so.

In the first place, while courses on the history of the Holocaust and its assorted implications have proliferated in the past few years, most of them are at institutions of higher learning with substantial Jewish enrollments. This gives rise to the suspicion that the courses have been instituted as some form of equal-time academia in connection with special black studies programs, women's studies, and the like—which then renders the subject just another example of the kind of ethnic gratification that has cheapened so much of higher education.

It is an illusion to believe that college-level textbooks are on the whole any better than junior or senior high school textbooks in explaining the history of the Jews and the Holocaust. One standard college-level textbook, for example, *The Origins of Modern Germany*, by Geoffrey Barraclough—a noted scholar on the subject—has been a staple of college and university courses for over twenty-five years. The text, which is supposed to be the history of Germany from 800 to 1939, never mentions Jews (despite the obvious impact Jews have had on the development of modern Germany), nor is there any mention of anti-Semitism (despite that phenomenon's impact on Germany's history, most notably the Nazi era). How any standard text on the history of Germany could fail to include both these historical facts is a matter of some astonishment, but no less astonishment must greet another standard college textbook, *The Columbia History of the World*, a collaborative effort by forty professors that opens at the beginning of the universe and ends in the 1960s. A grand total of three sentences in this magisterial work deal with anti-Semitism and Nazi racial policies, and another three sentences discuss the Holocaust. This is hard to understand; its parallel would be a history of the American South that failed to explain slavery.

Jews are also nearly invisible even in some of the specialized works on Germany and the Nazi era. For example, *Hitler: A Study in Tyranny*, a long-standard work on the Nazi leader's life by Alan Bullock, devotes only about 2 percent of the entire book to Jews and anti-Semitism—an extraordinary statistic, considering the fact that anti-Semitism was a force that dominated Hitler's life and political career. Or take British historian A. J. P. Taylor's *The Origins of the Second World War*, which decides that Hitler was no more wicked than any other statesman of his era (this judgment would be of some interest to Winston Churchill), and that Hitler was guilty of a "terrifying liberalism." Taylor goes on to assert in his respected study, used in many modern history courses, that Hitler's "inspiration" was the pulp literature produced by Karl

May, who around the turn of the century churned out potboil-
ers about American cowboys and Indians.

This assertion, of course, affords deep insight into Hitler's
political ideas, to say nothing of anti-Semitism and the Jews,
and its insight can be compared with the insight afforded by
several ventures into Hitler and psychohistory, a popular
adjunct to college-level modern history courses. One such venture, Rudolph Binion's *Hitler Among the Germans*, claims
that Hitler's mother had been "traumatized" by the deaths of
three of her earlier children. She "incestuously" breast-fed
Hitler "passionately," in the process passing her trauma to him.
Additionally, Hitler's mother died shortly after being treated
by a Jewish doctor, an experience that compelled Hitler to hate
Jews. (This theory leaves unexplained the question of why
Hitler hated all Jews, not just Jewish doctors.)

Unfortunately, all this takes place at a time when the Jews have
been experiencing a pronounced indifference. One of the forms
that indifference has taken is the trivialization of the Holocaust. Contemporary rhetoric has the distressing habit of not
only trivializing the very word—"holocaust of the slums" is
among the currently popular phrases—but also universalizing
it; there is the habit of equating Auschwitz and Hiroshima, just
to cite one example.

Taken as a whole, the treatment of Jews in lower and
higher education would serve as effective refutation to the old
canard of history always being written by the victors. No
greater crime can be perpetrated against a people than to deny
them their history. It is fair to say that something very much
like that has come to pass, at least among the younger generation of this country; there is no escaping the fact that only a tiny
percentage of the junior and senior high school students in this
country have any concrete idea about who the Jews are and
their history.

That fact serves to dishonor many things, not the least of

them the memory of the famous historian Simon Dubonow who, as the Nazis took him from the Riga Ghetto in 1941 to be gassed at Buchenwald, called out: "Brothers! Write down everything you see and hear. Keep a record of it all!"

Dubonow's injunction has to a great extent been fulfilled, but as he never could have imagined, it may do little good if no one is listening.

CHAPTER SEVEN

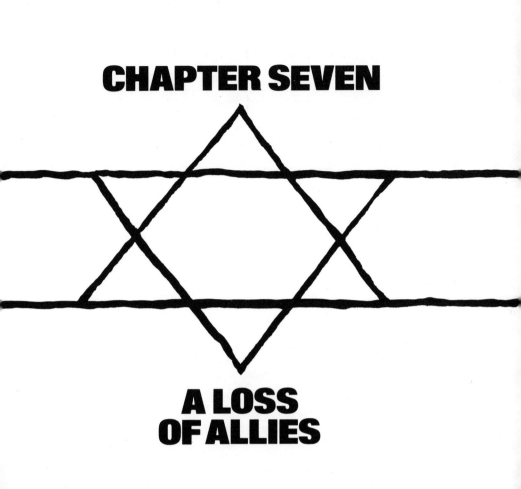

A LOSS
OF ALLIES

*Every Jew in America over thirty years old
knows another Jew that hates Negroes,
and if we hate Jews, that's just even, baby.*

Dick Gregory

*You Jews have created one eternal legend—
that of Judas.*

Josef Stalin

In the spring of 1967 the irrepressible Thomas P. Hoving, then director of the Metropolitan Museum of Art in New York City, announced that the museum would hold a show on Harlem. In his typically flamboyant style, Hoving noted that the show would have no paintings or sculpture, but would be "thirteen-room, multi-media environment of sight and sound, including photomurals, film projections, videotapes of Harlem street sounds and the voices of Duke Ellington, Langston Hughes, Malcolm X, and the king of soul songs, James Brown... [which] had nothing to do with art in the narrow sense—but everything to do with this museum and its evolving role and purpose in what we hope is its emerging position as a positive force in modern society."

This somewhat breathless announcement gave no hint of trouble to come, but that's about all the exhibit—named "Harlem on My Mind" when it finally opened the following year—wound up bringing, not only to Hoving and the museum, but to the city administration and the black and Jewish communities. Indeed, "Harlem on My Mind" was an event that coalesced, seemingly, all the black-white and Jewish-black tensions that had been simmering for a long time. And it is as good a starting place as any to examine how blacks and Jews, the supposedly inseparable allies during the great civil rights struggles, became estranged (and on some levels bitter enemies). Or, put another way, how the American Jewish community somehow lost what had been regarded as its most important ally. It will also tell a great deal about how the Jews lost their other great ally in this country—the left political movement—since the two events overlap to a certain extent; they also share some common dynamics.

How all that came about is a matter of some importance to American Jews, because for all the talk about "Jewish power" and the supposed clout of a "Jewish lobby," the fact is that Jews constitute only about 3 percent of the American population, a figure that is steadily shrinking because of a low Jewish birthrate. Historically, Jews have made the most progress in this country when their concerns—under the headings of justice, equality, brotherhood and freedom—were linked with the hopes and aspirations of other minority groups. The civil rights struggle, in which blacks and Jews found common cause, is just one example. Another would be the informal alliance between Catholics and Jews during the presidential campaign of John Kennedy, when many Catholics, upset over the anti-Catholicism that candidacy caused in many parts of the country, began to get an idea of what anti-Semitism was all about. But in the social upheavals of the 1960s, all those alliances seemed to be coming apart all at once.

The most serious event was the rupture between blacks and Jews, an occasion which returns us to the "Harlem on My Mind" exhibition. It is difficult to imagine anything that did more to sum up, in one incident, all that was wrong with black–Jewish relations. The first problem, it turned out, was the very name chosen for the exhibition—"Harlem on My Mind." It came from an old tune by Irving Berlin. Black groups immediately objected on the grounds that using a title taken from a song composed by a white Jewish songwriter, to represent the history of a black community, demonstrated condescending paternalism. Perhaps, but that was only the beginning of the controversy. Black groups also objected to the whole idea of the exhibition, partially because Harlem community leaders were not consulted about how the exhibit was put together, and also because Harlem artists and sculptors were not represented. (At the same time, patrons of the museum from the white establishment regarded the show as a carnival, and the main spokesman for the establishment, *The New York Times*, sniffed that the whole idea was "an exercise in social evangelism.")

Evangelism to whom? Certainly not to the Jews, who discovered that the exhibition's catalog, a 255-page volume that was being printed as a mass-market paperback, contained some serious anti-Semitic slurs. The catalog's introduction read, in part:

> *Behind every hurdle that the Afro-American has yet to jump, stands the Jew who had already cleared it. Jewish shopkeepers are the only remaining "survivors" in the expanding black ghettos... the lack of competition in the area allows the already-exploited blacks to be further exploited by Jews... Psychologically speaking, blacks may find that anti-Jewish sentiments place them, for once, within a majority. ..our contempt for the Jews makes us feel more completely American in sharing a national prejudice.*

Almost unanimously, the Jewish community reacted in fury and demanded that the catalog be withdrawn. New York City Mayor John Lindsay announced that he would not allow any "racial or religious slurs" in his administration, a pledge which did not seem to have much impact on Hoving, who answered criticism expressed by the Jewish community by saying, "If the truth hurts, then so be it." Jewish leaders became even more infuriated, and Hoving—claiming that he was "under unbelievable pressure, so great I don't think one person could stand it"—offered an apology, plus a disclaimer to be stuck inside the catalog from the author of the introduction saying that "any racist overtones which were inferred from the passages quoted out of context, are regrettable." That didn't do much to bank the fire, and Hoving wound up withdrawing the catalog from circulation (16,000 had already been sold), then announcing that the controversy was "distracting the public from judging the exhibition on its merits."

What "merits" Hoving meant were hard to fathom. The blacks were angry because in their view the exhibition presented a distortion of life in Harlem; the white establishment was angry because their museum had been turned into a circus; and the Jews were angry because the exhibition's catalog contained gross anti-Semitism (not to mention Hoving's apparent conviction that such anti-Semitism was wrong only to the extent that it caused a controversy which disturbed the esthetically placid waters of the museum). It was the anti-Semitic aspect of the whole affair that was most disturbing, not only because it had actually happened, but also because neither city officials nor the museum director nor the leadership of the black community seemed to understand how biased it was.

"Harlem on My Mind" was, in an important sense, a microcosm of everything that was wrong with black-white (and more specifically, black-Jewish) relations at an important turning point in modern American history. The civil rights revolution was over, and black priorities were changing. It was now time for blacks to move into the economic mainstream, to consolidate their victories in the legislative arena with new community efforts to gain their "slice of the pie"—time to convert the apparatus that had given them the Civil Rights Act into machinery that would give them economic freedom, as well. That is why they were so deeply offended by the "Harlem on My Mind" exhibition, in their eyes a patronizing reminder of a part of their history they wanted to put behind them. But there was a more significant clue to the future course of events. The deafening silence by almost all the leaders of the black community toward the anti-Semitism in the catalog of the exhibition demonstrated quite clearly that the blacks were intent on striking out on their own in their new direction—a drive that no longer required the help of the Jews. Indeed, as we shall see, the Jews came to be seen by much of the black leadership not as former allies who were no longer useful, but often as outright enemies to the hopes and aspirations of blacks.

"Harlem on My Mind" took place during a time of fundamental change in the thinking of black leaders, during which they sought to remove the black community from the coalition of labor, liberals and Jews that had won the civil rights struggle for them. Their theory, best expressed by the "black power" slogan, argued that blacks had to withdraw from any coalitions with whites—especially Jews—and form themselves into a cohesive bloc. As long as the blacks moved toward economic equality, the argument ran, their drive would be subject to manipulation by white forces that were not nearly so delighted by blacks demanding economic equality as they were about blacks demanding civil rights. Civil rights, after all, had no direct impact on the white coalition outside the south, since it had no economic impact. This argument particularly concerned the Jews, since many black leaders felt the Jews would do the most to obstruct any black demands for economic equality; it was argued that since the Jews dominated so many of the professions and civil service—precisely the targets blacks had in mind for their new drive—the Jews would fight to maintain their economic dominance.

Thus, "black power" was born, and it turned out to be a tragic misreading of American political realities. None of the three main ethnic groups that had won important footholds in the American mainstream since before and after World War II—the Jews, Irish and Italians—ever made the mistake of demanding "Jewish power" or "Irish power" or "Italian power."

They learned, the hard way, that the secret of urban capitalism was that ethnic minorities had to work with each other, at least to the extent of capturing the wellsprings of the Democratic Party, which gave the ethnic minorities real political power, especially the Irish. The black leadership came to be dominated by the young firebrands of the civil rights struggle who failed to learn this lesson, and once they removed themselves from the liberal coalition, that coalition began to fracture. In turn, this fracturing has had the most profound effect on American politics since it was, to a large extent, responsible for the rise of the conservative opposition, which had been captured by the new Republican Party. The black leadership also made a second mistake: forging an alliance between American black nationalism and Third World movements, an alliance that not only has gained nothing for American blacks, but has also tended to exacerbate the already strained relations of blacks and whites. (And it also put them in a deep hole: without allies, the blacks proved susceptible to a vigorous counterattack by the conservatives.)

Shortly after World War II, blacks and Jews joined together in a joint attack on discrimination, not because they necessarily had common interests but because they had common enemies. And while the respective leaders of both groups talked of common cause and brotherhood, on a more personal level, especially in the cities, blacks and Jews were not communicating very well. In fact, when they were required to deal with each other in day-to-day issues such as rents, or credit, or residential integration, or who was sitting next to whom in the classroom, the blacks and Jews had hardly anything to say to each other. Blacks, while accepting the help Jews offered them in the pursuit of civil rights, nevertheless did not quite understand such phenomena as moderately wealthy Jews, with large suburban homes and late-model automobiles, talking about "the poor" or "the downtrodden." Blacks and Jews really were talking to each other only at the leadership level; the vast majority of Jews and blacks lived in totally different worlds.

There is a common assumption among Jews that anti-Jewish hostility among the black community did not begin until the late 1960s. Actually, there was considerable tension between the two groups long before, beginning in the 1930s. In the words of one noted study of the time, the tension was caused by "unequal status, friction-generating contacts between merchants and consumers, between landlords and tenants, between housewives and domestics." The Reverend Adam Clayton Powell, Jr. put it more succinctly in 1935 when, following riots in Harlem, he announced: "The Jews own New York, the Irish run it, the Negroes enjoy it." As historical analysis, Powell's summation was quite wrong, of course: the Jews didn't own very much in that Depression year, an Italian named La Guardia was mayor and, as the riots in Harlem demonstrated, the Negroes weren't exactly dancing in the streets. Still, Powell's phrase passed into popular mythology, and continues to be stated to this day, in slightly revised form.

Black nationalism was in nascent form during that period; during World War II, the black press occasionally featured strong anti-Semitic writings, usually along the line that Hitler had done at least one right thing—"put the Jews in their place." But that was the exception; almost all black leaders, Powell among them, strongly condemned anti-Semitism. ("The Jew doesn't wrong us any more and probably much less than any other group," Powell wrote at one point.) After the war, black and Jewish groups joined in a formidable coalition for the great civil rights battles. Jews played a prominent role at such agencies as the NAACP, and in 1950, four years before the United States Supreme Court's historic 1954 decision outlawing school segregation, Jewish groups had filed court briefs seeking to strike down the doctrine of "separate but equal." The Jewish role in the vanguard of the civil rights movement reached its height during the struggles in the South. Jews were beaten or jailed in such battlegrounds as Selma and Mississippi, and two Jews were among the civil rights workers murdered in Mississippi in 1964.

Judged in one way, it seems extraordinary in retrospect that this pronounced Jewish involvement in the civil rights struggles did not serve to immunize Jews against black anti-Semitism. But some more perceptive observers, notably Dr. Kenneth Clark, the prominent psychologist and leading analyst of black-white relations, discovered that lurking beneath that surface were the old Jewish-black tensions—and a growing resentment among blacks about the role of Jews in the civil rights movement. As early as 1958, Clark detected trouble. For some years, he noted, blacks increasingly were focusing on Jews as symbols of their problems with whites, since Jews were the most visible whites they knew. It was perfectly fine, Clark said, for Jews to be talking about greater civil rights for Negroes, but the vast majority of blacks were more concerned about such things as a 1946 incident, when Jewish housewives in the Bronx were accused of holding black domestics in virtual peonage. And, Clark acidly noted, a much-heralded 1945 conference on "Judaism and Race Relations," held by the Central Conference of American Rabbis, was hardly impressive to blacks. "The question arises," Clark said, "as to what Jews and others would think if a conference of Negro leaders were to devote a round table to the problem of Jews in the United States."

The fact is that Jewish community leaders chose to overlook (or sometimes failed to recognize) the signs of the black community's estrangement from American Jews. Also unrecognized was the rise of black nationalists within the black leadership and the growing militancy of the younger generation of black leaders, for whom such things as civil rights marches were dead history. True, the most prominent black leader, Martin Luther King, Jr., was publicly committed to a continuing alliance with the Jewish community (King firmly suppressed any expression of anti-Semitism within his movement), but King was not speaking for the new generation of militants rising to power in the black community, the H. Rap

Browns, the Stokely Carmichaels, and the leaders of such groups as the Black Panthers.

The explosion came in 1966, when an anti-Semitic outbreak seemingly occurred throughout the entire spectrum of black organizations. There were several sparks that ignited this outbreak, the most significant being the publication in the *Liberator* (a small but influential publication by the Afro-American Institute of New York, that was something of a bible for the black intelligentsia), of an article called "Semitism in Black Ghettos." It charged that blacks were being systematically exploited by merchants and landlords, most of them Jewish. In language that became familiar in subsequent black extremist literature, the article said:

> *What the brothers know, is what they see: the landlord, the corner butcher, the grocer, and the cat from the credit or collection agency. In most cases, these cats are Jewish. It follows that the first line of resentment against slum housing, inferior grades of meat, spoiled food and vegetables is directed against the* living person *who perpetuates these conditions. In general, it is that segment of the Jewish population which had grown rich exploiting black Americans for decades. [Emphasis in original.]*

Ossie Davis and James Baldwin resigned from the advisory board of the publication in protest over this article, but it was a gesture lost in the wave of militancy that swept across the black community. In that same year, the Congress of Racial Equality began to betray unmistakable symptoms that it had also succumbed to militancy—and in the process had turned bitterly anti-Semitic. The Mount Vernon, New York, chapter of CORE, locked in a nasty fight with the local school board over school integration, charged that Jews on the board were deliberately sabotaging efforts at integration. At one point a CORE leader charged at a public meeting: "Hitler made one mistake—he didn't kill enough of you!" CORE headquarters suspended the Mount Vernon chapter. But soon after, leadership of this influential civil rights organization, the second largest such group in the country, was taken over by militants. (By 1973, CORE director Roy Innis was doing such things as visiting Uganda, where he praised Idi Amin and expressed admiration for the dictator's plan to erect a statue of Adolf Hitler.)

Innis—who at one point said that "we have no records to prove if Hitler was a friend or an enemy of black people"—was only one of the militants who rose to prominence at that time. Another, Ron Karenga, head of the California-based US (United Slaves), called Christ a "dead Jew," a rhetoric exceeded by Charles X. Kenyatta, head of the Mau-Mau black nationalist organization, who blamed the Jews for the deaths of John Kennedy, Christ, Malcolm X, plus the congressional revocation of the seat held by Representative Adam Clayton Powell, Jr. "The slaves of black Afro-America thank Hitler," Kenyatta said at one point, "for destroying six million Jews. They hope he will reappear in America!"

The year 1966 also marked two important developments in the rise of black militancy. One was the election of militant Stokely Carmichael as chairman of the Student Non-Violent Coordinating Committee—Martin Luther King's prime shock troops for the civil rights struggle in the South. In the halcyon days of the struggle, the committee included hundreds of Jewish volunteers. But no more; Carmichael and his successor, H. Rap Brown, converted SNCC into a "black power" organization, and only a year later the group had also acquired a pronounced anti-Semitism. The organization's newsletter, in an article on "the Palestinian problem," was replete with anti-Semitic and anti-Israel statements, including a cartoon showing a hand marked with a Star of David and a dollar sign tightening a rope around the necks of Gamal Nasser and Muhammad Ali. (It turned out that most of the material was lifted straight from Palestine Liberation Organization propaganda publications.)

Theodore Bikel, one of SNCC's most prominent supporters, resigned in protest, but one can only wonder whether Bikel and other prominent Jewish supporters of the organization had been asleep up to this point. They could not have failed to notice a highly-publicized article Carmichael wrote for the *New York Review of Books*, around the time he became chairman of SNCC, in which he analyzed black "resentment" toward Jews by claiming, "It was . . . the exploitation by Jewish landlords and merchants which first created black resentment toward Jews—not Judaism." They also must have missed the David Susskind television program which featured three leading "black power" advocates, who spent most of their time complaining about "Jewish exploitation" of blacks.

However much Jews might have been shocked by this sudden explosion of anti-Semitism, a fair number of black leaders were not surprised, for they had known a fact many Jewish leaders had chosen to ignore: anti-Semitism was endemic in the black communities and it remained only for the new generation of black leadership, particularly the black nationalists, to exploit it. As James Baldwin observed, "Georgia has its Negroes; Harlem has the Jew." That was Baldwin's way of trying to explain how the Jews had become the scapegoats for the black frustrations following the high hopes raised by civil rights legislation and the "war on poverty," expectations that were soon to be dashed. Many blacks became convinced that the Jews were not only primarily responsible for their frustrated goal of a new economic order for the black community, but that the Jews were also responsible for the white condescension the new generation of blacks found so objectionable. Plainly, blacks resented the steady stream of "advice" on how to solve their "problems," in their view an onerous burden placed on them by a white culture that was dominated by Jews. This resentment was best summed up by one of the most influential books ever published within the black community. Harold Cruse's *Crisis of the Negro Intellectual*, which said at one point:

> *In fact, the main job of researching and interpreting the American Negro has been taken over by the Jewish intelligentsia to the extent where it is practically impossible for the Negro to deal with the Anglo-Saxon majority in this country unless he first comes to the Jews to get his instructions.*

Cruse's book, published in 1967, had immense impact throughout the black leadership, and it signaled the dominance of the black intelligentsia movement by cultural separatists and black nationalists. It also signaled a new militancy, reflected not only in strident rhetoric, but a wave of violence that struck America's urban ghettos; by the summer of 1967, there had been riots in a dozen cities. The violence featured a number of anti-Semitic aspects, including destruction of Jewish-owned businesses, and calls by militants to "get the Jew." (In a New York rally, H. Rap Brown talked of "Uncle Sam and Uncle Shylock," and a new black slang word, "Goldberg," appeared, meaning Jews.)

The riots caused President Johnson to appoint the Kerner Commission to study the problem of black-white relations in this country, and it was only after the committee was appointed that Johnson realized that it did not have a single Jew as a member—although Jewish businesses were the prime victims of the violence. He hurriedly appointed a Jew as the commission's director, and the group went on to make the not very startling discovery that America was moving toward two societies, one black and one white. That was precisely the goal of the new militant black leadership, best reflected in one of the more disturbing anti-Semitic incidents during this period, the New York City school troubles of 1968 and 1969.

The troubles arose from the conviction among a number of black separatists that black children did not succeed as well as children of other ethnic and racial groups because Jews dominated the teaching profession and the educational establishment. This conviction led to such developments as the creation of the Afro-American Teachers Association in New York City, which charged that Jewish teachers were "educationally castrating" and "mentally poisoning" black students, as part of a master plan to ensure that the black students failed—as the education establishment had been insisting they would fail for so many years.

This ultimately led to the idea of "special demonstration schools" that would be staffed by black teachers who "understood" the special problems of black students. To mollify the militants, three "experimental" schools were set up under the control of black-dominated governing boards—who immediately clashed with the powerful Teachers Union when several white teachers were fired. The union went on strike, and the resulting controversy soon developed into a test of wills between blacks and whites, with strong anti-Semitic overtones.

Given the black militant's desire to take over the levers of power, the clash was almost inevitable, and it was equally inevitable that anti-Semitism would become the most prominent feature, since both the union and the educational establishment had long been dominated by Jews. (The educational professions were one of the most traditional upward routes for immigrant Jews and their descendants in New York City.) No one, however, could have anticipated how ugly the anti-Semitism would become: a poem attributed to a fourteen-year-old black student and read over a local radio station said, "Hey Jewboy, with the yarmulke on your head/you paleface Jewboy, I wish you were dead." (Another black student, in a second radio show said, "Hitler did not make enough lampshades of you Jews.") Some of the ugliest anti-Semitism was produced by one of the most prominent black nationalists, playwright LeRoi Jones (who later changed his name to Imamu Amiri Baraka). Baraka, who dominated the black community organizations in Newark, New Jersey, in a 1966

poem had signaled his deep antipathy toward Jews. The poem
referred to "slimey bellies of the owner Jews" and "jewlady's
mouth." Another Baraka poem called Jews "little arty bas-
tards." These poems were no aberrations on Baraka's part; he
has consistently been among the most anti-Semitic of the black
nationalist leaders. At one point he had a traveling troupe of
actors called Spirit House Movers and Players that gave performances at various schools. In one performance at a Harlem
school, the performers delivered anti-Semitic diatribes, casti-
gating blacks for accepting slavery and for "going to white,
dirty, Jewish-owned bars." (In a 1972 book that collected
Baraka's essays, there were a number of anti-Semitic slurs,
including a claim by the author that black history was "Cohen-
edited Negro history.")

What Baraka and the other black militants and nationalists exhibit is a demonstration of classic anti-Semitism—
scapegoatism, blaming Jews almost exclusively for the problems of American blacks. It is unquestionably true that some
Jews exploit blacks in the ghettos, but that's not because
they're Jews; they exploit, not because of their religion, but
because they're exploiters. And it is also true to say that black
children were, and have been, victims of the American educational system that is not educating *anybody* very well, least of
all minority students. Teachers bear a large part of the blame,
to be sure; with no idea of discipline and trained in such
nonsense as "educating the whole child," they have failed to
realize that such clichés have no meaning to kids from broken
homes in Harlem. The central tragedy for the black leadership
lies in a failure to realize that the failure of the educational
system has almost nothing to do with the religion of those
running the system; by the same token, exploitation of blacks
economically is a social, not a religious, phenomenon.

In the end, black militance failed, not because of its anti-
Semitism, but because it finally could not deliver the goods to
the black community; blacks soon turned away from a militancy that while rhetorically interesting, did not seem to

increase anybody's paycheck very much. The militants subsequently have drifted into a new anti-Semitism—anti-Zionism, part of the militants' continued fascination with Third World movements. The nationalists have been insisting that an "Afro-American" movement, which would ally itself with the blacks of Africa and elsewhere, is the best road to "liberation" of American blacks. It is this attempt to link up the struggle of American blacks with the Third World struggle that has led the militants directly into anti-Zionism, since Israel remains a special villain in the eyes of Third World theorists, who identify closely with the Palestinians.

The first hint of the new direction that the black militants were taking came during the complicated comings and goings of certain Black Panther leaders, especially Eldridge Cleaver and Huey Newton. As early as 1969, Black Panther publications were calling Zionism "kosher nationalism," and, in their characteristic invective, calling supporters of Israel "Zionist fascist pigs." The new direction of the Black Panthers—whose famous epithet "pigs" had heretofore been reserved for such representatives of the white power establishment as policemen and judges—signaled an interesting linkup between the left movements (also stridently anti-Israel) and black militants. In 1970, for example, a new black group called Committee of Black Americans for Truth About the Middle East took out a half-page ad in *The New York Times* to denounce Israel and Zionism. It turned out that the group was funded by the Socialist Workers Party (Trotskyists). A year earlier, the student newspaper of Wayne State University in Detroit fell under the control of black radicals, who in short order began printing a number of anti-Israel articles; by 1973 the paper, still under black radical control, questioned the need for a Jewish state, and doubted that six million Jews had been exterminated during World War II. (This material was accompanied by an illustration showing a Star of David superimposed over a swastika.)

This sort of anti-Semitism has been unfortunately preval-

ent throughout much of the black community, and it is no
wonder that during the past three years black-Jewish relations
have broken down almost completely. That breakdown has
had an important effect on national politics since, as noted
earlier, blacks and Jews are the two key components of the
liberal coalition. The symptoms of the breakdown are everywhere. In Michigan, Coleman A. Young, the black mayor of
Detroit, and Morley Winograd, the state's former Democratic party chairman, split over Coleman's demand last year
that a newly-vacant seat on the Democratic National Committee be given to a black. At the same time, blacks in Florida
blamed Jewish state legislators for refusing to enact a special
sales tax surtax to pay for the cost of cleaning up a black
neighborhood in Miami wrecked by black rioters in 1980. In
Washington, D. C., that city's black mayor publicly claimed
that if the young murder victims in Atlanta had been Jewish,
the federal government would have acted more quickly in
helping local authorities solve the crimes. And black-Jewish
antagonism also erupted last year at a meeting of the Democratic National Committee, when a prominent black political
leader, Mayor Richard G. Hatcher of Gary, Indiana, tried to
remove a Jewish member of the committee and replace him
with a black man. Hatcher also denounced a plan to reduce
from ten to eight the number of blacks scheduled to be given
at-large memberships on the committee; some black leaders
complained privately that "the Jews" were behind the move.

 This political infighting is reminiscent of the Andrew
Young affair. Another flashpoint between blacks and Jews, it
concerned the controversy over Young's flirtation with the
Palestine Liberation Organization and his eventual dismissal
when revelation of the contact became public. Blacks openly
blamed the Jewish lobby for pressuring Young to resign. The
affair caused a great deal of tension between the black and
Jewish communities, but nothing compared to the tension
generated by a much more visceral issue, one that threatens to

create a division so deep between the two groups that it may never be healed.

The division is caused by an issue known as affirmative action, although the term doesn't quite describe all the ramifications. Affirmative action was born during the late 1960s, when the federal government pressured the construction industry to accept the so-called "Philadelphia Plan," which established racial quotas for the hiring of construction workers. The activation of this plan caused no great political ripples, least of all in the Jewish community—but that turned out to be a colossal tactical blunder by the Jews, who failed to understand that the Philadelphia Plan was only a crack in the door, a wedge the government would eventually use to try and solve every problem of discrimination afflicting American society.

The Jewish community's motives for not vigorously protesting the Philadelphia Plan were varied, one of which may have been the fact that the plan violated the rights of the Italians, an unfashionable minority, and aided the blacks, at that time a fashionable minority. But as the Jews learned to their cost, fashions change rapidly in this society; by 1977, the federal government had a new law which requires that 10 percent of all federal work contracts be set aside for business firms operated by members of minorities. The Jewish community discovered that the government's definition of minorities did not include Jews, who had now become an unfashionable minority.

But there was worse to come. Upon the advent of the Carter administration, the government moved to expand the quota system further, this time into the higher-level professional positions (such as tax adjuster or customs agent) in the civil service. The civil service has long been the traditional preserve of Jewish upward mobility—and a preserve the Jews had won through many decades of work, which is to say merit, a factor the government apparently no longer considered worthy of consideration. The Carter administration's first target in its drive to get more minorities into the government civil service apparatus (partially a political payoff to strong minority support for the Carter presidential candidacy, especially among blacks), was the Professional and Administrative Career Examination (PACE), a standardized test used to select candidates for technical jobs. The minority pressure groups wanted the test eliminated entirely, since, they argued, its high standards discriminated against the minorities. The administration compromised by agreeing that at least 20 percent of all such jobs had to go to minorities, regardless of merit. (The Reagan administration has since eliminated this ridiculous provision.)

To achieve such a quota, the government bureaucracy has had to devise complicated arrangements, not only to decide who is (or is not) a minority group member, but also exactly how assorted quota systems are to be carried out. The implications of this determination process have unsettling echoes of Nazi Germany and modern-day South Africa, witness this formula, contained in a Department of Health and Human Services ruling on April 1, 1980:

$$\frac{d/T + L}{EOs}$$

This formula, issued under the department's "Operational Management System," aims to fulfill "opportunity targets" (the "T" in the formula above), taking into account "current deficiencies" ("d" in the formula), "expected loss" (L), with a "target hiring rate percentage" expressed in terms of "employment opportunities" (EOs).

There is some question as to how many people actually understood this formula, and an even more important question is how many understood its implications. Obviously, since the federal government was devising arcane scientific formulae to determine how quota goals were to be met, the next step was to apply the same science toward determining who was a minority. And that is exactly what happened. On June 13, 1980, the

Department of Health and Human Services approved a directive ordering every component of the department to determine the precise percentage of "under-representation" of minorities in the civil service, and then devise ways of filling those positions with minority-group members to the precise percentage of minorities in the American population. But this puts a premium on identifying who is a member of a minority group. The government solved this problem with a new form, of course, this one known as Standard Form 181. First produced in July 1980, entitled "Race and National Origin Identification," the form sets out complicated rules for determining who is black, Hispanic, American Indian, Eskimo, and other minorities. (It refrains from setting out any rules for determining one particular minority, women.) The form and the system it represents would delight the Nazi racial theorists of the Third Reich, who spent their time deciding who was "one quarter Aryan," or "50 percent Jewish," and so on.

The comparison is not meant to be inflammatory; consider that in August 1980, the Administrative Office of the United States Courts, under congressional order to determine the numbers of minorities serving in the federal judiciary, ordered that henceforth all federal court employees and judicial officers were to be identified in records by "race/national origin." The new guidelines ruled that employees had to be listed in various subgroups, in addition to their race—and the subgroups included "Arabic" and "Hebrew." Further, the guidelines went on to say that all employees' subgroup listings had to be based on "ethnic, not religious factors," a ruling that reads like something out of the Nazi race theorists, who insisted that Jews were a race, not a religion.

Fortunately in this case, the insistence that "Hebrew" employees be so identified (for the first time in the history of the federal government), came to the attention of Senator Daniel P. Moynihan, whose opposition forced the government to backtrack and drop the idea.

Still, there are plenty of other such guidelines floating

around the federal government, and "affirmative action" remains the government's (and the federal courts') main weapon to combat discrimination. Aside from the question as to whether such a policy is the right weapon against the problem of discrimination or economic deprivation, the sad fact is that for all this talk of helping minorities, the Jewish minority is invisible. And it is an invisibility that works in two directions: first, by not including the Jews in any listing of official "minority," on the assumption, presumably, they are not aggrieved in any way; and secondly, in the name of helping other minorities, destroying a merit system that for many years has served as the best means of helping minorities, notably the Jews. Thus, it is not surprising to find Jews, as they survey the wreckage of this democracy's great merit system for its federal employees, drawing increasingly closer to another American minority with whom such an affinity would have seemed impossible even several years ago: the Italians. The reason for this growing affinity is obvious; the Italian community is still extremely bitter about the Philadelphia Plan, a bitterness that parallels the Jewish community's bitterness about affirmative action in the civil service. Both groups share a common experience: relegated to digging ditches for so many decades, it took the Italians many years before they were able to move up the rungs of the American economic ladder by dominating the construction business. Overnight, seemingly, they watched what they had worked so long to achieve being given away to another minority more fashionable than their own. It is an experience that has made them understand what happened to the Jews in civil service and other fields.

The experience of the Jews recalls the wisdom of the great pre-Civil War Jewish leader, Rabbi Isaac Mayer Wise, who warned his people against becoming involved in the Abolitionist movement. There was no doubt that the goals of the movement were worthwhile, Wise said, but he was very afraid of its "nature." It was a shrewd observation; in modern terms, we might say that Wise was warning against expressive politics, an

especially volatile brand whose direction can shift at a
moment's notice. This, to a large extent, is what happened with
the black civil rights movement: it was pure expressive politics,
and when the blacks became frustrated over their inability to
win economic freedom after civil rights freedom, they unleashed their fury in another direction—where the Jews happened to be. Much the same thing happened after the Civil
War, when the forces unleashed by the Abolitionist movement
turned on the Jews and resulted in the gross anti-Semitism of
America's so-called Gilded Age.

This is not necessarily an argument against Jewish involvement in civil rights. As others have pointed out, Jews could
hardly ignore involvement in the struggle for civil rights, given
their own struggles and the tradition of justice in their religion.
But it is fair to ask whether the Jewish community should ever
have gotten so deeply involved. It is also fair to ask the same
question about the deep involvement of the Jews with another
development of modern history—left-wing politics. Since the
left political movement was the Jews' other great ally—or
supposed ally—along with the blacks, it is worthwhile to examine how that presumed friend also turned away from the Jews.

Historically, Jews have always been associated with the
left-liberal side of the political spectrum, for the simple reason
that very early in its history the left supported the liberation
of the Jews. The left argued that once a free nation was
achieved, anti-Semitism would disappear, along with other
"petty bourgeois" prejudices. This vision, at a time when
Europe was divided into warring nationalisms, was a slender
reed of hope—literally about the *only* hope until the rise of
political Zionism just before the beginning of this century—
that the Jews had during an existence filled with pogroms,
discrimination and danger of imminent destruction.

Few Jews understood, however, that the left's utopian
vision hinged on the assumption that once their political ideal
was achieved, Jewish particularism would also disappear. In
other words, the Jews would become just like everybody else—

meaning that the continuance of Jewish particular customs (ethnic or religious) would be expected to disappear. That consequence got lost in the shuffle as large numbers of Jews joined the European leftist movements that proliferated after the revolutions of 1848. To be sure, the Jews had little alternative; on the other side of the spectrum were such things as the nationalistic German political parties, the anti-Semitic politics of the Austro-Hungarian Empire, or the even more anti-Semitic parties of Russia (excepting the Communist movement).

The Jews who immigrated to America brought their politics with them, and discovered in this country little to which they could respond politically. The Republican Party of the late nineteenth century was strongly allied with the anti-immigrant nativism movement; the other parties included agrarian and social reformers, but among them were native anti-Semites who spoke of the "control by the Rothschilds" of banking and commerce. East European Jews in effect created their own politics, playing major roles in the small Socialist and Communist movements in this country. Socialism held the greatest appeal for many American Jews, especially in the 1930s, for only that movement seemed to offer any effective resistance to the Nazi menace.

In the process, a rather curious Jewish radical was created: to accept socialism, he had to accept its hostility to Zionism. The hostility arose first because the East European-left had opposed it for fear it would drain away the oppressed Jews of the Russian Empire (an important source of leftist strength in Europe), and later because Zionism was regarded as an "outmoded expression" of nationalism. Anti-Zionism, then, was a prominent feature of the left political movements right from the very beginning, a fact which later generations of Jewish radicals tended to forget.

The most forgetful generation seemed to be the generation of Jews who enlisted in the so-called "New Left" movement that burst upon the American scene in the 1960s. The movement began first as a campus phenomenon, then broke away from the established left and announced a hostility to all establishments. In the beginning, the New Left movement lacked any clear political program of what it wanted—except for an end to the war in Vietnam—but the need to find that necessary ideology finally led the New Left to join up with various dropouts from the Old Left, notably Maoist communism and "liberation" movements. What, then, was the resulting ideology? Elitism, really; the conviction that the movement represented the only political visionaries in America, the sole enlightenment pointing a way to a great dream, the only people capable of embarking on this great revolutionary course. The corollary was the equally firm conviction that only a fantastically clever, powerful group, which had untold powers of manipulation, prevented "the people" from realizing that they should join the New Left. There was no small matter of generational rebellion at work here; there were a great many young Jews who did not accept the seemingly schizophrenic existence their parents lived. In their view, their parents were leading double lives: an affluent life-style on one hand, while on the other, an instinctively left-liberal political view of the world. To the younger generation of American Jews, Jewish life in this country was therefore hypocritical: they had been raised on the left-liberal doctrines of their parents, who in turn seemed to leave those convictions at the voting booth.

When Vietnam, the one single issue that imposed some sort of unity over the disparate elements of the New Left, finally ended, the movement turned on the Jews. This development, of course, was inevitable. First, there was the case of Israel; so long as Israel opposed the Arabs—seen by the New Left as largely the victims of Western imperialism and the oil companies—then Israel was a leading figure in the New Left's pantheon of villains. Further, Israel was opposed to a particular favorite of the New Left, the Palestinian liberation move-. ment. Thus, American Jews who supported Israel were imperialists opposed to "just liberation." There was also another

factor: the New Left was enamored of the black radical movement, including its pronounced anti-Zionism and anti-Semitism.

Domestically, the New Left found Jews a natural target.
In the vision of a rotten society that the New Left saw, Jews
dominated the teaching profession, played an important role in
business, were disproportionately represented at elite colleges
and similarly seemed to dominate the media. To the New Left,
all these areas were particular symbols of the darkest villainy,
since in the logic of that movement it was in these areas that the
mysterious forces of repression did their dirty work. And, in
view of the fact that Jews played important roles in these areas,
then it followed that the Jews were to a large extent responsible
for the presumed evil they did. In the final analysis, the New
Left has attacked virtually every American institution important to Jews: the civil service system, the principle of merit and
nondiscrimination in government service, the merit system for
college admissions, the authority of the teaching profession,
private business, institutionalized professions (especially the
law), and college and university faculties. It is no wonder that
in Cuba, whose revolution is considered the ideal model for the
New Left, almost all the Jews fled the country shortly after
Fidel Castro came to power; while Americans debated the
extent of Castro's Marxist convictions, the Cuban Jews
instinctively sensed what his revolution meant.

To the New Left, ideological anti-Semitism is a distrac-
tion, so overt anti-Semitism is a rarity. But the New Left does
regard Jews as obstacles to the great revolution soon to occur,
especially Jewish involvement with the hated Establishment
and the support of American Jews for the "imperialist" state of
Israel. For that reason, the New Left pleads guilty to "anti-
Zionism" which they insist is different from anti-Semitism. The
argument is not especially persuasive, since the New Left's idea
of an ideal Israel would be a Palestinian state within the present
borders of Israel, with the Israelis relegated to a minority
within that state—which the New Left regards as the "correct"

solution to the Middle East problem, the "inevitable result" of the "correct" revolutionary forces they see at work. Left unsaid, naturally, is what would happen if the Palestinian or Arab majority in this new state would do to the hated Israeli minority what the New Left claims the Israelis have done to the Palestinians. To the New Left, the only factor blocking this inevitability is the intransigence of American Jews, who remain the chief villains "oppressing" Palestinians.

This anti-Zionism is also a prominent feature of the Old Left, defined as the traditional Communist and Socialist movements. They, too, share a pronounced antipathy toward the Israelis, but the difference is that the Old Left has a virulent anti-Semitic bias which it makes little effort to conceal. To understand why that is so, we must examine the real inspiration for all of it, the Soviet Union.

It is not fashionable today to draw exact parallels between Soviet communism and the various movements it has spawned throughout the world. And while no one can believe in the old myth about monolithic Communist politics, it is also true that Soviet Communists exert an influence on similar-minded movements elsewhere that is strong and pervasive. It is no accident that as the Soviet Union's official policy during the past decades turned progressively more anti-Semitic, the Old Left in this country and elsewhere also became more anti-Semitic.

In the Soviet Union, history is ideology, or as a Soviet historian once put it, "politics projected into the past." That belief has special impact on how the Russians have regarded the Jews, once important factors in the very creation of Soviet communism (Trotsky being the most noted example). Through the years of Lenin and the Stalin dictatorship, the Jews were portrayed and regarded by the Soviets as ambiguous figures of history, to be used ideologically as the occasion demanded. Officially, they were regarded as nearly invisible throughout most of the Stalin era; Russian Jews were told nothing of the Nazi crimes against the Jews because at least until the day of the German invasion in June 1941, Stalin worked assiduously to placate Hitler. (When Jews were rounded up in German-occupied areas in Russia, they had no idea they were to be murdered, because not a word of the Nazi atrocities had been permitted in the Soviet media.)

The Soviets made much of the concentration camps they liberated, but the extensive publicity Moscow produced about the subject did not mean they had developed a new sympathy for the sufferings of Jews. In fact, the Soviets wanted to use the atrocities as anti-German propaganda, part of its justification for remaining in the eastern occupation zones. Only a year later, Stalin unleased an "anti-cosmopolitan" campaign, an anti-Semitic drive that sought, in effect, to blame Russia's disasters early in the war on the Jews. (It was also designed to obscure the problem of the 1,500,000 Jews in Russia murdered by the Nazis; obviously, the Jews could not have been in the least responsible for the Soviet Union's near-defeat if so many of them were murdered.)

The curious thing about this is that while at home Stalin was cracking down on the Jews, overseas his policy was quite different. Stalin believed that the creation of Israel meant that the new state would align itself with "revolutionary socialism," since the Zionists had struggled against British colonialism. To that end, the USSR was the second major power, after the United States, to recognize Israel in 1948, and the then-Soviet ambassador to the United Nations, Andrei Gromyko, made a speech in which he said that the failure of the Western powers to protect Jews against Nazi terror "explains the aspirations of the Jews for their own state. The denial of this right to the Jewish people cannot be justified." Shortly afterward, Soviet officials supported unlimited Jewish immigration to the new state and criticized Arab states for invading Israel. A book published in Moscow under official auspices in 1948 actually called the Arab League a manifestation of "the reactionary ruling circles helping England."

In the light of subsequent events, this enthusiastic support for Israel and the Jews (excepting Russian Jews) is surprising, and it explains why the Old Left in this country and elsewhere took a remarkably benign view of Israel shortly before and after its creation. But when it became clear that Israel had no use for Moscow—especially Stalin's hint that it disassociate itself from the United States—the Soviet party line changed dramatically. The Russians then suddenly discovered that in fact the Arabs had been right all along, and they were not, as previously assumed, under the domination of "Western imperialist interests." Further, the perfidy of Israel in its alliance with the United States was now discovered to be part of an insidious Zionist plot to take over the Middle East. No one knows exactly why Stalin changed his mind about Israel, but one reason may have been the paranoia induced by the sight of the first Israeli ambassador to Moscow, Golda Meir, arriving in the capital city to the tumultuous welcome of nearly 80,000 Russian Jews. It was a welcome of indescribable emotion that may have convinced Stalin that he had still another enemy in his midst to be stamped out.

This shift in Soviet thinking was signaled by a wave of trials against "counterrevolutionary elements" in the Soviet Union and Eastern Europe, the accused being predominantly Jewish. Stalin then turned on Israel, launching an extensive "anti-Zionist" campaign within the Soviet Union; untold thousands of Jews were arrested and killed or deported to Siberian labor camps to die a slow death. By 1953, shortly before his death, Stalin personally became convinced that the Jews were the most dangerous minority in the world, and he was determined to stamp them out. One of the more dangerous forms that conviction took was Stalin's belief that Jewish doctors were trying to poison him—and by extension, many non-Jewish Russians. He had hundreds of doctors arrested, and only his death prevented a plan to publicly hang a number of Jewish doctors in Red Square as a preliminary to an extensive slaughter of Jews in the Soviet Union. (Soviet émigrés to this day remember seeing trains of cattle cars readied to deport Jews to death camps in the Soviet Union; they were scheduled to be loaded the very morning of Stalin's death.)

There was a brief lull under Khrushchev, who sought to

use Stalin's pogroms against Jews as another count in the lengthy indictment he had drawn up against the dead dictator—and to consolidate his own power. Once Khrushchev had won that power, however, the party line returned to anti-Semitism, and all talk of how the Jews had suffered ended. Some party functionaries got caught in the switch. The Soviet historian Aleksandr M. Nekrich had written a book explaining that Stalin was wrong when he blamed Jews for the lack of Russian preparedness in 1941, and that in fact the fault lay with Stalin himself. But by the time the book was published the party line had changed again, and all copies were destroyed; Nekrich wound up in disgrace for his terrible "error."

In 1967, following the complete victory of Israel over its Moscow-supported Arab enemies, the Soviet line took another twist, this time propounding a theory that "Zionists"—the Soviet code word for Jews—were actually responsible for "Hitlerism" and that the Holocaust was the creation of Zionists. This bizarre assertion, which blamed the victims for the crime, quickly found its way into the rhetoric of nearly every left organization in the world. In a pattern that has often been repeated, the left carefully emulated every twist and turn in the Soviet party line; the Soviets had no sooner announced that "anti-Zionism" was the "correct" way of viewing the Middle East, than the leftists also began talking about "Zionist crimes." Just to cite one example, the Socialist movement in the United States held its national convention right around the time in 1971 that Moscow's anti-Zionism campaign reached its height, during which the movement decided that "Zionism and the state of Israel . . . is the enemy of the Palestinian people . . ." (A year later, the *Militant*, main publication of the Socialist Workers Party in the United States, called condemnations of the Palestinian Liberation Organization for the murders of Israeli athletes at the Olympics "hypocritical"). The Progressive Labor Party, another prominent Old Left group, at the same time circulated pictures of Golda Meir retouched to look like Adolf Hitler, and in 1973 a coalition of Old Left groups charged that American Jews were guilty of "racism" toward Arabs, and that Zionism was a "racist ideology."

The Soviet campaign—emulated by Old Left groups in nearly every detail—has since hit new lows. Recently the Soviets have unveiled *The Protocols of the Learned Elders of Zion* as part of their campaign, and an extensive series of presentations in the Soviet media now openly accuse Jews of striving for world domination, attempting to control international banking, manipulating the Western press and, for good measure, trying to infiltrate Masonic lodges (for what purpose is not made clear). The Soviets have even gone so far as to justify the pogroms against Jews carried out by the czars, accusing Russian Jews of being "agents and soldiers of Zion inside the USSR." (Recently, there has been still another twist: Soviet propaganda now accuses Jews of owning all American arms manufacturing companies.)

This hatred, as we have noted, finds an echo in the left political movements, which share the Soviet Union's growing anti-Semitism. But there is another, more ghostly echo: just a few miles from Kiev, there is a large, open field called Babi Yar. On September 29 and 30, 1941, when Babi Yar was a huge ravine, Nazi killing-squads slaughtered 33,771 Jews and covered over the bodies. Ultimately, during two years of occupation, over 100,000 people were murdered and buried at Babi Yar, almost all of them Jews. Not until 1976 was a monument erected at the site of this terrible crime. The official Soviet government monument is in the standard Soviet "heroic" style, and contains a brass tablet noting the crime of the "German fascist invaders."

But there is no mention of any of the Jews who died there.

CHAPTER EIGHT

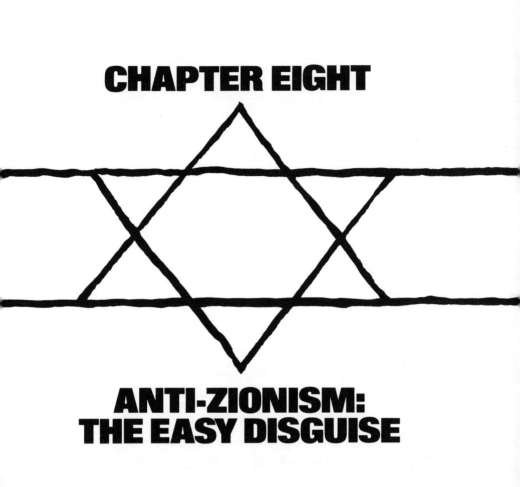

ANTI-ZIONISM:
THE EASY DISGUISE

A drop of oil is worth a drop of blood.

Georges Clemenceau

*There's a helluva lot more Arabians
than there is Jews.*

Billy Carter

On a warm spring night in 1978, the living embodiment of what has been called variously "the Israel lobby," or "the Jewish lobby," or "Jew power," sat on a bench in the reception lobby of the chamber of the United States Senate. He sat there, not as the representative of what is sometimes darkly referred to as a great, mysterious force with the power to cloud men's minds, but as the representative of a losing cause.

His name was Morris J. Amitay, and at the time he was head of the American-Israel Public Affairs Committee, the official name of the so-called "Jewish lobby" in this country. He had concluded several hours of intense lobbying, trying to convince senators to vote against a $4.8 billion Middle East arms package, which included sixty F-15 fighters for Saudi Arabia. Those planes, the Israelis and the leadership of the American Jewish community complained, would give the Saudis—Israel's bitterest enemy—sophisticated weapons capable of attacking Israel. Worse, in their view, was the fact that the sale showed that the administration of Jimmy Carter had embarked on a policy of "tilt" toward the Arabs so as to protect American oil supplies in the Persian Gulf.

The argument against the sale, advanced by Amitay in face-to-face meetings with senators as he tried to convince them to vote against the proposal, finally failed. The Senate approved the package, and in the process the "Jewish lobby" suffered its first major defeat since becoming a domestic political force to be reckoned with during the maneuverings that accompanied the creation of the state of Israel about thirty years before. But the significance of the vote lay beyond that: for the first time, the United States government had embarked on a policy of treating what it called "moderate" Arab states— Egypt and Saudi Arabia—on an equal footing with Israel. Moreover, it had been decided that the security of Israel would henceforth be linked to the security of the Arab states that the United States was trying so hard to woo.

From there on, the American Jewish community has become more alarmed as it has seen a long succession of similar defeats, ranging from the attempt by the American government to open a "dialogue" with the Palestine Liberation Organization, to the plan to sell advanced radar-warning planes to Saudi Arabia. In the Jewish view, this represents at least an erosion of the traditional American support for Israel, its only firm ally in the entire Middle East; worse, it represents what appears to be the beginning of an American attempt to abandon Israel in the name of a more "balanced" or "pragmatic" foreign policy in the Middle East, for which read "oil." These developments, combined with the increase in "anti-Zionism"—earlier it was seen how that particular brand of anti-Semitism has become endemic to certain religious groups, black organizations and elements of the political left—have convinced American Jews that Israel is in the greatest danger in its history, for the simple reason that America remains Israel's greatest (and really only) lifeline. Without that lifeline, Israel would not last: it is the American Jews, most responsible for Israel's creation, who must fight for its continued existence.

On the surface this equation seems odd, for American

Jews, after all, do not live in Israel; except for a small number, the Jews in this country appear to have no intention of ever emigrating there, as the doctrine of Zionism would seem to suggest. Further, the historical fact is that the Zionists fought with the American Jewish community throughout the early part of this century, unavailingly, to convince American Jews that the only real solution to the problems of Jews was the creation of a Jewish state in what is now Israel. So why do American Jews care so much about Israel? The answer is composed of a series of paradoxes.

The first paradox is that Zionism is to a large extent the only real single unifying theme of American Jewry. The majority of American Jews are neither observant nor devout in the orthodox sense; their religion, highly secularized, focuses not on the specific religious aspects of Judaism, but more on the community aspects, the idea of shared heritage and nationhood. Israel is the chief symbol of that shared heritage, and so it is Israel that is the focus of much Jewish concern. Zionism—in its simplest form the doctrine which advocates a national homeland for the Jewish people as their God-given right and the injunction that all Jews should return there—is the underpinning on which Israel rests. So many American Jews are Zionists, although they do not emigrate to Israel, for the most part. (As Golda Meir once remarked to a group of young American Jews who expressed their concern to her about the survival of Israel, "Then why didn't you move here?")

Meir was illustrating the dilemma of American Zionism, a dilemma that is best illustrated by the fact that American Jews consider themselves Jews even if they hardly ever go to temple, even if they marry outside the faith, even if they don't believe in God—but only a tiny minority of Jews believe they can remain Jewish while opposed to the idea of the state of Israel. Indeed, only Zionism has survived as an ideology within American Judaism; such competitors as Yiddishism, anarchism, and the Jewish Socialist Bund have all disappeared into the dustbin of history. The American form of Zionism amounts not only to a belief, but a wide-ranging apparatus of support, particularly money. (In one day, during the crisis that preceded the 1967 Middle East war, American Jews gave $100 million in donations to Israel, a feat unmatched in the annals of charity.)

American Jews are the only special interest group in the United States that is largely defined by its foreign policy, a policy that essentially says: Zionism is correct in its claim on behalf of the Jewish people, that those people are entitled to a return to the land of Israel. And it is the land of Israel which, in the words of prominent American Zionist Arthur Hertzberg, "is the almost universally shared central purpose of American Jewish life." And this amounts to a major paradox: a "central purpose" in American Jewish life, at a time when American Jews seem to be increasingly drifting away from traditional Judaism.

It is not especially surprising that the relationship of American Jews with Israel is packed with contradictions, for the rise of Zionism itself is a series of contradictions. Zionism is the stepchild of a number of accidents, all of them stemming from events of the nineteenth century. Historically, however, Zionism really was born long before the Jewish people's *Diaspora* (the great scattering) in 586 B.C., the date of the Babylonian exile. According to the Bible, the Jewish prophets had predicted an exile and a return, a process that was to be led by a Messiah. But that Messiah did not come, and the Jews were exiled again in A.D. 70, when Jerusalem fell to invading Roman armies. The Jews scattered all over the earth, outcasts everywhere, barely surviving massacres as they awaited the coming of the Messiah who would lead them back to Zion.

But the Messiah still did not come. What did come were several unlikely leaders, foremost among them an assimilated Austrian Jew named Theodore Herzl, who in the 1890s propounded the then-revolutionary idea that the problem of anti-Semitism was insoluble so long as the Jews lacked a homeland;

as stateless people, they would suffer increasingly from the growing political anti-Semitism of Europe, and would eventually disappear. Herzl's vision of a new all-Jewish state amounted to his idea on how to end anti-Semitism, for in his view, once all the Jews were removed from Europe, then anti-Semitism would disappear. That turned out to be quite wrong (as modern events demonstrate), and Herzl died without seeing his dream realized. The rest of the story is well-known: how a Jewish chemist named Chaim Weizmann convinced the British government to support the idea of a national homeland for the Jews; how the British reneged on that agreement; the trials of the early Zionist settlers; and their final triumph—in the ashes of the Holocaust. The Holocaust was the one central event most responsible for the creation of the modern state of Israel, and the one event that not even the most fervent Zionist could have believed would ever happen.

Nor could the Zionists ever have imagined that Israel would ultimately become, as it is today, the focus for modern anti-Semitism. That development is relatively recent; in 1958, then-Foreign Minister Golda Meir of Israel was telling the General Assembly of the United Nations in a speech (heavily applauded), how much Israel appreciated the support of so many of its member states. "Many of these countries," she said, "are without direct interest in our area. But their appreciation of the moral, social, historic and religious factors involved led them to profoundly held convictions which they have maintained with staunchness and courage. . . . It is a satisfaction and a joy that with many of the new countries that have joined the United Nations in the meantime we are linked in bonds of friendship, of understanding and of mutual aid."

In the light of subsequent events, these words have an ironic ring: only seventeen years after Meir spoke them, the United Nations had come so far as to equate Zionism with racism and invite Palestine Liberation Organization Leader Yasir Arafat to address the world body—a speech marked by the clear indication that the speaker was wearing a gun as he spoke to an organization supposedly dedicated to the cause of world peace. Somehow, the gun was appropriate at a time when the politics of racial antagonism, radical Moslem fundamentalism and clashing national ambitions—not to mention the rivalry of the major powers—had become in fact the real business of the United Nations, the place where the modern state of Israel was born.

The issue of the Palestinians and whether their cause is just will not explain what has happened. However much anybody wants to believe that the Palestinians' plight is cause for some concern, it obviously bears no resemblance to the very real plights of the Cambodian refugees, the Vietnamese boat people, the Soviet Jews and the many victims of the torture chambers of Latin America. But, despite these very real victims of some very tyrannical states, the military training camps supposedly dedicated to "national liberation" in Syria, Libya and Lebanon have no recruits preparing themselves for the day when they will overthrow the tyrannies responsible for these horrors. No, the camps are full of Palestinians, Germans, Japanese and others, all working for an internationale devoted to destroying Israel, as though Israel was responsible for the tide of refugees everywhere in the world.

But in the modern lexicon of hate, Zionists have become the world's pariahs. They have become pariahs for much the same reason that Jews have been pariahs for centuries: they inspire fear, the fear of a small accomplished elite whose success is out of all proportion to their numbers. This is the central paradox of Zionism: the more successful it became, the further it strayed from its original goal of ending anti-Semitism. It is no accident that most modern anti-Zionism can be dated from the 1967 war, for that was the one single event which underscored, in a dramatic way, the triumph of Zionism. The Israeli victory in that war proved that both main trends in Zionist thought had been proven right. One, the so-called "practical Zionism," was the prominent feature of the early Zionist settlers in Palestine, who sought to create the fact of their cause by buying barren land and reclaiming it with Jewish settlers. The second, most often known as "political Zionism," sought to establish the "legitimacy" of Zionism in political terms. The United Nations Partition Resolution of 1947, which in effect created an independent Jewish state whose borders encompassed the areas of greatest Jewish settlement, in one swoop confirmed both trends at once, most importantly conferring a political legitimacy that has been cemented by the agony of four wars.

The question of the political legitimacy of Israel (and the Zionist movement) leads us directly into the question of the role American Jews have played. That role has been critical, and since it is under increasing assault, it bears some examination.

Political Zionism first came to the United States during the 1880s, when it accompanied some of the first great waves of Russian Jews entering this country. The idea was received coolly by the American Jewish establishment (the normally far-seeing Isaac M. Wise called it "Ziomania"), but by 1897 Zionism had become a fairly serious movement among some American Jews. The Federation of American Zionists had 8,000 members in 1900, despite the opposition of the Jewish radical movement—which pronounced Zionism "reactionary nationalism" contrary to the Socialist goal of "internationalism"—and the Orthodox and Reform Jewish movements. The Orthodox opposition was the most serious, since it was founded on religious grounds. The Orthodox believed that the arrival of the Messiah was the absolute prerequisite to the reestablishment of the Jewish people in the Holy Land. The Reform movement, meanwhile, denounced Zionism on the grounds that the messianic concept of a return to Israel was outmoded; of much more concern should be establishing a home for Jews in America that would be free of bigotry.

Despite opposition, the Zionists suceeded in playing a key role at the 1919 peace talks in San Remo, Italy, where the conference to decide the future of Palestine took place. The

American Zionist leaders worked closely with President Woodrow Wilson in ensuring that the Balfour Declaration—a statement by the British Foreign Office that Great Britain would support the establishment of a Jewish national homeland in Palestine—would be incorporated in the final peace treaty. This was a critical piece of diplomacy since, without incorporation into the peace treaty, the Balfour Declaration was only a slip of paper.

In subsequent years the Zionist movement in the United States won the allegiance of most of the Jewish community, and more importantly, was able to mobilize pro-Jewish Christian sentiment and congressional support. This was the real beginning of what later became known as the "Jewish lobby," a term that passed into American political parlance in 1947, when organized Jewish support helped convince President Harry Truman to support the idea of an independent Jewish state. (Some years later, Truman was introduced at a ceremony as "The man who helped create the state of Israel." Angry, Truman replied, "What do you mean, 'helped create'? I am Cyrus, I am Cyrus!" Truman was referring to the biblical king of Persia who had made it possible for the Jews to return from Babylonian captivity.)

It is important to realize that Zionism has played a significant role in the development of American Judaism. While for its original progenitors Zionism was primarily an answer to political anti-Semitism, it also promised Jews a return to the roots of their history. In the American version of Zionism, there was no intent to settle in Israel, for the most part, but there was an intent to fight to bring a Jewish state into existence and help all Jews everywhere who wanted to settle there.

Zionism has resulted in a unity among American Jews that otherwise would not have been possible, given the deep divisions within Judaism among Conservative, Orthodox, Reform and unaffiliated factions. Zionism as an ideology allows American Jews to assert their Jewishness without being bound to a religious establishment.

Whatever disputations and reservations existed were removed by the experience of the Holocaust, an event that compelled some of the most Orthodox Jews to support Zionism and the idea of a Jewish state; some Orthodox, in the Talmudic tradition, devised an ingenious explanation to explain how Orthodox believers could now accept the idea of Israel. The creation of Israel in the wake of the Holocaust was a "gift from heaven" that Jews could accept, and while the Messiah had not yet come, the new nation of Israel was undoubtedly a good omen of his imminent return. The unity that Zionism imposed on the American Jewish community—which still remains remarkably diverse—welded those elements into a powerful political force whose main effort has been to ensure the continued existence of the state of Israel, and to make certain that the original commitment made to Israel at the dawn of its creation remains strong.

Essentially, this is what the "Jewish lobby" is all about, and it is a phenomenon unparalleled in American politics. It would be difficult to imagine, say, a similar lobby of Irish-Americans or Italian-Americans or, despite their best efforts, a similar lobby of Arab-Americans. The reason is that the relationship between the United States and Israel—sire and progenitor—is unique, unmatched by the relationship of this country with any other nation in the world. This uniqueness is the bedrock on which the Jewish lobby operates and is the real reason for the historic American foreign policy concern for Israel, not, as is often supposed, because of the supposed power of American Jews.

More fundamentally, it is not possible to be a friend of Israel and an anti-Semite at the same time, for the simple reason that Judaism and Zionism, especially since the Holocaust, have become so intertwined that they are not only synonymous, but inseparable, as well. Thus, anti-Zionism, which is to say anti-Semitism, is directed against Jews rather than against the political entity that is known as Israel; the nation of Israel is a Jewish state, not a Zionist state. Zionism finally built the state that Jews sought, not the other way around. Or, put another way, the Holocaust built Israel, and it is Israel that is the repository of what remains of the Jewish civilization of Europe that Hitler destroyed. He destroyed much: a vital, civilization that had enriched the lands of Europe for nearly 1,500 years, a civilization that enriched its lands of exile with an ancient religion, a culture, and an ethical system.

These amount to the components of Israel's legitimacy, and it is this legitimacy that anti-Zionism seeks to attack. Taken as a whole, anti-Zionism insists that the state of Israel never had a right to exist, since it was "seized" from the "legitimate national aspirations" of the Palestinian people, and that Israel is in fact the creation of "Western Zionists" who sought to checkmate Arab nationalism. None of this is historically true, and illustrates that anti-Zionism is as irrational and wrong-headed as the classic symptoms of anti-Semitism. In fact, a reading of the vast literature produced by anti-Zionists is persuasive that anti-Zionism is centrally animated by anti-Semitism, and there is not too much point in trying to claim (as many do) that anti-Semitism and anti-Zionism are two very different things.

This is no mere overstatement; the fundamental fact is that anti-Zionists of all stripes deny the legitimacy of the idea of a national Jewish homeland, deny there was ever any reason for it, and deny that the Jews have any right to support it. In other words, Zionism must diasappear, and along with it, the state of Israel. The root of this idea is the classic idea of all racists, that there is a biological determinism which in the case of the Jews prohibits them from Zionism, since Zionism is "artificial." It is the racism that lies behind such statements to the effect that there are many more Arabs than Jews, or that Jews somehow forced themselves upon the modern Middle East.

The state of Israel and the fortunes of the millions of Jews in the rest of the world are so inextricably linked that it is inconceivable that the bond could ever be broken between them. However, all forms of anti-Zionism seek to do precisely that, claiming that there is some sort of distinction to be made between their animus toward the state of Israel and what they claim is their benevolent attitudes toward Jews in general. It amounts to saying that they cannot abide Israeli Jews, but have nothing but affection for non-Israeli Jews. The claim won't work with most Jews, whose historical memory recalls a time in pre-war Europe, when German Jews and others made the tragic mistake of assuming that Nazi hatred for Polish Jews could not possibly be turned against themselves, since they were so "different" from Eastern European Jews. (It is also a mistake that will not be repeated in Israel, which has more recent events to serve as signposts. Claims that a "secular democratic Palestine" can be created while maintaining the rights of Jews are made a mockery by events in nearby Lebanon, where the Christian minority and the Moslem majority in that democratic secular state have been slaughtering each other for years.)

Zionists have argued that there is a basic truth of Western civilization: even emancipated Jews will never be accepted as equals, except to a certain extent in the United States. There, American Jews have had their own problems (nothing like the sufferings of European Jews, however), but they have shared a common symptom of anti-Semitism—opposition to the Zionist idea. There is some merit to the argument, expressed by Hannah Arendt, that anti-Semitism itself, or at least the more powerful forms of it in this century, has been to a great extent the reaction to what has sometimes been called "the great awakening" of Jews and Jewish nationalism at about the same time. This may be a chicken and the egg argument, for it is clear that the central anger of all anti-Semites is directed at the unwillingness of Jews to rid themselves of all characteristics of national life, except for religion. And anti-Zionists refine that anti-Semitism one step further, arguing that the idea of Israel represents the most telling indication that the Jews will never give up their national idea.

In modern forms, anti-Zionism has a chief accusation to make against Jews: they are guilty of "divided loyalties," which is the idea that Jews suffer from a fundamental conflict of interest. In all cases, the anti-Zionists say, the Jews will always put the interest of Israel above their own nationality's. This is a special feature of anti-Zionism in America, which tends to focus on the Jewish lobby as prime target, accusing it of bending every effort to help a foreign state, severely warping American foreign policy in the process, while ignoring "political realities" in the Middle East.

Harry Golden once considered the logical extension of this charge and decided, in the event of a war between Israel and the United States, that he would commit suicide. An interesting statement, but it doesn't quite answer the implications of what the anti-Zionists have been saying, nor does it address any of the considerable complications that form the relationship of American Jews to Israel and to their own government in that connection—and the unique relationship of America to Israel.

To begin with, anti-Zionists fear and distrust the American Jewish community—an ever-evolving, highly-organized society of about 6,000,000 people that has achieved the highest economic, educational and political levels in the entire history of the Jewish people. They are welded together by a virtually unanimous support for the state of Israel, not only politically, but also financially (over $4 billion worth of Israel bonds have been sold in the United States since 1951, the third most popular security sold in this country). They have also been instrumental in the American government's decisions to give large amounts of military and other forms of aid to Israel; since 1976, the United States has given Israel nearly $15 billion in military and economic aid.

In terms of numbers, the actual "Jewish lobby" only amounts to a relatively small number of people, but since they represent a united ethnic minority, the impact is out of proportion to numbers. There are about 11,000 dues-paying members of the American-Israel Public Affairs Committee, the main Jewish lobbying group—although an old political aphorism asserts, with some foundation, that the Jewish lobby is actually composed of all the millions of American Jews. At any rate, there is nothing sinister about how the group operates. Like every other lobby, it uses the weapons of public statements and private sessions with legislators to influence public opinion and political action. But the Jewish lobby has a reputation for political acumen and sophistication that makes it among the most effective lobbies in Washington.

The strength of the Jewish lobby stems from the fact that Jews in America are disproportionately activist in politics. Although they do not represent a majority in a single one of the country's more than 400 congressional districts, an estimated one-third of all contributions to the Democratic Party come from Jews. Further, Jewish voters have an important impact on elections; in New York, a major electoral state, Jews compose about 35 percent of the voters in a primary election, and Jewish voters will cast about 25 percent of the votes in a general election. That amounts to powerful political ammunition when representatives of the Jewish lobby try to influence Congress or the White House, but politicians are also aware than an even more powerful emotion fuels the Jewish lobby, even more powerful than the issue of Israel: guilt. Older American Jews have arrived at the conclusion that perhaps they did not act strongly enough to save the Jews of Europe. They feel that they might have exerted more pressure against the Roosevelt administration to open American immigration quotas, or undertaken some action that might have compelled the United States to take in the European Jews threatened by the Holocaust. (In 1938, the United States refused to expand its immigration quotas to take in the Jews of Austria and Germany, and a year later an ocean liner filled with Jews expelled by the Nazis from Europe was refused entry to this country.)

In the past three decades, since the creation of the state of Israel, the American Jewish lobby has had a long run of successes. Aside from American aid to Israel, the lobby has been directly responsible for various legislation including: an amendment to laws involving United States–Soviet trade that compels Moscow to allow freer emigration for Soviet Jews; laws forging strong military links between this country and Israel; resolutions calling for reexamination of American membership in the United Nations in event of the expulsion of Israel; the blocking of American aid to the United Nations Educational, Scientific and Cultural Organization (UNESCO), because of its actions against Israel; laws prohibiting participation by American businesses in the Arab boycott against Israel; and cuts and modifications in proposed military aid to Arab nations. The lobby has also managed to exert strong influence on the direction of American politics and can demonstrate its political muscle almost at the drop of a hat. When some time ago Senator Charles Percy of Illinois advocated direct negotiations between Israel and the Palestine Liberation Organization, he was bombarded with an outpouring of 20,000 letters and telegrams, the vast majority of them highly critical, and almost all of them from Jews around the country who had been alerted by Jewish leaders about the necessity of making their feelings known to the senator.

This all sounds very impressive, but beginning shortly after the 1973 Arab oil embargo, the Jewish lobby has found its influence diminishing in official Washington, as a series of events coalesced to reverse the longstanding honeymoon between this country's officialdom and Israel. Those events include the growing power of Arab oil (and the influence it represents), the changing strategic picture in the Middle East, a change in American official perceptions of our interest in that area, and a general anti-Zionism that seems to have broken out all at once. Because of its high visibility, it is the Jewish lobby that has borne the brunt of these changes.

The oil boycott was, of course, a seminal event, for it established at once a new and vital factor in the Middle East equation: the critical dependency of the United States on Middle East oil. Judged in cold, strategic terms, Israel's interests seem insignificant compared to the reality of the bulk of the world's oil supplies lying beneath the desert kingdoms of the Arabs. In turn, this meant that almost overnight the political concerns of the Arab states—which seem to be almost exclusively focused on their insistence that Israel must be cut to size—became a matter of the gravest concern. And that, in turn, led to another significant development: a deduction by the American government, particularly in the State Department, that the Arab nations now represented a critical strategic factor.

The conviction was first articulated during the Nixon administration, when the first American wooing of the Arabs took place. It took the form of pronouncements that the United States was now pursuing an "even-handed" policy in the Middle East, meaning that the foreign policy concerns of Israel and the Arab states were to be regarded as co-equal by this country. What that meant was that henceforth, in addition to guaranteeing the security of Israel, the United States would also guarantee the security of certain Arab nations—Saudi Arabia above all—from what was presumed to be imminent Soviet attack in the Persian Gulf. The problem, of course, is that judged strictly in strategic terms (which is the way the White House regarded the situation), there is no way that Israel and the Arab nations can be regarded as co-equal. Obviously there is no similarity between a commitment that is basically moral (Israel), and another that is made because of critical strategic factors (Arabs and oil).

In the eyes of American policymakers it is here that the real tilt against Israel began. Once they made their minds up that the security of the oil beneath the sands of Saudi Arabia and other Arab states was a paramount consideration, then there was no way they could have an "evenhanded" policy in the Middle East, for the simple reason that the Arab states regard Israel as a pariah state, in existence only because of American support. And the price of the so-called "new relationship" between the Americans and the Arabs has been Israel, because there is nothing else that the Arabs care that much about. And so, very carefully, American administrations began to edge away from support of Israel, making it clear publicly and privately that their commitment to Israel was something less than total.

The change in American outlook is best summed up by the situation in Saudi Arabia, where a vast web of mutual dependence has grown during the past eight years, to the point where both nations are locked into a relationship that extends very deep. The reason for this is, of course, oil. In 1976, for the first time, Saudi Arabia passed Canada and Venezuela to become the largest supplier of crude oil to this country. The Saudis will provide nearly one-third of all oil imports into the United States this year; further, they have agreed to American requests for higher production rates to help stabilize oil prices in world markets.

Beginning in 1974, the United States embarked on a major program to forge stronger ties with the Saudis and, where possible, to create some new ones. Many of the links are business ties—at the moment, about 700 American companies do about $35 billion worth of business in Saudi Arabia—and others include everything from labor manpower training programs, another program to develop Saudi science, plans to develop Saudi water and agricultural resources, and even a program sponsored by the United States Census Bureau to "develop Saudi statistics."

More disturbing has been the pell-mell race by the United States to see how fast we can arm the Saudis to the teeth. That effort began with a relatively modest $300 million in 1972, shot up to $6.5 billion in 1979, and by now the United States has sold over $35 billion worth of arms to Saudi Arabia—all this for a country whose armed forces total all of 73,500 men. The equipment ranges from ordinary rifles to the best in the American arsenal—F-15 fighters, the most advanced in the world; the U.S. Army's main battle tank, the M-60; first-line tactical missiles; and the airborne warning and control system (AWACS) plane, a flying radar detection system that includes the very latest electronic warfare equipment. Additionally, American military and civilian contractors are constructing $24 billion worth of military and military-related projects, including naval bases and airfields in Saudi Arabia.

Against what threat? The threat, American policymakers have insisted, of a Russian invasion into the Persian Gulf, an invasion that would have as first priority the rich oil prize of Saudi Arabia. This assertion led the Carter administration to sell the F-15 fighters to Saudi Arabia, supposedly stripped-down models that would pose no threat to Israel. But upon taking office, the Reagan administration proposed that the Saudis be sold a few options for the planes—such as bomb racks, fuel tanks, new air-to-air missiles and aerial refueling aircraft. That would make very good offensive weapons that much better—and provide them with the fuel and capability to reach Israel. In the Reagan view, such an eventuality was not possible because the United States would not permit it—although it has not been explained what would happen if the Saudis suddenly decided to throw out all the American advisors, and announce they would do with all their advanced military equipment whatever they wanted to do, including an attack on Israel. The weapons, after all, have been bought and paid for by the Saudis, and it is difficult to imagine how the United States proposes to control all that hardware and accompanying military facilities if the Saudis ever get the idea to use the stuff in a way the United States does not exactly approve.

The significance of all this now has come down to a battle of the lobbies—a major effort by the Reagan administration to convince Congress and the American electorate that a Saudi Arabia as an armed camp is critical to United States interests, a position opposed by an increasingly nervous Jewish lobby, which argues that the American arming of the Saudis is out of all proportion to their legitimate defense needs, and underscores the American tilt toward the Arabs. In the administration's view, the Saudis face dire threats to their existence, including a possible major Soviet assault (as indicated by the Soviet invasion of Afghanistan), increased tensions with Iraq and Iran, and the danger of attack from the Soviet-supported countries of Ethiopia and South Yemen. In this dire view, the Saudis are surrounded on nearly all sides by fierce enemies, and only the American military pipeline keeps the wolves at bay.

This argument simply does not stand up. How an armed force of less than 75,000 men, however modern their American weapons, is supposed to combat a Soviet invasion is a mystery. Further, Iraq and Iran have been bleeding each other to death in a protracted war, and F-15 fighters and AWACS planes are no use against guerrillas operating in the mountains of Yemen. And as for another American assertion—that its bonds with Saudi Arabia serve as a "moderating influence" on the Saudi regime—the evidence suggests otherwise. For example, during the Islamic Conference sponsored by Saudi Arabia early last year, the Saudis called for a "jihad" (holy war) against Israel and openly condemned the superpowers for interference in the Middle East. (It is also worthwhile noting that Saudi Arabia thus far has refused to agree to a standard stipulation in United States laws governing arms sales, that such equipment will not be used against this country "or its allies," which in the context of the Middle East, obviously includes Israel.)

There is also a preponderance of evidence to suggest that the Saudis are hardly moderated by anything, including American arms sales or closer ties with this country. The Saudis are still leading the Arab offensive against the Camp David accords, and remain the leading source of funds for the Palestine Liberation Organization.

That being the case, why is the Jewish lobby having such a hard time (nearly total failure, actually) in convincing Congress that the mindless military buildup of Saudi Arabia has to stop? Because since at least the time of the Arab oil embargo in 1973, the Jewish lobby has been encountering a growing anti-Zionist trend, which most often takes the form of expediency: arguments to the effect that the "new realities" of the Middle East argue for a diminution in the American relationship with Israel. This is the more moderate form of the argument; there are officials, especially those Foreign Service officers assigned to Arab countries, who go even further, arguing that the American-Israel relationship creates "imbalance" in the Middle East, jeopardizing long-term American interests which should be firmly allied with the oil-producing states.

In the process, there is a chasm that is growing wider between the leaders of the Jewish community and the leaders of the American government, who plainly find the Jewish lobby an inconvenience. How far that gap has been deepening can be gleaned from a private meeting between then-Secretary of State Cyrus Vance and representatives of the American Jewish community in 1977, during which Vance sought to assure them that recent actions by the Carter administration did not mean the United States was turning against Israel. The Jews were not placated since they had only recently been confronted with evidence that the drift against Israel that they perceived was in fact so. One piece of evidence was the administration's decision to include acceptance of the role of the Palestine Liberation Organization in the Middle East peace process, which implied that the United States was about to do something the administration had vowed it never would do—officially recognize the PLO.

In reply Vance defended the administration, claimed that the PLO was not to be recognized, and made a few generalities

about the Middle East peace process. This was hardly reassuring, and at one point one of the Jewish leaders stood up and
said, "The Carter administration has done more to unify the
Jewish community in the past year than has been done in past
history."

In retrospect, the meeting can be considered extraordinary, not only because of Vance's seeming insouciance about
the Middle East, but because it underscored the abrupt change
that had taken place in the relationship between the Jewish
lobby and government officials. Once open and easy because
both sides seemed to share common goals, the relationship has
now become testy, and Jews increasingly find that what they
have to say is not very welcome in the corridors of power. More
significantly, last year the Jewish lobby found itself challenged
openly by an administration for the first time.

That confrontation amounted to a fight the Reagan administration deliberately picked with the Jewish lobby over the
issue of the sale of AWACS planes to Saudi Arabia. There
remains some doubt as to how that proposal came about—the
administration said it was acting on its own behalf, although
the Saudis said the idea had practically been forced on them by
the White House—but the ultimate effect was to create a
confrontation that turned ugly. Part of the problem was that
the administration decided to bet all its political chips on the
proposed sale, arguing that something like a crisis of Western
civilization was at hand. For example, here is how Joseph W.
Twinam, Deputy Assistant Secretary of State for Near Eastern
and South Asian Affairs, characterized the possible result if
Congress were to reject the AWACS sale:

> The result, inevitably, will be that our regional secur-
> ity will be undermined. The chances of Soviet politi-
> cal coercion and military intimidation will grow as
> the prospects for continued Western access to oil will
> diminish . . . Israel may pay as large a price as we if
> this sale is defeated . . . it will face . . . a Saudi Arabia

which is less responsive to United States influence,
less willing to work with us in the search for a lasting
peace, and less able to resist the pressure of radical
forces from inside and outside the region. Indeed, if
the sale is defeated, the only winners will be those
who would benefit from regional turmoil and cur-
tailed Western influences and curtailed Western
access to oil.

As the proposal reached Congress, there was an obvious new
twist to the administration's strategy—hinting, sometimes not
so subtly, that AWACS was in the national interest and only
the selfish interests of the Jewish lobby prevented this most
vital matter from winning immediate approval. Reagan enlisted the aid of three ex-presidents and a slew of former
officials to lobby for the sale, and one of them, ex-President
Richard Nixon, publicly claimed that "some parts of the Jewish community" were trying to sabotage the sale. No one in the
Reagan administration rebuked Nixon for this sideswipe at
American Jews, leading to the suspicion that he was acting as
point man for the administration, saying publicly what administration officials were saying in private. As a matter of fact,
some reports indicate that in private, sentiments among those
officials were bitterly anti-Israel (one report described the
atmosphere as "poisonous"), with special venom reserved for
American Jews. Another report described a private meeting
between Reagan and Republican senators, during which Reagan is supposed to have advanced the argument that the senators could not defeat the AWACS proposal, because such an
action would make it appear to Saudi Arabia that America was
susceptible to Israel and American Jews.

It is not known why the administration decided to pick a
fight with the Jewish lobby at that particular time on that
particular issue, but there appear to be two main considerations. One was the perception that the Jewish lobby had crested
and that the tilt away from Israel was in full swing; following

the lobby's major defeat in 1978 over the sale of jet fighters to Saudi Arabia, the Jewish lobby lost a series of other battles. Thus, it was time to confront the power of the lobby and "put it in its place" once and for all, so that the new reorientation of American foreign policy in the Middle East could continue.

The second consideration was the belief that the Jewish lobby was especially vulnerable at that time because it was busy attempting to justify several controversial actions by Israeli Prime Minister Menachem Begin, including the bombing raid on the Iraqi nuclear reactor and another bombing raid directed at the Lebanese capital of Beirut. Indeed, there was in fact deep division within the American Jewish community about Begin's hawkish policies in general, a division that had been papered over. Despite the deep misgivings about Begin within American Jewry, the Jewish community is always careful to present a united front on the theory that such divisions only provide ammunition for enemies of Israel (and American Jews); further, such arguments traditionally are kept "inside the family."

There is some question of how valuable such a policy is. Certainly it did no good during the AWACS controversy; the proposal took no account of Begin's policies and concentrated instead on the theory that what was good for Saudi Arabia was good for the Middle East. The point was that Begin or no, Israel was hardly considered as a factor by the sale's proponents. Much of their testimony before congressional committees, in fact, concentrated not only on the wondrous benefits AWACS would bring, especially to the Saudis, but also how positively innocent the plane was. A parade of witnesses did so much downgrading of the plane and its capabilities, that Senator Henry M. Jackson was moved to observe, "I get the impression that it [the plane] is a piece of junk. I've never seen such a downgrading to this system." Senator Howard Cannon noted, "I did not realize that in funding this airplane when it was first proposed some years ago, that I was supporting a system of so little importance."

What then is the sense of the Jewish lobby working so hard to present as favorable an image of Israel (and its policies) as possible? Not much, really; as most people seem to be aware, if some Israelis are heroes in the defense of their homeland, there are also criminals and prostitutes; if it is true that Israel is a nation devoted to democratic ideals, it is also true that Israel deals with repressive Latin American regimes and has close links with South Africa; if Israel represents the triumph of Judaism, it is also true to say that the nation's religious affairs are run by a petty religious dictatorship of the Orthodox rabbinate; and if it is true that Israelis are devoted patriots to the Jewish state, then it is also true to note that nearly 250,000 Israelis have voted with their feet, leaving Israel to live and work in the United States. (It is also true that the overwhelming majority of emigrating Soviet Jews choose to go to the United States, despite the Israeli visas that got them out of the Soviet Union.)

One of the problems that has made the American Jewish lobby susceptible to the counterattack by the Reagan administration has been its insistence on having it both ways: on one hand trying to recapture its influence with the government, while on the other hand either pretending that problems with the way Israel conducts its policies do not exist, or trying to gloss over them. Certainly nothing was gained by downplaying the problems stemming from the Israeli occupation of the West Bank. During one particularly bad period in 1976 and 1977, the evidence seems persuasive that Israeli occupation authorities did actually engage in torture of Arab prisoners. The Israelis finally stopped these abuses, but one wonders how much more quickly they might have been halted had the American Jewish community openly condemned them. By the same token, it is fair to wonder how many of Israel's bad mistakes in its occupation of the West Bank might have been forestalled if they had been more widely publicized among American Jews.

The argument that such open discussion of Israel's faults provides ammunition to Israel's Arab enemies is specious, for the Arabs customarily do not bother with such formalities as facts when discussing Israel. Consider, for example, the speech given by the Jordanian delegate to the United Nations, Hazem Nuseibeh, before the General Assembly in December 1980:

> *The representative of the Zionist entity is evidently incapable of concealing his deep-seated hatred toward the Arab world for having broken loose from the notorious exploitation of its natural resources, long held in bondage and plundered by his own people's cabal which controls and manipulates and exploits the rest of humanity by controlling the wealth and money of the world ... It is a well-known fact that the Zionists are the richest people in the world and control much of its destiny.*

It should be remembered that this speech, replete with ancient anti-Semitic libels, was spoken in the chamber of the world body (not in some Arab radio propaganda broadcast) by the representative of what American officials call a "moderate" Arab state. Presumably, Jordan is as moderate as Saudi Arabia, whose leader, King Faisal, several years ago was quoted as saying that he heard "absolutely truthful" reports to the effect that five children had been murdered in France by Jews, who then used the dead children's blood for Passover seders.

The attempt to present Israel in the most favorable possible light has had little impact on the problem of the growing estrangement of the Jewish lobby and the government, especially Congress, because the central objection is that the lobby even exists, not how rosily the image of Israel is presented. How far that feeling has spread was indicated by an article written last year by a leading Republican moderate in Congress, Senator Charles McC. Mathias, Jr. of Maryland, in *Foreign Affairs* magazine. The article, entitled "Ethnic Groups and Foreign Policy," criticized various ethnic pressure groups—

the Jews among them—for imposing foreign policy positions on Congress.

"I know of few members of either house of Congress who do not believe deeply and strongly that support of Israel is both a moral duty and a national interest of the United States," Mathias wrote in his article, but then went on to say that the "Israel lobby" (meaning Jewish lobby) has tried to influence the direction of American policy in the Middle East "in a manner not consonant with the national interests of the United States." In one example cited in suppport of his thesis—the role of American Jews in pressuring President Truman to recognize the state of Israel—Mathias is guilty of bad history. He says, for example, that "Truman came down repeatedly on the side of his political advisers who warned of the risk of alienating Jewish voters," and that Truman first endorsed the creation of a Jewish state on October 4, 1946, the day of Yom Kippur and one month before the congressional election. However, the fact is that Truman recognized the state of Israel only after being advised to do so by the State Department, which argued that the United States could not afford to be the second nation to recognize Israel; the Russians, it was argued, were about to extend recognition, and for the United States to appear to be following the Soviet lead would be unthinkable. As for Truman's action in 1946, the fact is that Truman only issued a statement saying that the partition plan advocated for Palestine "would command the support of public opinion in the United States." The statement, in fact, disappointed Jewish and Zionist leaders in the United States, who were hoping for a more direct statement supporting their cause.

The tenor of the Mathias article, while apparently quite reasonable, nevertheless is suggestive of a basic antipathy toward ethnic politics (or lobbying) in general, with specific emphasis on the Jewish lobby. It is part of a continuing pattern of official and quasi-official annoyance at the existence and activities of the Jewish lobby, which in their view "complicates" Middle East policy. A more direct expression of that annoyance can be found in a widely-noted article appearing last year in *Time* magazine. Written by the magazine's diplomatic correspondent, Strobe Talbott, it is strongly redolent of the official State Department position on Israel and its American supporters, and there is sound reason to believe that it accurately reflected official American thinking.

"His [Begin's] country does not need the U.S. for its survival, but the sad fact is that Israel is well on its way to becoming not just a dubious asset but an outright liability to American security interests, both in the Middle East and worldwide," Talbott wrote, and a no more clear summation of how American officialdom now regards Israel could be found. And also the Jewish lobby: "His [Begin's] fellow Jews in America make up only 2.7 percent of the population. Begin recognized that American Jews wield influence far beyond their numbers but he also knew that there is considerable pent-up irritation in the U.S. with the power of the pro-Israel lobby..."

Talbott concluded by saying, "It is high time for the U.S. to engage Israel in a debate over the fundamental nature of their relationship. If that means interfering in Israeli internal politics, then so be it. Israel has been interfering skillfully and successfully in U.S. politics for decades, and will be doing so again..." The State Department reportedly loved the article.

All of this is a tribute to a number of things, not the least of which is the potency of the new oil politics, as practiced increasingly by the American government. It rests, sadly, on the delusion that piecemeal abandonment of the American commitment to Israel will blunt the Arab appetite. It will not, nor will the new anti-Zionism bring any more oil for this country. And it will not impose any sort of peace in that volatile area; Syria will still try to dominate in Lebanon, Iraq and Iran will still shoot at one another, Jordan will still fear Syria, and Saudi Arabia will still fear everybody. And the price of oil will continue to go up.

But however much support for Zionism erodes, one constant above all will remain: that short of a general conflagration, the Jewish people will never be homeless again. Zion, if only as an idea, is a fact of history, and no amount of anti-Zionism will ever change that.

CHAPTER NINE

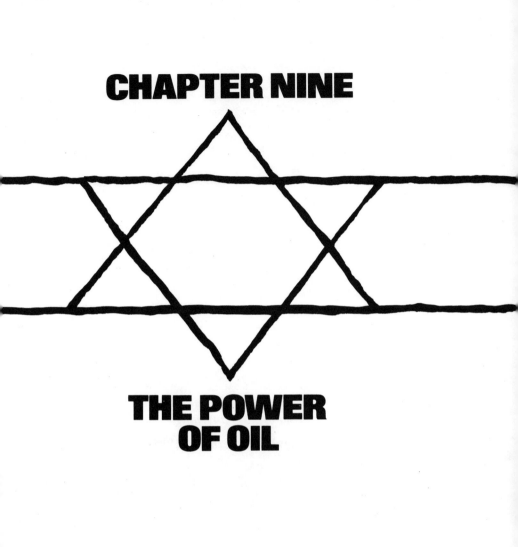

THE POWER
OF OIL

*For the defense of Saudi Arabia,
we will do anything.*

Zbigniew Brzezinski, 1980

For the sophisticated Frenchmen who run the gambling casino at the Hotel Majestic in Cannes, there had been no occurrence in that legendary playground of the jet set to shake their equally legendary blasé attitude toward the excesses of the idle rich. Not, that is, until a night in 1974, when an event transpired at the casino that stunned even the worldly Frenchmen.

Into the casino swept Prince Fahd bin Abdul Aziz, member of the Saudi Arabian royal family, complete with entourage and several young women. The Prince, clearly, was ready for a night of heavy gambling. From what appeared to be an inexhaustible bankroll, he proceeded to buy chips as though they were mere pennies; hundred-dollar chips were either thrown with abandon at waitresses and croupiers, or recklessly bet. The Hotel Majestic is accustomed to high rollers, but even their wildest dreams had never prepared them for Fahd. In about six hours Fahd lost around $2,500,000, a disaster which did not seem to bother him unduly: at the end of the night he simply shrugged his shoulders and left the casino, entourage in tow, and accompanied by the devout wishes of the management for his imminent return.

This event attracted a good deal of attention in the world press, and set off much bemused clucking about the profligacy of newly-enriched oil barons spending their new millions in the world's fleshpots and gambling casinos, like small children suddenly let loose in a toy store with thousands of dollars to spend as they wished. There have been many such incidents in the past eight years, plus other excesses such as the Saudi sheik who sought to buy the Alamo as a birthday present for his son, or another Arab oil millionaire who contracted with the University of Houston to send two professors to teach his daughters in Saudi Arabia at a cost of $3 million, undoubtedly the most expensive college education in history.

These incidents have all served as causes for some amusement, but the sensational headlines obscure the fact that there is something much more significant at work here than the assorted pecadillos of nouveau-riche oil barons who can't find ways to spend their money fast enough. The fact is that they represent exceptions; actually, the vast bulk of the Arab oil profits are not being gambled away in the world's casinos, but are being used to carry out an economic war against the Jews.

In the Arab view, this war has been going on for over thirty years since the creation of the state of Israel. In a modern parallel to the Thirty Years War that nearly devastated Europe in the seventeenth century, the Arabs regard their dispute with Israel as a "permanent state of war." Although four separate outbreaks of fighting would seem to have established Israel's legitimacy as a state, the Arabs continue to believe that Israel is a pariah state, an alien identity to be eliminated by every weapon available. And for some years now, the most potent weapon in the Arab arsenal has been economics.

It is the economic power provided by oil that fuels the entire Arab economic war, boycott included. There should be no mistake about the intent of the Arabs: to destroy the state of Israel and to cut off Israel's support from Jews—and non-

Jews—everywhere. That intent, of course, is not new; it has existed from the first moment of Israel's creation. However, it was never an especially effective weapon until the oil crisis of 1973, when world economics was stood on its head.

There are really two economic weapons. The most serious is the leverage provided by oil, a vital commodity whose proven reserves, by accident of geology, lie for the most part beneath territory owned by Arab nations. The second weapon is the economic boycott, an attempt to destroy Israel *and* the world Jewish community by economic strangulation.

This is not an extremist deduction; Arab powers no longer even bother to make a distinction between "anti-Zionism" and "anti-Semitism," making it clear that they are against Jews everywhere, period. Their battleground is the entire world, wherever they perceive "Jewish power" has created a threat or worked to support Israel. Since the main battleground at the moment is the United States, it is worthwhile to examine how that war is being conducted here, its impact on American Jews, its role in the new anti-Semitism and how, tragically, the Arabs found so many willing allies here in their fight to destroy the Jews.

There is an old Arab adage which says, "You can't drink your own oil," often cited in the years before 1973 when some of the more extreme Arab confrontationists tried to convince other Arab oil producers to seize the Western-dominated oil production companies and set the pricing themselves. Even as late as 1972, King Faisal of Saudi Arabia was warning the confrontationists that using the oil weapon against the West to derive more income and force changes in Western policies toward Israel would be "dangerous". In Faisal's analysis, the United States would simply cut its exports from the Persian Gulf, and then the Arabs would be left without the income from the oil, income vital to the Arab war effort against Israel. (In those days, the Egyptian war machine, among others, was almost totally funded by such Arab states as Saudi Arabia, which provided the cash to buy Soviet and European weapons.)

The confrontationists—notably Colonel Muammar el-Qaddafi of Libya—gradually got the upper hand, mostly because the Western oil companies that dominated the Arab producers became increasingly greedy. By January 1973, in fact, the average price of a barrel of crude oil was $2.59, and even with many millions of barrels being produced, clearly the Arabs weren't deriving the potential benefits this precious natural resource had conferred on them. It was just as clear that the Western producers were ripping them off, the better to build a vast industrial machine with cheap oil.

The break came during the Yom Kippur War in 1973, when an emboldened Arab oil cartel for the first time decided to use the oil weapon to help achieve Arab victory on the battlefield. On October 18, twelve days after the war had broken out, Saudi Arabia cut its oil production and threatened to stop shipments of oil to the United States altogether. Other Arab producers followed suit, and the resulting embargo set off a near-panic in the totally unprepared United States. The cease-fire between Israel, Syria and Egypt ended the ostensible reason for the boycott, but by December the Organization of Petroleum Exporting Countries (OPEC) demonstrated its new power by sharply increasing the price of oil—the price was raised to $11.65 a barrel (a price that seems nearly nostalgic in view of today's costs). By January 1974, the oil bill for the developing countries, especially the United States, was nearly $30 billion, $18 billion more than the previous year.

That was one aspect of the new realities of oil politics. But there was a second one that has turned out to be much more significant—the economic power represented by vast piles of surplus billions of dollars, the Arabs' profits from increased oil prices could be used as a weapon. Money is a very formidable weapon. In 1974 the Arab oil producers had about $50 billion in surplus money; by last year, that total had grown to over $300 billion. The bulk of this surplus money has been invested, mostly in the United States, which offers the world's best investment opportunities and the kind of economic infrastructure some of the Arab nations, particularly Saudi Arabia and Kuwait, would like to replicate in their own countries.

In the process, the Arabs have opened a new battlefront in the Arab-Israeli war—the boardrooms and counting rooms of America. There has been some spectacular publicity accompanying this investment effort, including the purchase of controlling interest in two large California banks, an Atlanta hotel and shopping center complex, a resort island off the coast of South Carolina, an unsuccessful attempt to buy two large coal-producing companies, and a large interest in an Arizona cattle ranching operation. But these represent only a small part of the overall Arab investment effort; most of it is carefully concealed behind a maze of secrecy and third-party operations that make it difficult to arrive at a definitive conclusion on just how much Arab money is invested in this country.

But it is not difficult to see that the Arabs have not had to work too hard to press their petro-dollars on reluctant American business; actually American businessmen have been pressing themselves on the Arabs, eager to take advantage of what might seem to be a bottomless reserve of Arab dollars simply laying around waiting to be taken. The American government has not only abetted this frantic scramble for the petro-dollars, it has also participated. As early as 1974, the government sought to make sure that the petro-dollars—at least most of them—wound up in the United States. In that year, then-Secretary of the Treasury William Simon made a pilgrimage to Saudi Arabia and convinced the Saudis to buy United States government bonds in an attempt to bail the government out of a bad cash squeeze caused by inflation. (One imagines the irony with which the Saudis greeted this request, since their oil price increases were and are to a large extent responsible for the soaring inflation in the American economy).

Since 1974 the American government has done everything possible to ensure greater Arab investment in the American economy, investments which the government has protected by allowing a veil of officially-protected secrecy to conceal their extent. And well they might, for there are indications that Arab investments are playing a growing role not only in the American economy, but in other world economies, as well. By May 1976 the Arabs owned about 20 percent of the world's entire monetary reserves, and two years later, when the Arabs decided that the English pound was no longer worth keeping, their dumping of billions of dollars worth of pounds on the monetary market nearly caused the pound to collapse. It was rescued only after an elaborate propping-up operation conducted by other nations, especially the United States.

There is much to be uneasy about with all this petro-dollar money flowing into the American economy. The most important question is how much of the power that this investment represents will be used by the Arabs as a weapon against Israel and its supporting apparatus from the world Jewish community— most significantly in the United States. Is this weapon being used? Yes, although at a low scale for the moment; more significantly, it turns out that the question comes down not so much to an attempt by the Arabs to effect changes in American Middle East policy, but the efforts by the Americans to anticipate that possibility by making that policy themselves. Thus, we find American companies voluntarily participating in the Arab boycott against Israel, refusing to hire Jews so as not to antagonize Arab business interests, and adopting a more pro-Arab (and often anti-Israel) policy to attract Arab business.

Even before the oil boycott hit, some American companies were adopting an expedient, although subtle, anti-Semitism to woo the Arabs. In June 1973, for example, the Mobil Oil Company took out a large ad in *The New York Times* that was headlined, "The U.S. Stake in the Middle East." Carefully worded, it amounted to a call for the United States to turn away from Israel:

> *We must learn to live with the peoples of these two countries (Saudi Arabia and Iran)... if we want to continue to enjoy our present life style... then we*

*will have to understand the changed and still-chang-
ing conditions in the Middle East... nothing less
than clear thinking, a sense of urgency, and a grasp of
what is at risk can lay the base for achieving a durable
peace in the Middle East.*

An even more direct example of this sort of Arab-wooing took place six months later when the chairman of the board of Texaco, Maurice Granville, delivered a speech in Scottsdale, Arizona. Granville told his audience that he was conveying to his countrymen an appeal from the Saudi Arabians "to review the actions of their government with regard to the Arab-Israel dispute and to compare these actions with its stated position of support for peaceful settlement responsive to [the] concerns of all the countries involved."

The prospect of petro-dollars has lured a wide range of business interests and former government officials to set up operations to snag these riches. The former officials who are involved with significant Arab investment operations in this country include former Texas Governor John Connally, former presidential adviser Clark M. Clifford, former Senate Foreign Relations Committee Chairman J. William Fulbright, and the most execrable of the lot, former Vice-President Spiro Agnew who, as noted earlier, has adopted anti-Semitism as his chief selling tool with the Arab oil producers.

It is no accident that a growing anti-Zionism and anti-Semitism has been emanating from this steadily enlarging community of American business interests who concentrate on Arab investments. Fulbright, whose Senate career was marked by many effusions of support for assorted downtrodden peoples, now no longer saw much merit in the grievances of the Israelis, a Middle East minority. Others have spoken much and often about the necessity of a more "realistic" Middle East policy by this country that takes into account desires of the Arab oil producers. Speeches often reflect an anxiety that American foreign policy support of Israel might anger the

Arabs, which in turn would compel them to withdraw their billions of investment dollars from the United States. It is an anxiety that has found some haven even in Congress, witness this statement by Senator Charles Percy during hearings in 1975 on Arab petro-dollars in American banks: "If Saudi Arabia and Kuwait withdrew their bank deposits, the biggest single loser would be the city of New York, and I would say the American Jewish community, centered in New York, would be the largest loser . . ."

This amounted to a warning to the American Jewish community to forget about trying to raise too many questions about the power of Arab money in this country. It is only one of the reasons why the Jews have become progressively nervous about the petro-dollar problem. They are concerned, for instance, about the fact that twenty-one of the largest American banks now have over $19 billion of OPEC money, about $15 billion of it from Arab oil-producing states. "Money buys influence" is an old principle of American economics, so it is perfectly logical to wonder about the role of such major American banks as Citibank of New York, which in 1976 was revealed to be holding $1.7 billion in deposits from Kuwait, alone.

Such concern has been pooh-poohed by the American businesses most directly involved with Arab investments. Their argument is that the Arab investment strategy is very conservative, that the sole aim of the investments is to receive good returns, and that the Arabs, whatever their rhetoric, are in fact pragmatic economically, having no desire to influence American Middle East policy or threaten the American Jewish community with the power of those billions of petro-dollars.

The problem with this assertion is twofold. In the first place, the Arab regimes which now direct the investment strategies and decide how the petro-dollars are to be spent are for the most part in the hands of highly conservative sheikdoms. What happens when another generation, not nearly so pragmatic, comes to power—or seizes power forcefully? What happens if more doctrinaire Arab politicians take power, or Moslem fanatics such as those who triggered the 1969 revolution in Libya that brought the fanatic Qaddafi to power? Secondly, how does the United States government propose to ensure that the Arab billions are not used to force changes in American foreign policy, in a blackmail operation similar to the one that caused such drastic increases in oil prices? Mere reassurances are not enough, for as we shall see subsequently, the American government does not even know at this point how much Arab money is in the American economy, which makes any assurance that it can control or monitor all that money a mockery.

American Jews have not been reassured by any action of the U.S. government on this subject to this point; in fact, many events are cause for some alarm. There is, for example, the case of Charles W. Robinson, a California businessman who among other things had put together a deal to move iron ore from Brazil to Saudi Arabia for a giant new Saudi steel mill. In the Nixon administration, Robinson became Undersecretary of State for Economic Affairs in the State Department, where he ran afoul of Assistant Secretary of State Thomas O. Enders. It so happened that Enders was author of a hard-line plan calling for a united front of oil-consuming nations against the depredations of OPEC. This distinctly displeased Robinson, whose duties included developing American policy for the State Department on Arab investments in this country and policy on American relations with OPEC. Robinson, strongly pro-Arab, was upset when, during a conference in Paris, Enders made several public anti-OPEC remarks. Robinson rebuked him, saying, "We are clearly here to work with the OPEC countries and deal in a constructive way with common problems". He subsequently complained to Secretary of State Henry Kissinger about Enders, who was exiled to the post of American ambassador to Canada. (Some years later, Robinson became a partner in two big New York investment firms that handle Arab investments in this country.)

This incident indicates a disturbing drift, and explains why Jewish groups in this country have shifted the focus of their concern. Traditionally, there has long been tension between the American Jewish community and American business over the question of hiring practices, especially in the executive suites; historically, Jews have been excluded from corporate leadership in a number of businesses, especially banking and investment. Along with most areas of American life, Jews have made progress in breaking down the doors of discrimination in the corporations, but as a recent report by the American Jewish Committee noted, Jews are still excluded from the executive ranks of several large corporations. This is of some concern, of course, but a greater concern is intruding: discrimination against Jews not simply because of the old-fashioned antipathy toward Jews, but because of fear that business might not get the Arab trade if there are Jews in executive leadership positions. A few instances:

• A Maryland electronics firm, trying to win a large armaments contract in Saudi Arabia, began asking job applicants their religion (such a question is in violation of the Civil Rights Act). The company at first denied that such a question was asked, then admitted so after one of the forms was made public. The company then said that the revelation would not change the composition of its work force destined to be sent to Saudi Arabia: it still would not include any Jews.

• Two engineers employed by a large maritime consulting firm were told they could not have well-paying jobs in Bahrain because they were Jewish.

• A receptionist-typist for an oil company was fired because she was Jewish; the company took the action because of fears that her presence would upset the many Arab visitors to the company's headquarters.

• An investment company trying to interest American

investors in the Middle East told clients about to take a tour of
that area to supply in advance a signed statement by a clergyman ("preferably on church stationery"), attesting that the
bearer was Christian.

• A large architectural firm, trying to win substantial contracts with Arab countries, reprinted its stationery in order to
remove twelve Jewish names from the letterhead.

Worse, several American government agencies have either
abetted this discrimination, or discriminated against Jews
themselves. The worst offender has been the U. S. Army Corps
of Engineers, which since 1964 has been constructing over $24
billion worth of civilian and military facilities in Saudi Arabia.
In most cases, the Corps subcontracts these vast construction
projects to civilian firms, with the Corps retaining full supervi-
sory duties for the work. In 1975, a congressional investigation
revealed that the original 1964 agreement with the Saudis
stipulated that Saudi Arabia would have the right to veto any
American contractors recommended by the Corps—obviously, a clause giving the Saudis the right to bar Jewish firms or
firms that employed Jews.

But it turned out that the problem was much worse than
that. Corps officials admitted that they not only cooperated
with the Saudi exclusion policy against Jews, but the Corps
itself had decided (even without prompting by the Saudi
government) to bar any Jewish soldiers and all Jewish
employees of American companies from going to Saudi Arabia
to work. The officials said they were only following orders of
the State Department—which signed the 1964 agreement on
behalf of this country—and that they did not even consider
applications by Jews for work in Saudi Arabia.

This disclosure created some measure of discomfort for
the Ford administration, which hastened to reassure that it was
indeed committed to equality and would not tolerate anti-
Semitism. President Ford himself issued a ringing statement,

and the Secretary of the Army announced that his organization would not participate in any anti-Semitism, whether "by proxy" or otherwise. These statements were all very heartening, but there is some question of how much was rhetoric, and how much was real. Only a year after the declarations, as a matter of fact, the Pentagon signed an agreement with the Vinnell Corporation, a group of ex-Army Special Forces and Central Intelligence Agency personnel, to train troops of the Saudi National Guard (the name for the Saudi Arabian army). The agreement, signed by the very same U. S. Army that only a year before had vowed it would never again participate in any anti-Semitic arrangements contained this clause: "All personnel shall be from countries recognized by the SAG [Saudi Arabian Government] and have no history of personal contact or interest in unrecognized countries."

In other words, no Jews. The incident caused Congress to lose patience, and it ordered the Ford administration to stop such practices. Congress threatened to block several billion dollars in American military sales to Saudi Arabia unless the Saudis stopped discriminating against American Jews—and this country ceased acquiescing to that discrimination. (Congressional investigators discovered that the Saudis were also barring American blacks because of fears that some of them might be Black Muslims, a sect greatly feared by the Saudis, who refer to them, incongruously, as "white Muslims.")

Again, administration officials promised they would end such discrimination, and accepted an anti-bias clause written by Congress. Since then, something of a veil of mystery seems to have settled over the situation. In 1977 there were reports of Jewish businessmen being permitted to visit Saudi Arabia, and two years ago there were other reports suggesting that a new Saudi hospital used some medical equipment that was manufactured in Israel. The Saudis themselves do not discuss these reported incidents, and American officials are even less willing to discuss them, or any other aspect of how the Arabs are handling the question of American business and Jews. What appears to be happening is that neither the Arabs nor the Americans want a repetition of the undue publicity of several years ago, so both sides have worked out some sort of quiet understanding. It amounts to handling the problem on a case-by-case basis, with both sides arriving at a deal on particular cases—depending on how willing American representatives in various Arab countries are to insist on exceptions to what is still a fundamental Arab policy not to have any dealings with Jews. We are still left with the current visa regulations of the Kingdom of Saudi Arabia, for example, that require: "Non-Muslims should produce a Certificate of Religion, e.g., Original Marriage Certificate if married in the church, or Baptismal Certificate, or Letter from Church on Church Headed Paper and bearing the Church Seal."

We are also left with the fact that many businesses (with the connivance of the American government) continue to cooperate with Arab anti-Semitism by not seeking any Israeli business, or making sure they have no Jewish connections or at least no highly visible Jewish employees, especially in the executive ranks. It is nearly impossible, however, to establish just how much of this is going on; how can it be established that a Jew was fired from a job or was not promoted because a particular business wanted to make sure it would not offend potential Arab business? It can't be done, although it should be noted that the recent project on anti-Semitism in the American business community (alluded to earlier in this chapter), found that Jews were mostly excluded from the executive ranks of the energy, heavy machinery, construction and banking industries; by interesting coincidence, those just happen to be the industries that do the most business with the Arab world.

In the long run, however, this sort of overt anti-Semitism may pale in significance when stacked beside a much more potentially dangerous development, the steadily growing piles of Arab oil billions now being invested in American business. Again, we find that it is not so much a case of Arabs trying to use that money to buy influence or control, but American business bending over backwards not to "offend" the source of all this vast wealth. According to the most recent Commerce Department accounting, foreign investments in the United States grew more than 20 percent last year, with investments by predominantly Arab OPEC countries rising nearly 50 percent. According to that accounting, total foreign investment in this country now approaches $66 billion—defined as book value of a foreign direct-investor's equity in U. S. business in which at least one foreign person owns, directly or indirectly, at least 10 percent of the voting securities.

Taken at face value, this does not appear to be much cause for alarm; after all, even $65 billion in the vast American economy, while not a drop in the bucket, nevertheless doesn't represent anything like imminent control. But the problem is that the Commerce Department figures in fact represent only the visible tip of an iceberg. For one thing, American regulations require public recording of investors only after their stock exceeds 5 percent of the issued stock of any given corporation. Moreover, the Commerce Department figures measure only what they can *find*; as we shall see, there is a great deal they are not finding.

One of the things they are not seeing is the true extent of Arab investments in this country. Under the agreement worked out by former Treasury Secretary William Simon in 1974, the United States agreed that it would never list publicly a detailed breakdown of Arab holdings in the United States. Thus, the most recent Treasury Department figures list only the combined totals for all thirteen OPEC members (about $70 billion, including government securities, corporate bonds, stocks and bank accounts). Without a breakdown, it is difficult to say how much money Saudi Arabia, Kuwait, the United Arab Emirates and other Arab nations have in this country.

According to one study by the *Mideast Report*, an economic and political magazine, Arab investments in fact total over $200 billion in this country, with less than a third detected by American government agencies because of highly sophisticated third-party and foreign syndicate operations designed to conceal just how much Arab money is actually pouring in. Concerned over these reports, the House Committee on Banking's Subcommittee on Commerce, Consumer and Monetary Affairs last year held hearings in an attempt to get the real figures from government officials—and came up against a stone wall. Treasury Department officials flatly refused to give a country-by-country breakdown of foreign investments by Arabs (citing the 1974 agreement), insisting that revelations of their investments would cause the Arabs to withdraw all that money. The same argument was made by various business interests, who claimed disclosure would balk what they considered "indispensable" recycling of petro-dollars (although they left unmentioned the motive of very fancy fees banks and investment houses in this country collect for husbanding Arab investments).

What that amounts to is a $60 billion discrepancy between what the United States government says is the total Arab investment in this country and the actual figures, as partially reflected in the American balance of payments accounts. The figures simply do not jibe, and what's worse, it is obvious that the government's policy of allowing the Arabs secrecy in their American investments has led to a pronounced dearth of knowledge on the subject. One interesting indication on how far this lack of knowledge extends occurred during the hostage crisis when Treasury Department officials, under orders to freeze Iranian assets in this country, tried to find out what assets there actually were. It took several months to find that the Iranians had about $11 billion in assets, and most experts agree that the real total was closer to $16 billion.

At the moment, there are only indications—clues, really— of the extent of Arab investment in America. One indication is the statistics on total foreign assets in this country: in 1974 they were reported at $196 billion; by 1980 they were $481 billion. Actually, in truth the figures may be higher, but there are inadequate reporting and accounting controls, not to mention the many indirect channels through which Arab money can be invested here. In fact, according to one estimate prepared by Paul A. Volcker, chairman of the Federal Reserve System, about $75 billion in OPEC foreign holdings had not been discovered by the government's detection process, and the Treasury Department found about $40 billion unaccounted for in its estimates on OPEC surplus funds.

Nongovernmental sources deduce that there is at least $100 billion worth of Arab holdings in the United States, a deduction they arrive at by taking the Treasury Department's official figure of $51.3 billion of total Arab investments by the end of 1980, adding the $6.2 billion known to have arrived here in the first four months of last year, then adding the $20 billion of Arab money deposited thus far in foreign branches of American banks, and finally adding the approximately $20 billion of Arab money flowing into this country from offshore banks and other sources. That brings the total to nearly $100 billion, which is probably approximately correct (or certainly a lot more accurate than the American government's official figures). Where does all the money go? How much influence does it buy?

Let's begin with the Saudis. Saudi Arabia funnels its money through an organization known as the Saudi Arabian Monetary Agency (SAMA), which receives $320 million *each day* in oil revenues, and is then supposed to figure out ways to invest it. This is no simple task, for the Saudis now receive about $120 billion a year in oil revenues, creating a surplus of more than $100 billion. SAMA generally follows a conservative investment policy, buying safe U. S. Treasury bills and notes (it now has about $30 billion of those), plus another $15 billion in loans to major American corporations, including $650 million to American Telephone and Telegraph, $200 million to U. S. Steel and $300 million to IBM. (The interest on such loans is called "service fee" by the Saudi Arabians, since the Koran forbids the charging of interest.)

Up to this point the Saudis have generally refrained from

using any muscle all that money represents, but that may be changing: last year SAMA agreed to lend money to the International Monetary Fund (IMF) for which they demanded (and got) a permanent seat on the fund's executive board. That board, which decides which nations will get monetary help from the international aid agency, may now possibly acquire a new anti-Israel trend as well as a new member—the Palestine Liberation Organization. The Saudis for some time have demanded that the IMF give observer status to the PLO, and it is a virtual certainty they will now use their new clout in the international organization to bring in the PLO. When that happens, the potential for mischief is nearly incalcuable.

In the United States there have only been a few instances of outright anti-Semitism associated with Saudi influence, a tribute not only to the Saudi conservatism and low profile in connection with its American investments, but also to the fact that the Saudis' American apologists usually carry out the dirty work. Take, for example, the wave of grants and contracts underwritten by the Saudis and a number of American oil companies recently, mostly to American universities for "Middle Eastern studies" or "Islamic studies." The Saudis seldom have to say that Jews are to be excluded from such studies; frequently the universities themselves decide not to "offend" their benefactors by making sure that such things as Hebrew studies and Jewish biblical history are excluded from Middle Eastern studies, although it is reasonable to wonder how any such course of study could possibly fail to include Hebrew civilization. But, in too many cases, this is precisely what has been happening, and it should be noted that the offenders include not only the universities, but also some construction and oil companies, bankrollers of some of these courses, eager to curry favor with their best customer, the Saudis.

Often the anti-Semitism is quite blatant. Last year, for intance, an Israeli professor at the University of Texas was blocked from permanent appointment to the history department, following pressure by the university's Middle East Center (funded by Arabs and American oil companies with significant business ties to Saudi Arabia), on the grounds that the Israeli's appointment would "antagonize" Arab benefactors of the center. Some years earlier there had been an even more blatant case, this time at the University of Southern Califoria, which received a $1,000,000 donation from Saudi Arabia to establish the King Faisal Chair of Islamic and Arab Studies. At first blush the donation seemed to have no strings attached, but it then developed that, on closer reading, there were several conditions. One was that the first occupant of the Chair would be one Professor Willard A. Beling, and successive occupants would be chosen only in consultation with the Saudi Arabian Minister of Higher Education. Beling, as it happened, was a long-time executive with ARAMCO (Arabian American Oil Company), who had organized a conference in 1978 to "pay tribute" to King Faisal. And it was during this conference that it was "suggested" to the representatives of forty American corporations in attendance at the conference that they might like to contribute money to help establish a Middle East Center at the University of Southern California. Further, the businessmen were told, the Saudis would be "delighted" with such a move; the businessmen needed no further hint and dutifully coughed up the money (with the understanding that the Center would be headed by Beling, whose academic credentials, by the way, do not include any in Islamic or Arab studies). Further, the funding would be administered by the Middle East Center Foundation—whose president was Beling himself.

Fortunately this squalid performance soon reached the ears of several Jewish organizations, and the resulting publicity forced the University of Southern California to decline the offer. This moved the executive of one of the firms involved in funding the original proposal to announce that the idea had been killed because of "distortions" by the "Jewish press."

There has also been some unwelcome publicity (at least from the Saudi standpoint) attendant on the activities of a number of interesting Saudi businessmen with strong American connections. Chief among them has been Adnan Mohamed Khashoggi, who first came to notice in 1973 when, thanks to his business partnership with Prince Talal bin Abdul Aziz (one of the King of Saudi Arabia's sons), he earned about $50 million in commissions from the Chrysler Corporation for helping to sell Chrysler products in Saudi Arabia. Khashoggi has since become notorious for his appetite for luxury, including a private Boeing 727 with five television sets and bedroom suites, plus luxurious homes and apartments around the world.

Despite frowns from the Saudi royal family, which dislikes such publicity, Khashoggi has gone his flamboyant way. He struck up a friendship with Richard Nixon in 1967, a relationship the Saudis sought to exploit in 1973 when Khashoggi, acting on behalf of the Saudi royal family, tried to convince Nixon to halt the airlift of arms to Israel during the Yom Kippur War. Over and above that, Khashoggi has been very busy in American economics. By 1976 he had fifty-three subsidiaries operating under the umbrella of his Triad Holding Corporation, based in Luxembourg for tax reasons. Armed with all that oil money, he bought: controlling interest in the National Bank of Walnut Creek, California (an acquisition eagerly abetted by the Bank of America, which was eager for Middle East business); a Japanese steak house in San Francisco; a Colorado company that manufactures truck trailers; a $250 million business complex in Salt Lake City; and is the largest stockholder in an Arizona cattle operation. Khashoggi had one brush of trouble with the U. S. Justice Department, which wanted to know about his dealings with various American arms manufacturers, including a $45 million "fee" for helping to arrange the sale by Lockheed to Saudi Arabia of $850 million worth of arms. (Khashoggi said this sort of business was "forced" on him by American companies avid to tap into the vast Saudi Arabian market.)

This assertion generated much amusement, but there was nothing very amusing about some of the uglier aspects of other Khashoggi deals in this country. One especially ugly incident involved the large First National Bank of San Jose, California. Khashoggi offered $21.83 a share for stock then selling for $16.50 a share. The board of directors approved what was to be a $15 million deal, but the offer (which had to be approved by the bank's stockholders) alarmed the Jewish community in California, which lobbied fiercely against the sale. It was enough to squelch the deal—banks are not fond of publicity— and Khashoggi was enraged at having to withdraw the offer. "Zionists," he claimed, "were trying to use the deal to create a new wave of hatred for the Arabs among the American public. I decided not to give them that satisfaction." To underscore their anger, the Saudis and Kuwait removed from any international underwritings involving petro-dollars a number of "Jewish-controlled" firms, such as Lazard Frères, S. G. Warburg, and the Rothschilds.

Much more subtle was the Saudi attack to gain control of the Commonwealth Bank of Detroit, once among one of the nation's most prestigious, but which by 1973 had fallen upon hard times because of poor investments. In 1974 an angel appeared in the guise of a wealthy Egyptian businessman who wanted to bail out the bank. In fact, however, he was only a front man for the Saudis, but he succeeded in lining up the city's business elite behind the sale, most notably Henry Ford (who was eager to curry favor for the Arabs at that point because of his desire to reopen a Ford assembly plant in Egypt).

The sale went through in 1975, aided in no small part by unofficial help from the Treasury Department, which was delighted to see a troubled major American bank bailed out. Jewish groups were less happy when they discovered that the real powers behind the bank takeover where Ghaith Rashad Paraon (a Saudi Arabian businessman who among other things had quietly picked up 1,000,000 shares of Occidental Petroleum, the eleventh largest oil company in America), and Sheik Kamal Adham (closely connected to the royal family by marriage, and head of the Saudi Arabian Intelligence Service that had strong ties with the American CIA). The resulting controversy not only caused strong protests by Jewish groups, but also a severe drop in deposits by Americans alarmed at Arab control of American banks.

What controls was the American government instituting to make sure that wouldn't happen? None; as a matter of fact, behind the scenes the government has encouraged even greater Arab investment, which is in turn aided by help from the American business establishment. In the Detroit bank deal, the law firm of John Connally handled the legal end, which in turn brought into play a wide range of establishment-connected contacts who also helped. For much the same reason, there was not a flicker of interest from the government when the Saudis bought a 37.6 percent share of a Houston industrial contractor. Nor was there any interest when the Kuwaitis bought 16 percent of Reynolds Securities Inc. (the Arabs' first big move into Wall Street). But when the Kuwaitis also bought the 3,500-acre Kiawah Island resort off the coast of South Carolina, the authorities actually fell all over themselves trying to convince the Kuwaitis to buy in. Overriding the protests of Jewish groups that the Arabs were "trying to buy America," officials of South Carolina tried to convince Kuwait to build a refinery in the state and attempted to create a whole series of joint Kuwait-South Carolina industrial projects. (It should be noted here that the then-Governor of South Carolina, John West, was later appointed ambassador to Saudi Arabia.)

It can be argued that these incidents only represent reasonable investment opportunities, and lack political impact. But there is steadily increasing evidence that the Arabs are beginning to convert the clout their economic power in this country represents into real political power. Aside from the Saudi attempt to balk arms shipments to Israel in 1973, as noted earlier, there was also an attempt by the Saudis to buy influence in the Carter administration. That took the form of a $2.4 million purchase of stock in the troubled Bank of Georgia from Bert Lance, a Carter intimate. Obviously, it was a bad deal: the purchase, carried out by a Saudi businessman, bought 120,000 shares at a price three times what Lance originally paid for them. Unless the Saudis knew of an oil deposit lying somewhere in the ground underneath the bank, the deal made no sense. But it made plenty of political sense; the Saudis were making a very direct bid for influence with Carter by helping to bail out his old friend.

In other cases it is Americans who offer political influence on a silver platter. Many American entrepreneurs in the public relations business have lusted after the Arabs, offering expensive campaigns to "sell" Americans on the virtues of Arabs. One special example is Raymond Mason, chairman of the Charter Company, a Florida-based oil business conglomerate whose properties included *Family Weekly*, a Sunday newspaper magazine with a 6,000,000-plus circulation. (It has since been sold to CBS Publications.) Mason, believing that the American media was "slanted" against Arabs, first considered the idea of buying a controlling interest in *The New York Times*, and then proposed a $7.7 million public relations campaign for the Saudis in this country. Neither of these ideas came to pass, but Mason had a favorable story prepared on Saudi Crown Prince Fahd for *Family Weekly*, and had it shown to the Saudi royal family before it ran.

Not everybody in American business lusts after Arabian dollars, of course; the executors of the estate of J. Paul Gettty last year rejected a $982 million bid from Kuwait to buy a 14.6 percent share of the Getty Oil Company. And a number of other, less-publicized companies have resisted any Arab takeover attempts, even when—as is most often the case—the money offered is very attractive.

Still, there are more than enough American corporations and other business enterprises only too willing to cooperate with the Arabs, including some of the uglier implications of anti-Zionism/anti-Semitism. And, combined with what amounts to official American government indifference, the

unfortunate trend is all upward; the deals are not only getting
bigger, but the slices of the American economy falling into
Arab hands are also getting bigger. Only recently, Kuwait
spent $2.5 billion to take over Santa Fe International, a leading
oil drilling and production company, plus a $185 million share
in a Hawaiian oil refinery, as well as participation in a United
States oil exploration group; the Kuwaitis are planning to soon
start buying American gasoline stations as part of a vertical
investment strategy to control the sale of oil, from oil well all
the way to the gas station.

There is another even more ominous development: the
Palestine Liberation Organization has begun to invest in
American corporations. The investments, carried out in the
greatest secrecy and presently on a low scale, are part of a $100
million PLO investment venture that seeks to raise funds for
the organization and sever the lifeline now extended primarily
by Saudi Arabia. (The Saudis contribute the bulk of the $70
million given each year by the Arab nations to the PLO.) The
PLO portfolio includes investment property in the Middle
East—hotels, shipyards, and oil tankers—and is now being
diversified into blue-chip corporations, especially American ones that have extensive Middle East dealings. The
investments, made with intricate arrangements to conceal their
origin, are mainly through the Arab Bank Limited. Based in
Jordan, the bank has assets of $4 billion and ties with the
banking community in nineteen countries, including the United States.

In this connection, mention should be made of an important by-product of this Arab economic offensive—the Arab
economic boycott. The boycott is not new; it was actually first
promulgated in 1922, when the Fifth Arab Congress called on
all Arabs to boycott Jewish businesses. The Arab Congress
was especially exercised about the sale of land to Jewish settlers
in Palestine, and its failure to block these sales was later to have
momentous consequences in Middle East politics. At any rate,

the creation of the state of Israel led to the formation of the Arab League Boycott Committee, headquartered in Damascus, Syria, where it remains to this day.

In its early days, the Arab boycott—which, in its simplest form, prohibits any Arab from doing business with anyone who had any business relationship with Israel or its Jewish supporters—was known as something of a joke. It boycotted actress Elizabeth Taylor's films after she converted to Judaism; banned showing of Walt Disney's "Snow White and the Seven Dwarfs" in the Arab world because one of the horses in the film was named "Samson" (somehow this was regarded as Jewish propaganda); and also boycotted any performances of what they thought was a musical group called "Red Orchestra," led by a Jew. (In fact, the name was given by the Germans to a noted Soviet spy ring of World War II; its leader had survived the war and emigrated ultimately to Israel.)

The jokes stopped in 1973, when the new power of oil suddenly put teeth into what had been up to that point a largely empty bluff; the boycott had been inefficiently administered, incompetently directed and generally ignored, partially because American business with the Arab world was at a comparatively low level. Actually, there are two parts to the Arab boycott. The so-called "primary" boycott in effect constitutes an agreement by all Arab states not to trade with Israel in any way. It is the "secondary" boycott which accompanies this "primary" boycott that is the more dangerous—it is aimed at all companies, organizations and individuals that do business with Israel in any form. Those that do are excluded from Arab markets. This secondary boycott has a corollary: Third World firms who do business with other firms that, in turn, have a business relationship with Israel, are boycotted from any Arab business. The companies even face boycott if they deal with a company that has no business relations with Israel, but does have Jews on the board of directors or in executive positions.

The changed economic circumstances caused by the oil crisis meant that almost overnight the Arab market, which had once been considered a relatively minor one suddenly became a major target, especially for American business. Which also meant that the boycott became a significant business factor. And again, in a pattern that seems to be repeated endlessly, it was discovered that the Arabs did not have to do much pushing to get American business to cooperate with the boycott—the businesses often have done the boycotting themselves in an effort to win favor with the Arabs. They cut off any business contact with Israel, work hard to ensure that they are "clean" (no Jewish executives or contact with Israel) with the Arabs, and hire middlemen who steer them through filling out the complicated questionnaires the Arab Boycott Office requires of businesses seeking markets in Arab lands. Here is a sample of a typical business declaration which, up to only a few years ago, was required by the Arabs:

WE HEREBY SOLEMNLY DECLARE THAT THE COMPANY IS
NOT A JEWISH COMPANY NOR CONTROLLED BY JEWS OR
ZIONISTS AND IT HAS NO RELATIONS WITH ISRAEL...

A 1974 agreement on economic cooperation between the United States and Saudi Arabia modified this provision; current editions eliminate the reference to Jews, but retain the reference to Israel. (The Saudis willingly agreed to this change because they see no distinction between Israelis and Jews, anyway.)

Whether the words are "Israelis" or "Zionists" or "Jews," the intent of this boycott paperwork is clear beyond any doubt: a boycott against Jews everywhere, part of an ongoing attempt to use Arab influence—particularly the new influence of oil politics—to destroy Israel and its Jewish supporters. Jewish groups long ago sensed the danger in the boycott, even as far back as 1954, when they carried out their own boycott against the Brown & Willamson Tobacco Company, which was refusing to sell cigarettes to Israel for fear of antagonizing Arab customers. After Brown & Williamson's share of American tobacco sales dropped from fifth to tenth place, the company got the point and began selling to both Arabs and Israelis. Years later, the Jewish community participated in a boycott of the Coca-Cola Company for its alleged reluctance to establish plants in Israel; Coca-Cola lost $5,000,000 worth of sales and, despite threats of closure of its bottling plants in Arab countries, opened an Israeli operation.

But there is some question whether such selective counter-boycotts by the Jewish community in this country would be effective today; the problem is that the range of American firms actively or covertly cooperating with the Arab boycott is so wide that there are simply too many targets. Oil companies and banks have been especially notorious compliers with the boycott. The more odious examples include a 1975 contribution of $50,000 by the Gulf Oil Corporation to help finance an anti-Zionist propaganda campaign by Arab organizations in this country (the company later apologized for it); and the signing of a statement by the Getty Oil Corporation the same year that large amounts of oil-field equipment it was selling to Kuwait "are not of Israeli origin nor do they contain any Israeli materials."

Banks, sensitive to the rise and fall of political barometers, have been especially cooperative with the Arab boycott, notably after billions of dollars in Arab petro-dollars began to flow into their vaults. Jewish-owned banks, which normally would have been involved in major international bond issues and other such transactions, found themselves frozen out by the rest of the banking community whenever Arab money was involved. The banking establishment even went a step further, stepping into politics. A delegation of bankers joined oilmen during one meeting to try to convince President Nixon to adopt an American Middle East policy "more friendly to Arabs," and Chase Manhattan Bank President David Rockefeller later led a delegation of American businessmen praising criticism (by Henry Kissinger) of Israeli "intransigence." (It should be noted that in 1975 the Chase Manhattan Bank refused to open a branch office in Israel.)

The anti-Zionism of the American banking industry became so notorious that the Anti-Defamation League was finally compelled to announce that twenty-five U.S. banks had been carrying out an "economic war against Israel in collaboration with the Arabs...[in] violation of U.S. anti-boycott policy." The banks, it was discovered, had been bending over backward to demonstrate their refusal to do business with Israel, part of an attempt to secure exporters' letters of credit—for which Arabs demanded proof of boycott compliance. Several of the banks were prominent in Arab-American chambers of commerce (groups which are suspected of playing key roles in the boycott by helping to "arrange" compliance).

The role of oil companies and banks was one of the major reasons for the growing disquiet within Congress concerning the extent of compliance by American business with a boycott that was fundamentally anti-Semitic. It did not take congressional committees long to discover that, among other things, fourteen American banks had acceded to at least 18,000 requests to participate in boycott restrictions. Further, two major securities firms had excluded "Zionist" banks from underwriting syndicates. These and other revelations led to an attempt to pass legislation making it illegal for American companies to participate in such boycotts. During 1975 and 1976, there were at least two dozen bills introduced, all of them balked by stonewalling tactics of the Ford administration, plus a strenuous propaganda assault from a coalition of oil companies and business groups. According to their testimony, any such law would leave the United States vulnerable to economic reprisals by the Arabs, create vast oil shortages, set off a recession accompanied by massive unemployment and, in the words of the Mobil Oil Company, turn this country into "a second-rate economic power." The Commerce Department saw no harm in the Arab boycotts, arguing that American

businessmen should be free to make "economic decisions based
on their own business interests," which is about as clear a
license for anti-Semitism (or any other kind of discrimination)
as has ever been uttered by an American government body.

Finally, after nearly two years of debate, President Jimmy
Carter signed a compromise anti-boycott law in June, 1977, at
the same time carefully reassuring the Arabs by saying that the
new law would not affect the primary Arab boycott against
Israel—which, as Carter accurately noted, is a right accorded
every nation. (Including, he might have added, the United
States, which for nearly three decades has carried out a primary economic boycott of Cuba.) While the bill was laudatory
on its basic merits, it contained a number of gaping holes,
chief among them being the provision giving the Commerce
Department authority to monitor American compliance with
the law and to impose fines on any U.S. business found comp-
lying with the Arab boycott. Which meant, of course, that the
Commerce Department would have to catch the violator first.
Secondly, the law offers a large loophole: it says that no
American company can comply with an Arab request not to
sell such-and-such brand of widgets to Israel, but there is
nothing wrong with the Arabs asking for a particular brand of
widgets they know is made by a company that has no business
connections to Israel—or employs no Jewish executives.

By last year it was clear that the American anti-boycott
law had turned out to be somethng less than a raging success.
Figures from the Commerce Department showed that about 60
percent of American companies operating in the Middle East
cooperated with the Arab boycott in one degree or another;
one report quoted a Commerce Department official as saying
privately that "an arrangement can be made" between Americans and Arab customers to comply with the law—one common example is for American companies to sign an Arab
statement to the effect that a particular product is made
entirely in the United States or some other country; obviously,
this is another way of saying that the material has no connec-

tion with Israel. Some American companies do get caught—
Rockwell was fined $71,000 in 1980 for providing Arabs with
information on other companies restricted from doing business with Israel—but on the whole, all parties concerned with
the issue have managed to work out quiet arrangements. And
what enforcement now exists has been threatened by department budgetary cutbacks by the Reagan administration, stim-
ulated in no small measure by a more sympathetic attitude
toward the problems of American businessmen.

What we are left with is a very dismal picture, indeed. It
amounts to an especially pernicious form of expedient anti-
Semitism; with the exception of some of the Arab fanatics who
figure in this account, there is not a single anti-Semite who can
be found. They are instead upright, honorable men, talented
and intelligent enought to have built business empires.Their
crime is a terrible one: selling souls for dollars, acting in effect
as though whatever profits are to be made in Saudi Arabia or
Kuwait (or here, from Arab oil dollars) are worth any price—
up to and including Israeli and American Jews. These men are
sophisticated enough to understand that the Arab boycott
amounts to nothing less than an attempt to obliterate a people
with whom the Arabs happen to have a political argument.

The history of the modern era suggests that as the military
war against Israel failed, so too will the economic war fail. But
for the economic war to succeed, it takes only normally decent
men to let it happen.

CHAPTER TEN

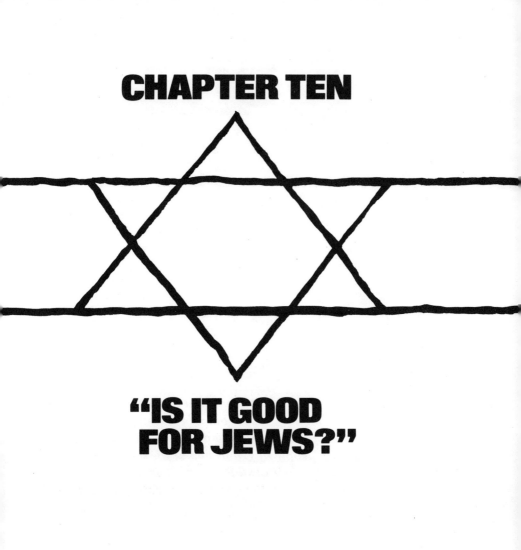

"IS IT GOOD
FOR JEWS?"

The Jews are a small people but a great people.
They are an ugly people but a beautiful people.
They are a people that builds and a people that destroys.
They are a people of genius and at the same time
a silly people. By their obstinancy they can drive through
a wall, but the hole in the wall remains gaping at them.

Chaim Weizman

It began with the ceremonial firing of a cannon salute, and then the procession of dignitaries, led by a grand marshall on horseback, moved solemnly to the local Episcopal church, where the honored man of the hour dedicated a cornerstone. Dressed in an elaborate ermine robe, the man—Mordecai Emanuel Noah—proclaimed "Ararat—the City of Refuge," a speech that drew warm applause from the assembled dignitaries. Then the cornerstone was put away, to await the building of Ararat on Grand Island in the Niagara River.

This event took place on the morning of September 12, 1825, in the city of Buffalo, New York. Ararat was never built, and Mordecai Noah died some forty years later, having failed to achieve his dream of a homeland for the Jews right here in America. He died a puzzled man, never understanding why the small American Jewish community of the time felt there was no necessity of a "refuge" for Jews.

It is interesting to speculate what would have happened if Noah—playwright, politician and later judge—had succeeded in his dream of building what amounted to a Zion in America.

Would the fact that Jews all lived on an island have lessened to any degree native anti-Semitism? Would the anti-Semites have thought any more of the Jews, now that they were all contained on a large island on a river between Canada and the United States?

Probably not, for anti-Semitism in all its guises is fundamentally irrational; it is irrational when Jews are accused of draining blood from the bodies of Christian children to make Passover bread; when Jews are accused of murdering Christ; when Jews are accused of poisoning wells to cause the Black Plague; when Jews are accused of dominating the world economy; when Jews are accused of constituting a satanic plot; when Jews are accused of being responsible for expensive oil. Anti-Semitism really has little to do with status or non-status of Jews, and it is for that reason that American Jews, the crowning (and most accomplished) glory in the history of Judaism since the days of the biblical David, also feel the sting of anti-Semitism.

The new outbreak of anti-Semitism which has been discussed at some length in this work is at once frightening and puzzling—frightening because such hatred historically is the harbinger of greater hatred to come, and puzzling because despite the vast library now extant on the history, causes, manifestations, and proposed cures dealing with anti-Semitism, it is a phenomenon that remains just slightly out of reach. There is much disputatiousness in studies of anti-Semitism, and there is no academic discipline that hasn't tried to grasp it—psychology, history, sociology, social psychology, psychiatry. All to little avail, because there is too much about anti-Semitism that makes no sense. (This is currently exemplified by events in Poland, where the tiny remnant of what was once a large Jewish community is subjected to a massive government campaign accusing them of being "Zionists" responsible for the tensions between Poland and the Soviet Union—this despite the fact that few Jews are prominent in the Solidarity movement, and Jews have been almost completely purged from all phases of intellectual life in that country.)

There is perhaps more disputatiousness than ever before on the subject of anti-Semitism, especially in this country, both because it is a topic of increasing concern and because the contemporary outbreak comes at an especially unpropitious time for American Jews. Bereft of its traditional allies, its commitment to Israel under increasing assault, and the object of official indifference, the American Jewish community is confused and divided. These confusions and divisions center almost exclusively on the future direction of American Jews. Where are they headed? Are they in danger of disappearing? Can they find new allies? Can they be held together? And those divisions are reflected in the reactions of the American Jewish community to the new anti-Semitism: in varying degrees, every-one seems aware of the danger, but there is no unanimity on what to do about it—or even a common understanding of exactly where the threat lies.

For at least the past seven years, Jewish organizations in this country and the more than dozen publications they rep-resent have been debating, analyzing and examining the new anti-Semitism, without a definitive answer—much like the famous analogy of Bushmen trying to describe an elephant they have seen for the first time. Folk wisdom may have more to say on this subject than all these learned sages; as one letter-writer put it recently in an Anglo-Jewish weekly, "Today Israel and the Jewish people are besieged by many enemies: Arafat, Khomeni, Jesse Jackson, the Klan, the Nazis, the radical left, the far right, the United Nations, Russia and Moslem world . . . a pro-Arab President of the United States and an anti-Israel State Department . . ."

This cuts to the heart of the issue, and while the writer may be accused of pessimism, he has hit the nail on the head: what counts, really, in any discussion of anti-Semitism is not its causes or its dynamics, but its *implementation*, for implementation is the cutting edge of the sword. This underscores the wisdom of an older generation of Jews, who were accustomed to considering all events in the light of that ancient question: "Is it good for Jews?"

It is a question that is not asked nearly so often these days, to a large extent because American Jews have been spending so much time in their recent history trying to find out who they are, and where they are going. They debate, at great length, about the declining Jewish birthrate (the percentage of Jews in the American population has been steadily declining since the 1920s); the rate of intermarriage (some estimates place it as high as 40 percent); whether Jews are too visible or invisible (one recent study says that Jewish family incomes are 72 percent above average); whether American Jews are Jewish enough; and whether the Jewish community leaders truly represent all the disparate elements of that community.

American Jews, in fact, have been suffering from a prolonged identity crisis, to quote a popular cliché of modern psychology. It is a reflection of the problem of Jewish modernity. As Jews moved out of the ghettos into the secular world outside those walls, Judaism lost much of its theological assurance; the religion that once served as the catalyst for survival in a time of pogroms and bigotry lost at least some of its meaning as the Jews became increasingly taken up with more secular concerns. American Jews, the most acculturated, secularized and powerful Jewish community in history, represent the final step in that historical road. American Jews have a divided identity; they seek, in effect, to be just like everybody else and, at the same time, to be quite different. The paradoxes are everywhere to be seen. Jewish parents send their sons and daughters off to college, where they will live and study mostly with non-Jews—and then the parents tell the children to marry Jews. Or the Jewish couple that attends temple perhaps twice a year and eats non-Kosher food at home—then makes elaborate preparations for their son's Bar Mitzvah.

This modernity problem is relatively recent. Most Ameri-

can Jews have a grandparent or other ancestor who knew
nothing about any such crisis. They arrived here as immigrants, settled in neighborhoods of people just like themselves,
spoke Yiddish just like everybody else they knew, and had no
doubts about their Judaism: it was a religion given to them by
God, and the road to salvation lay in following its command-
ments. Why were they Jews? That was a question for rabbis
and Talmudic scholars; for them, life was Jewish values, Jewish patterns, and Jewish memories.

Among modern American Jews there is the predominant
conviction that Judaism is no longer required as a defense
against the threat of the outside world. There are no major
bastions left in this country for the Jews to conquer; the continued exclusion of Jews at some private clubs is hardly an
issue (Jews form their own clubs, anyway), nor is there much of
a problem about the American economic mainstream being
closed to Jews; moreover, restrictions against Jews in higher
education and other areas are part of the past. What is left,
then, is a somewhat paradoxical relationship between modern
American Jews and their religion. As Arthur Hertzberg puts it:

> *Affiliation is very high, but going to synagogue or
> believing in God is lower [among Jews] than among
> any communion on the American scene. This can be
> explained only on the presumption that this genera-
> tion is safeguarding the mystery of Jewish identity,
> while being "absent without leave" for what it regards
> as its inconvenient details such as religious faith,
> worship and piety.*

This is a strong position, but it does indicate a deep concern
among leading American Jewish thinkers about the future
course of the American Jewish community. Assorted conferences of that community these days are filled with expressions
of doubt and worry about American Jews—the breakup of
families, increasing narcissism among young Jews, the extra-

ordinary success of cults in attracting Jews, skyrocketing divorce rates, the perceived decline in religiosity, and problems affecting the Jewish organizations themselves. (The overwhelming majority of members of Hadassah, the Jewish women's organization, are forty years of age and over; like many other groups, Hadassah is having trouble attracting members from the new generation of Jews.)

Fundamentally, the modern American Jewish community is loaded with contradictions and there are some who argue that this is simply the latest development in a long chain of contradictions, for Jews themselves and their very existence amount to a contradiction. As Isaiah Berlin notes, "The Jews are a peculiar and difficult people in many ways, not least because their history has contradicted most of the best-known and most admired theories of historical causation." By which he meant that according to the best-known laws or theories of history, the Jews—like many other minorities long since destroyed—should have disappeared. But they did not, and their remarkable survival in the face of oppression (and the re-creation of the state of Israel) confounds everything we are supposed to know about historical causation. Historians such as Arnold Toynbee spent a lifetime trying to understand how Jews have managed to survive—despite Toynbee's conclusion that they should have been wiped out 2,000 years ago—and Toynbee wound up explaining it away by saying that the Jews are "exceptional." Perhaps, but it may not completely explain why Jews have managed to survive a history that began with ostracism, passed to expulsion, and wound up in destruction— all for the single crime of being Jewish. And that survival has come despite the blindness of so many Jews; recall that in 1906, only generations before the Nazi gas ovens, German Socialist leader August Bebel was reassuring the Jews that religious persecution in so literate a nation as Germany was impossible.

What does all this have to do with modern anti-Semitism? A great deal, for there is a stark historical fact: the worst outbreaks of anti-Semitism have always come just at the time when Jews have been most divided, the situation of the Jews in pre-World War II Europe being the prime example. "New troubles cause one to forget the older ones," is an old Hebrew proverb, which is a way of saying that anti-Semitism constantly assumes new forms and directions, its threat ever-present. But the key to combating anti-Semitism is a relatively unified Jewish community that not only recognizes the danger, but understands how to fight it. We have seen how some forms of the new anti-Semitism have often gone unrecognized by Jews. How have some of the divisions among the American Jewish community affected its fight against anti-Semitism?

Any account of the subject must begin with the Jewish Defense League, which has turned out to be not only the most sensationalized Jewish response to anti-Semitism, but the most misunderstood, as well. To a great extent the League is part myth, part fact—the myth of a small band of "super Jews" who have single-handedly stood up for "Jewish rights" in ways unlike the organizations of the "Jewish establishment" (most prominently the Anti-Defamation League and the American Jewish Committee), who are too "accommodating" to anti-Semites, too willing to work behind the scenes, and too timid to confront anti-Semitism directly. That much is myth, but the fact is that the JDL sprang from some very deep divisions in the American Jewish community.

Partially, the divisions stem from generational factors: JDL members are for the most part young and intense; they openly consider their elders "defensive Jews" who are not aggressive enough in confronting anti-Semitism. More importantly, the JDL considers most American Jews to be obsessed with wealth and security, thus not "authentically Jewish." It is important to understand the JDL's roots—the economically lower and low-middle class Jews from the poorer neighborhoods of New York City. In their view, the Jewish establishment had turned its collective back on them; they called themselves the "forgotten people." They were truck drivers, taxi drivers, small business owners, low-ranking municipal servants, secretaries, clerks, salespeople—the very segments of the Jewish community that each day had to confront the new militancy of the blacks in urban communities from which, like many other Jews, they could not financially afford to flee to the suburbs. And while the leadership of the American Jewish community was talking about brotherhood and civil rights, many of these poorer Jews became victims of the great city crime waves unleashed by the disadvantaged. These Jews were also trying to survive in an eroding economy, and they scarcely understood such actions as the successful pressure brought by the American Jewish Committee on the Bureau of the Census to delete questions relating to income by ethnic grouping on the 1960 census for fear that the high levels of income among Jews would cause outbreaks of anti-Semitism.

Their frustrations amounted to an accident waiting to happen, and it was an Orthodox rabbi named Meir Kahane who articulated their concerns and in 1968 created an organization to represent them. Kahane, whose basic thesis was that *all* non-Jews are potential anti-Semites and that *all* Jews are potential victims, argued that the "forgotten Jews" needed a militant spokesman to fight for them, not only against the danger of imminent destruction, but also against what JDL members derisively called "WASH" (white Anglo-Saxon Hebrews). As Kahane once summed up the Jewish establishment: "The Judaism of Scott's parents [a prototypical Jewish family Kahane often used in his speeches] and the Jewish culture to which they wished him exposed, consisted primarily of two things: making sure their son came home with a Shirley instead of a Mary, and seeing to it that their offspring would be properly sacrificed to the great American Jewish god, the caterer, in that unique temple rite known as the Bar Mitzvah."

Kahane became a figure of much controversy, both within and outside the Jewish community, but however offensive many found his analysis of modern Jewish life, he nevertheless touched several wellsprings among a large number of Jews.

Several thousand joined the JDL, and some were soon wearing football helmets and carrying clubs, occasionally participating in confrontations with perceived enemies. JDL members thumbed their noses at the main-line Jewish organizations, at one point taking out a large newspaper ad that showed a picture of JDL activists standing outside a large Jewish temple in New York (which one leading civil rights militant had threatened to invade to demand reprations for American blacks from Jewish "oppressors") with chains, clubs and baseball bats. The ad was headlined, "Is This Any Way for Nice Jewish Boys to Behave"? The main-line Jewish organizations didn't think so, arguing that this sort of ethnic fanaticism was doing more harm than good, and hardly addressed the problem of anti-Semitism, latent or otherwise. But the criticism seemed to do little good; it appeared only to create a new publicity for the JDL and enroll new members. By 1972, JDL membership reached a high point of just over 15,000, with branch offices throughout the United States.

To Jewish criticism, Kahane had a stock answer which consisted, primarily, of an analysis of Jewish life in America: the Jews were still hated by most non-Jews, and they faced destruction unless they learned militancy and violently confronted all anti-Semitism in any guise. A 1971 speech he gave in New Jersey is typical, although the words on paper lack the fire and zest of Kahane's considerable oratorical gifts:

> *If there are racial problems, it's the Jew; drugs, the Jew; generation gap, the Jew; earthquake, the Jew—always the Jew! Nixon finally gets one Jew and he sends him to China! Every radical-right leader has the real reason: it's a Zionist plot to convince China to fight Russia. Halavay! [If only this were so]... Let us not be fools. Let's not repeat the mistakes of the Jews in a certain country which in the 1920s had a Jewish foreign minister... where Jews felt secure and*

safe and above all equal. And in Germany when
Adolf Hitler arose, they laughed at him and said . . . "He
doesn't mean us, he means the Ostjuden *(Eastern*
European Jews) . . . So, what is this?

The speech, and many others, demonstrated not only Kahane's
contempt for the leadership of the American Jewish community, but betrayed the beginning of a radical shift in JDL thinking. By that time the group had begun to advocate a radical
Zionism, arguing that the situation of Jews in America was so
bad, only mass emigration to Israel was a solution. In the
process, of course, Kahane and the JDL began to turn away
from their original bedrock of strength—the poorer economic
classes of Jews in urban areas. The group in fact became a
youth movement, concentrating on such issues as Soviet Jews
and defense of Israel—issues of especially great importance to
the younger generation of Jews, but not nearly so important to
the older generation of Jews still stuck in urban ghettos, for
whom economics and the dangers they faced every day were
more overriding concerns.

There were other contradictions. One was the conviction
by the JDL that it alone saw the "true meaning" of Jewish
history, an analysis in which the Jews of America were seen as
downtrodden victims of their own inertia and timidity by their
leaders, no better than the Jews of czarist Russia, huddling
afraid in their little *shtetls*. The JDL drew a comic-book history of the Jewish people, claiming that the Jews were giants of
the earth in biblical times, smiting their enemies without
mercy; but somehow, over the centuries, the Jews had become
timid. It was time to redress the balance and, in what became a
major embarrassment to the American Jewish community, the
JDL carried out a series of bombings and other radical acts,
especially against Soviet diplomats in this country. Since an
extensive law enforcement crackdown on the JDL some years
ago, the organization has become much more circumspect on
this score, neither claiming credit nor denying responsibility

for various violent acts. New groups, especially one calling itself "Thunder of Zion" (which has carried out several bombings), are widely suspected of being JDL front groups.

The slogan of "never again!" has become a prime staple of JDL lore, which to a great extent is a creation of the media. Indeed, the JDL has come to see itself as an organization almost exclusively determined by its image on television news. But this image is not nearly as historic as JDL likes to believe. Its bombing of the office of impresario Sol Hurok in 1972 (for his role in bringing Soviet artists to this country) achieved great publicity, but the one person who was killed and the twelve who were hurt in the explosion could hardly have been persuaded by that sort of tactic, nor was the Soviet Union, nor was the American Jewish community which was compelled to wonder how the bombing of Sol Hurok helped one single Soviet Jew. The fact is that, for all its talk of playing a historic role in American Jewry and "forcing" the Soviet government to release Soviet Jews, the JDL has never been responsible for the release of a single Soviet Jew, nor has it been in the least responsible for any diminution of anti-Semitism in the United States. The verdict is clear: Soviet Jews have been leaving the Soviet Union, not because Moscow is terrified of JDL attacks against its diplomatic missions, but because of the pressure exerted by the American Jewish community leadership which Kahane so rigorously condemns; it is that leadership which literally forced the American government to take action on the matter.

None of this is to say that the JDL has been entirely wrong. It has managed to highlight a number of contradictions among the American Jewish community on its approach to fighting anti-Semitism, or, put another way, JDL has questioned whether that community really knows who its enemies are. Last year, for example, Yeshiva University announced a dinner to honor a prominent industrialist—a dinner canceled only after it was pointed out that the man to be honored had been employing (and had interceded with the American government on his behalf) a notorious Nazi industrialist charged with building slave-labor factories at Auschwitz. Or a leading union president was honored by the Jewish Histradut organization for "distinguished service"—only a short while after calling a Jewish lawyer with whom he was negotiating a union contract a "kike." Or Orthodox Jewish organizations have been lobbying for tuition tax credits, despite the objections of other Jewish organizations—and warnings that private schools for Jews, federally supported, almost guarantee a fostering of anti-Semitism. Or Jewish groups are lobbying in New York for a dangerous bill authorizing police to seize a cult member for "deprogramming" (as civil libertarians noted, Jews obviously could be considered members of a "cult"). Or the Jacobo Timmerman affair, which ignited American Jewish organizations into unseemly debate over the extent and aims of anti-Semitism in Argentina—a confusion that seemed to raise the question: if American Jews cannot agree on whether the Jews of Argentina are or are not in danger, then how do they expect to recognize the danger to themselves? Or the plan by the Simon Wiesenthal Center in Los Angeles to present a multimedia program on the Holocaust that will travel to various cities across the country. The program, the center announced, would include "five screens, three film projectors, eighteen slide projectors, and multi-channel sound ... narrated by Orson Welles and Elizabeth Taylor," and would be a "stirring and illuminating work".

Indeed, no one need look any further than the continuing debate within the American Jewish community concerning Hannah Arendt, whose analysis of the Eichmann case—including charges that the Jews were too acquiescent in their fate and were betrayed by their own leadership—continues to inspire the most heated argument even now, a long eighteen years after its publication. An example of the strong reactions that work aroused was the headline in one local Jewish newspaper—"Self-Hating Jewess Writes Pro-Eichmann Seri-

es"—when Arendt's "Eichmann in Jerusalem" was first serial-
ized in *The New Yorker* magazine.

Arendt was trying to accomplish a number of things in her
work, among them the teachings of an important lesson—
important, at least, in the context of this work. In her view, the
Judenraete (Jewish councils), the groups of bankers, lawyers
and bureaucrats from the Jewish establishment appointed by
the Nazis to oversee the Jewish ghettos "deluded the herd," and
ultimately played a leading role in their destruction. Moreover,
she said, the anti-Semitism that finally resulted in the Nazi
genocide stemmed in no small measure from the fact that the
European Jewish community was preoccupied with interne-
cine rivalries—rivalries that prevented the Jews of Europe
from taking full advantage of the new philsophical and political opportunities that had arisen since the Enlightenment.

This summarizes (perhaps unfairly) an extremely complicated argument, but it is interesting how so much of it paral-
leled what such groups as the JDL had been saying, in other
ways. They, along with Arendt, saw (and they continue to see)
a great danger to American Jews because there is, in their view,
so little understanding of anti-Semitism. The JDL has never
approached the intellectual level of Arendt, of course, but if
some sort of dialogue could have been arranged between
Kahane and Arendt before her death, it is probable they would
have had much to agree on—but not Zionism; Arendt was
rigidly anti-Zionist, arguing that the concept of Israel was no
answer to the problems of anti-Semitism. One suspects that if
Arendt were still alive now, she would be thoroughly alarmed
at some of the more ominous developments presently emanating from the American Jewish community—developments
that could be interpreted as proof that too many American
Jews have forgotten the lessons of the past and seem determined to repeat the very mistakes that helped smooth the way
for disaster.

What would she have made, for example, of Kahane

himself, who recently (from his organization's headquarters in Jerusalem) took out ads in large-circulation Israeli newspapers advocating a five-year mandatory prison sentence to be imposed on "any non-Jew who has sexual relations with a Jewish female." (An unsettling echo of the Nazi Nuremberg laws?) She would also have been alarmed to read, in recent editions of Jewish newspapers in this country, the entertainment column carrying a Polish joke. When one Anti-Defamation League leader reminded the columnist that it was unseemly for a Jewish newspaper, of all places, to be publishing ethnic jokes, he then announced that all future jokes would be called "Chelm jokes," after a small town in Poland. The columnist was apparently unaware of the fact that shortly after World War II, Jews in Chelm were subjected to pogroms by townspeople, and a number were slaughtered on the streets. There is nothing very funny about Chelm. It is also disquieting to read a recent advertisement placed in many Jewish newspapers in this country by a group called Jewish Educated Women Electing Life and Survival (JEWELS), which attacks birth control and abortion, and goes on to advocate that Jewish women have as many babies as possible to counteract a declining Jewish birth rate—again, an unfortunate echo of another time, when Hitler and the Nazis encouraged German women to have babies in order to ensure the survival of the "Aryan race." Or other ads in the same newspapers, headlined "Thwart the Cults!" and going on to claim that "the Roman Calpurnius Piso (pen name of Flavius Josephus) and his family made up Christianity."

These incidents are among many which suggest that the American Jewish community may be changing in very fundamental ways. Aside from the problem of the "me generation," common to every ethnic and religious group in America, there is the feeling that Jews may not be as concerned as they once were with social justice and human rights. It was perhaps best expressed in a noted sermon by a New York rabbi, Gunter

Hirschberg, last year during services marking the start of the observance of Yom Kippur, the Jewish Day of Atonement:

> *It's a long time since I heard anything [among Jews] about the poor, the underprivileged, the plight of the minorities. It seems a pity. It seems a shame. It seems un-Jewish. My friends, Jewish morality is not a bleeding-heart philosophy. Turning the other cheek is not our cup of tea. We are commanded to love our neighbor as ourselves—but not more than ourselves. But Jewish morality is based on two brief sentences in the Talmud from Rabbi Hillel the Elder. The first is: "If I am not for myself, who is for me?" But this sentence is not meant to stand by itself. It must always be coupled with the next: "If I am only for myself, then what am I?"*

And that returns us to the question of anti-Semitism, for if Jews have trouble defining themselves, then it is clear that they will have trouble defining the nature of the threat lurking out there in the darkness—or sitting right beside them in plain view. The old answers simply will not do anymore. Certainly not the solution of Rabbi Menachem Mendel of Vorki who, when asked in Martin Buber's famous account what constitutes the true Jew, replied, "Three things are fitting for us: upright kneelings, silent screaming, motionless dance." And not the charming but hopeless solution of comedian Sam Levinson, who once proposed that anti-Semites be told that they would no longer be allowed to use certain "Jewish products"—such as insulin and polio vaccine, invented by Jews. (This is an inversion of the terrible racist dogma promulgated during the Nazi regime about "Jewish science," which led a generation of German scientists into an officially-sponsored attempt to disprove the theory of relativity.)

What, then, should the Jews of America do about anti-

Semitism? For one thing, stop studying it. At this point, the studies on the phenomenon and the associated studies on American attitudes toward Jews amount to a vast pile of paper that has not proven of much use. It should be recalled that in September 1964, a two-day conference to discuss these assorted studies arrived at the central conclusion that anti-Semitism had declined so precipitously in the United States that nothing short of a catastrophe could ever reverse that trend. That conclusion, of course, has turned out to be terribly wrong and, as has been demonstrated over and over again in this work, there does not seem to be much point in studying and restudying a phenomenon—anti-Semitism—that is not subject to measurement.

There is no question that the divisions now afflicting the American Jewish community render the Jews more susceptible to all the variegated forms of the new anti-Semitism. More importantly, the Jewish identity crisis discussed earlier is also injurious, for it undercuts what being Jewish is all about—not a way of preserving the past, but as a paradigm for the future, "a light unto the Gentiles," as the ancient Hebrews put it. There is no necessity for the Jews to be better than everybody else, only the conviction that they have as much right as anybody else to survive in this country, the only nation in the West in which there are no cathedrals where kings were once crowned. And no history of pogroms, needless to add.

All this leads to the question: will the American Jewish community survive? That's a difficult question, for anti-Semitism may not necessarily be its greatest enemy; the greater enemy may be the drift and internal divisions that weaken it, making it susceptible to the new virus. The antidotes are the traditional ones: unity, conviction, and the ability to recognize the enemy by any name it has chosen. It is well to remember that Moses did not form a committee to study the roots of Egyptian anti-Semitism when he was confronted with the sight of an Egyptian striking a Jew: "He smote the Egyptian and buried him in the sand." (Exodus 2:11.)

Perhaps the final answer lies not here, but somewhere else, in Prague, Czechoslovakia. There, the ghosts speak.

There is a magnificent synagogue in that city, one of the few surviving after the German occupation and the Holocaust that exterminated most of the country's Jews. Its existence is puzzling: why didn't the Nazis destroy that one too?

Because the Nazis intended that this synagogue would serve as a museum of Jewish life in Europe before it had been finally and totally exterminated. From all over Czechoslovakia the Nazis combed the camps and killing centers, seeking the most renowned Jewish historians they could find. The historians were set to work. Out of the vast piles of loot taken from synagogues all over Europe, they were ordered to select the best religious material and outfit the synagogue as a "typical" Jewish house of worship.

No one can imagine the sadness with which those unfortunates performed their task; they worked with what remained of European Jewish civilization, certain in the knowledge that they, too, would shortly be exterminated once their work was finished. And what work they accomplished—with exquisite attention to detail, they created what is probably the most magnificent synagogue ever seen. They used the most beautiful Ark hangings, magnificent Torahs with silver crowns, stunning ornaments, ritual dishes, charity boxes, and every possible aspect of a Jewish house of worship, complete and correct in every detail. The Nazis forced them to create a separate room in which a completely-equipped Passover seder was laid out; the Nazis built dummies with grossly hooked noses, dressed in Hasidic garb, to sit around the table.

And when the task was finished—the "chamber of horrors," as the Nazis phrased it—the historians were taken away and shot.

The museum remains today, saved from destruction only because the Nazis did not find time to blow it up in the last days of the war. Visitors come today to marvel at its beauty, at the lovely window on the east that catches the first rays of the sun each day, at the equally beautiful window on the west through which the first evening star can be seen—the traditional means by which observant Jews know it is time for prayer.

There is a legend about this synagogue. Every night, so it is said, the ghosts of the murdered Jews come through the great front doors. They stand silently, looking at the magnificence within, weeping in memory of the people who no longer worship here and whose ashes lie beneath the soil of Europe.

And then, one of them cries out, in a voice that he hopes will be heard by the Jews in every land:

Am Yisrael chai! [The Jewish people lives!]

BIBLIOGRAPHY

The literature on the subject of anti-Semitism is vast, and there is no attempt to indicate completeness in the following listing. However, it will cite the major sources used, along with suggestions for future reading, where appropriate.

Introduction:
The Socialism of Fools

Krasrilovka: Author's notes.
General anti-Semitism: Arthur Hertzberg, "*B. G. Rudolph Lecture in Judaica Studies*," Syracuse University, April 11, 1973; Paul E. Grosser and Edwin G. Halperin, *Anti-Semitism: The Causes and Effects of a Prejudice* (Citadel Press, 1979); Hannah Arendt, *The Jew as Pariah* (Grove Press, 1978).
Jews and anti-Semitism: Max I. Dimont, *Jews, God and History* (Simon and Schuster, 1962). For general discussions of prejudice, see the classic work by Gordon W. Allport, *The Nature of Prejudice* (Addison-Wesley, 1979), and two

justly famed anthropological studies by Ruth Benedict, *Race: Science and Politics* (Random House, 1940), and *Patterns of Culture* (Houghton Mifflin, 1934). See also Gertrude S. Selznick and Stephen Steinberg, *The Tenacity of Prejudice* (Harper & Row, 1969).

History of anti-Semitism: Edward H. Flannery, *The Anguish of the Jews: Thirty-Three Centuries of Anti-Semitism* (Macmillan, 1965). Other valuable accounts include Leon Poliakov, *The History of Anti-Semitism* (Vanguard Press, 1965); Dagobert Runes, *War Against the Jews* (Philosophical Library, 1968); and *Anti-Semitism*, produced by Israel Pocket Library of the Ketter Publishing House in Jerusalem (1974), an extremely valuable short account.

Wilhelm Marr and modern anti-Semitism: The unsurpassed account is Hannah Arendt's *The Origins of Totalitarianism* (Harcourt Brace Jovanovich, 1973 edition), especially the "Anti-Semitism" section. This classic work is very heavy going, but is indispensable for any understanding of how modern anti-Semitism is fundamentally a political phenomenon. Another insightful, but much less daunting account is James Parkes, *Anti-Semitism* (Quadrangle Books, 1964).

The Protocols of the Learned Elders of Zion: Norman Cohn's *Warrant for Genocide* (Harper & Row, 1966) is the classic account.

Approaches to studying anti-Semitism: There are any number of works that discuss anti-Semitism from the standpoint of various academic disciplines. Philosophy: Jean-Paul Sartre, *Anti-Semite and Jew* (Schocken Books, 1948); history: Hugo Mauritz-Valentin, *Anti-Semitism Historically and Critically Examined* (Viking Press, 1936), an important early work; economics: Werner J. Cahnman, "Socioeconomic Causes of Anti-Semitism," in *Social Problems,* Winter, 1957; psychiatry: Sidney Tarachow, "A Note on Anti-Semitism," in *Psychiatry* IX (1946); sociology: Bruno Bettelheim and Morris Janowitz,

Dynamics of Prejudice (Harper, 1950); social psychology: Neil J. Kressel, "Hating the Jews: A New View From Social Psychology," *Judaism* Summer 1981. On this subject, see also a different, but nevertheless interesting, account by R. N. Stanford et al, *The Authoritarian Personality* (Harper, 1950). For an attempt to link up all these disciplines in one study, see *The Roots of Anti-Semitism*, a valuable account by Ernest L. Abel (Associated Universities Press, 1975).

The new anti-Semitism: Earl Rabb, "Is There a New Anti-Semitism?" *Commentary,* May, 1974; J. L. Talmon, "The New Anti-Semitism," *The New Republic*, September 18, 1976; Arnold Foster and Benjamin Epstein, *The New Anti-Semitism* (McGraw-Hill, 1974). The latter work is actually the Anti-Defamation League's official view of the problem, with emphasis on cases in which the League has been involved.

Voltaire: Peter Gay, *The Enlightenment* (Simon and Schuster, 1973).

Anxiety of modern American Jewish community: Norman Podhoretz, "Is It Good for Jews?" *Commentary*, February 1972; remarks, Dr. Jack Wertheimer, assistant professor of Jewish History at the Jewish Theological Seminary, at Public Affairs Institute Day, April 9, 1981, sponsored by Nassau Hadassah organization; author's notes. See also Murray Zuckoff, "Anti-Semitic Resurgence Worldwide," Jewish Telegraphic Agency, April 5, 1981.

Appraisals of the new anti-Semitism by the American Jewish community: "American Jewish Committee Appraisal of Anti-Semitism Calm," *The Jewish Week-American Examiner*, March 29, 1981; and "ADL and AJC in Slight Disagreement on Extent of Anti-Semitism Rise," in the same publication, May 17, 1981.

Traditional Jewish appraisals of anti-Semitism: Koppel S. Pinson, editor, *Essays in Anti-Semitism* (Conference on Jewish Relations, 1964); Norman Podhoretz, "Issues," in *Commentary*, February 1972.

Gallup Poll: "Feeling Toward Jews Found More Favorable in a Survey by Gallup," *New York Times*, April 27, 1981.

Parallel with Weimar Germany: Walter Laqueur, *Weimar: A Cultural History* (Putnam's 1974). For examinations of the status of Jews in pre-Hitler Germany, see Paul W. Massing, *Rehearsal for Destruction* (Harper Brothers, 1949); H. G. Adler, *The Jews in Germany* (Notre Dame University Press, 1961); and the especially insightful study by Peter G. Pulzer, *The Rise of Political Anti-Semitism in Germany and Austria* (John Wiley and Sons, 1964).

History of Jews and anti-Semitism: Cecil Roth, *The Jews in the Renaissance* (Jewish Publication Society of America, 1959); A. M. Hyamson, *A History of the Jews in England* (Chatto and Windus, London, 1908); and Parkes, *Anti-Semitism*, op cit.

Chapter One:
History of an American Prejudice

Peter Stuyvesant: John Higham, "American Anti-Semitism Historically Reconsidered," in Herbert Stember, editor, *Jews in the Mind of America* (Random House, 1966); Max Dimont, *The Jews in America* (Simon and Schuster, 1978).

Historical revisionism: Jonathan D. Sarna, "Anti-Semitism and American History," in *Commentary*, March 1981, a very valuable account and the best expression overall of the revisionism of the history of Jews and anti-Semitism in this country. Another prominent example of revisionism is Michal N. Dobrowski, "American Anti-Semitism, a Reinterpretation," in *American Quarterly*, Summer 1977; see also his *The Tarnished Dream: The Basis of American Anti-Semitism* (Greenwood Press, 1979).

Early histories of anti-Semitism in America: Carey McWilliams, *A Mask for Privilege* (Little, Brown, 1948); Benjamin F. Eptstein and Arnold Foster, *Cross-Currents* (Doubleday, 1956); Morris U. Schappes, *The Jews in the*

United States (Citadel Press, 1958); Werner Sombart, *The Jews and Modern Capitalism* (Free Press, 1951); Oscar Handlin, *Race and Nationality in American Life* (Little, Brown, 1957); Oscar and Mary Handlin, *Danger in Discord: Origins of American Anti-Semitism in the United States* (Anti-Defamation League, 1948). See also Max Lerner, *America as a Civilization* (Simon and Schuster, 1957), passim. All the above works are not only out of date, but seriously flawed, as well.

Anti-Semitic representations in American literature: Solomon Liptzin, *The Jews in American Literature* (Bloch Publishing Company, 1966).

American anti-Semitism in the nineteenth century: John Higham, "Anti-Semitism in the Gilded Age: A Reinterpretation," in *Mississippi Valley Historical Review*, March 1957; Arnold Rose, "Anti-Semitism: Roots in City Hatred," in *Commentary*, October 1948; Leo Hershkowitz, *Tweed's New York* (Anchor Press/Doubleday, 1947); Louis Ruchames, "The Abolitionists and the Jews," *Publications of the American Jewish Historical Society*, December 1952.

Leo Frank case: Clement C. Moseley, "The Case of Leo M. Frank, 1913-1915," *The Georgia Historical Quarterly*, March 1967.

Beilis case: Arnold J. Band, "Kafka and the Beilis Affair," in *Comparative Literature*, Spring 1980.

Jews and immigration: Irving Howe, *World of Our Fathers* (Harcourt Brace Jovanovich, 1976), a marvelous and magisterial work, provides the best overall account of early Jewish immigration and history of the Jewish community in New York during the immigrant generations. See also Stephen Birmingham, *Our Crowd* (Harper & Row, 1967) for a fascinating look at the early German-Jewish families. See Robert Divine, *American Immigration Policy* (Yale University Press, 1957) for a more scholarly approach.

Early twentieth century anti-Semitism in America: Ruth Gay,

Jews in America (Basic Books, 1965); Michael Selzer, editor, *Kike!* (World Publishing, 1972).

Social discrimination: John Higham, "Social Discrimination Against Jews in America, 1830-1930," in *Publications of the American Jewish Historical Society*, September 1957.

Henry Ford: Albert Lee, *Henry Ford and the Jews* (Stein and Day, 1980).

Anti-Semitism in the 1930s: Donald Strong, *Organized Anti-Semitism in America* (American Council on Public Affairs, 1941); Milton Friedman, "Anti-Semitism and the Great Depression," *Newsweek*, December 16, 1974; David H. Bennett, *Demagogues in the Depression* (Rutgers University Press, 1969).

Father Coughlin: Charles J. Tull, *Father Coughlin and the New Deal* (Syracuse University Press, 1965); Sheldon Marcus, *Father Coughlin* is an especially valuable account (Notre Dame University Press, 1973).

German-American Bund: James V. Compton, *The Swastika and the Eagle* (Houghton Mifflin, 1967) shows how Hitler financed the Bund; Richard O'Connor, *The German-Americans: An Informal History* (Little, Brown, 1968) discusses the Bund's impact on the German-American community; the best overall account is Sander A. Diamond, *The Nazi Movement in the United States, 1924-1941* (Cornell University Press, 1974).

The "America First" debate: Wayne S. Cole, *The Battle Against Intervention, 1940-1941* (University of Wisconsin Press, 1953); Mark Lincoln Chadwin, *The Hawks of World War II* (University of North Carolina Press, 1968).

Post-World War II: Grosser and Halperin, op cit.

Chapter Two
A Callous Indifference

Poisoning of wells by Jews: Barbara W. Tuchman, "They Poisoned the Wells," in *Newsweek*, February 3, 1975.

Rise of anti-Semitism: Stanley Karnow, "*Anti-Semitism on* *the Rise?*" in *The New Republic*, December 14, 1974; remarks of Abraham H. Foxman, Associate Director, Anti-Defamation League of B'nai B'rith, on "First Estate," NBC television, New York, August 2, 1981, author's notes; "TheVirulent Disease of Anti-Semitism," *Christian Century*, April 24, 1974; Irving Spiegel, "Report by Anti-Defamation League Sees Examples of New Kind of Anti-Semitism," *New York Times*, March 6, 1974; "Plague-Bearers," *The New Republic*, April 20, 1974; Natalie Gittelson, "Anti-Semitism: It's Still Around," *Harper's Bazaar*, February 1972.

Rue Copenic incident, Barre quote: "Oops ! How's That Again?" *Time*, March 30, 1981.

Attitude studies on anti-Semitism: "Feelings Toward Jews Found More Favorable In a Survey by Gallup," *New York Times*, April 27, 1981; "Poll Indicates New Generation in U.S. Less Anti-Semitic," *"Jewish Week-American Examiner*, August 2, 1981.

Yankelovich study: *Newsday*, July 29, 1981.

Types of anti-Semitism: Remarks, Brooklyn College Professor Henry Friedlander, during forum on anti-Semitism, Brooklyn College Center for Holocaust Studies, Brooklyn, NY, April 2, 1981, author's notes.

Problems with surveys on anti-Semitism: Lucy S. Dawidowicz's "Can Anti-Semitism Be Measured?" in *Commentary*, July 1970, is a ground-breaking study whose devastating criticisms put much attitude-survey work in question; see also "How Does One Measure Depth of One's Bias?" in *Jewish Week-American Examiner,* August 9, 1981. For an attempt to explore some of the paradoxes of the more recent attitude-surveys about anti-Semitism, see Edward Labaton and Adam Simms, "Non-Causes of Anti-Semitism on Long Island," in *Newsday*, August 26, 1981.

Richardson incident: Bernard Weintraub, "Anti-Semitism Charges Cloud Reagan Nomination," in *New York Times*, April 16, 1981; "More Data Surfaces on Designee to HHS." *Washington Post*, April 19, 1981; "A Damning Whiff of Anti-Semitism," in *The Economist*, May 2, 1981; "Liberty Lobby Leader's Appointment to Major Office Arouses Protests," in *Jewish Week-American Examiner*, April 26, 1981.

Carto: *Jewish Week-American Examiner*, op cit.

Lefever controversy: Scott Armstrong, "Embarrassing Testimony Sank Lefever," in *Washington Post*, June 14, 1981, is the best overall summation on the Lefever case, especially the anti-Semitic aspects.

United Nations: The single most comprehensive account is by Sen. Daniel P. Moynihan of New York; it can be found in the *Congressional Record*, February 19, 1981. My account relies heavily on Moynihan's analysis and recollections.

Ikle and Jews: *Jewish Week-American Examiner*, May 31, 1981; author's notes.

Neumann: "Fall of a Disloyalist," *Newsweek*, August 10, 1981.

George Ball: Ball's thesis is found in three of his major articles: "The Coming Crisis in Israeli-American Relations," *Foreign Affairs*, Winter 1979-1980; "Israel—No More Blank Checks," *Manchester Guardian*, July 5, 1981; and "Plain Talk for Israel," *New York Times*, September 6, 1981.

Rep. McCloskey: "Questioning the Israeli Lobby, *Time*, July 27, 1981.

Abourzek: "The Relentless Israeli propaganda Machine," Sen. James Abourezk, *Penthouse*, January 1978.

Time magazine: "How to Lean on Israel," *Time*, October 3, 1977. *Newsweek* has also been guilty of similar animus: in a September 1981 issue, the magazine showed a Star of David festooned with lethal weapons. In referring to Israeli Prime Minister Menachem Begin, the magazine said, "Begin rhymes with Fagin."

High school courses on Holocaust: *Jewish Week-American Examiner*, April 12, 1981.

"Sixty Minutes": Letter, Barry Lando of CBS, April 5, 1981.

British Airways/Sabena: *Zionist Information News Service,* April 5, 1981.

Concentration camp vacation: *Jewish Week-American Examiner,* April 12, 1981. British officials revised the book following disclosure about the Nazi death camp "vacation."

Hilton hotels: *Zionist Information News Service,* May 24, 1981. A Hilton International directive ordering inclusion of Israel in the chain's brochures was issued August 1, 1980.

Begin and the Mafia: Based on an investigation by the author, winter 1980-1981. American government records are quite clear: there is no record of Begin entering America until 1948.

Chapter Three:
Casual Anti-Semitism

Obsession with polls and studies: Charles Herbert Stember, et al, *Jews in the Mind of America* (Basic Books, 1966); Ellen Willis, "the Myth of the Powerful Jew," *Village Voice,* September 3, 1979.

Office of War Information decision: Christopher Lasch, *The Culture of Narcissism* (Norton, 1978).

Denial of the Holocaust: Lucy S. Dawidowicz, "Lies About the Holocaust," *Commentary,* December 1980; Paul L. Berman, "Crackpot History and the Right to Lie," *Village Voice,* June 16, 1981.

Faurisson: John Shirley, "A Tale of Horror on the Berlin Express," *London (Sunday) Times,* March 29, 1981.

Butz: Seth S. King, "Professor Causes Furor by Saying Nazi Slaying of Jews Is a Myth," *New York Times,* January 28, 1977; "Of Attempts to Disprove the Holocaust," *New York Times,* February 16, 1977; "Of Nazis, Jews and Professor Butz's 'Painstaking Research'" *New York Times,* February 4, 1977; Dawidowicz, op cit.

Chomsky: Noam Chomsky, "Freedom of Expression? Absolutely," *Village Voice*, July 7, 1981.

Morris book and American Historical Association: "Revising Holocaust History: Malice in the Mails," *Christian Century*, July 1980.

Institute of Historical Review: Robert Lindsey, "Auschwitz Survivor Sues for Prize for Proving Germans Gassed Jews," *New York Times*, March 6, 1981.

Dawidowicz incident: Dawidowicz, op cit.

David Irving incident: Neal Ascherson, "A Bucketful of Slime," *London Observer*, March 29, 1981; David Irving, "An Author Defends Himself," *Newsday*, May 10, 1981.

Truman Capote: "Interview: Truman Capote," *Playboy*, March 1968; C. Robert Jennings, "Truman Capote Talks, Talks, Talks," *New York Magazine*, May 13, 1968; Andy Warhol, "Sunday With Mr. C: an Audio-Documentary by Andy Warhol Starring Truman Capote," *Rolling Stone*, April 12, 1973.

Hemingway, Pound, anti-Semitism: "The Eyes of Ez," *New York Review of Books*, April 30, 1981; *Ernest Hemingway: A Life Story*, Carlos Baker, passim. For effective refutations of "Jewish domination" of writing and publishing, see Philip Nobile, *Intellectual Skywriting* (Charterhouse, 1974): and Alain Finkielkraut, "The Ghosts of Roth," *Esquire*, September, 1981.

Vanessa Redgrave: Gary Giddins, "Vanessa Redgrave Violates the Gentlemen's Agreement," *Village Voice*, May 1, 1978. In September 1981, Vanessa Redgrave was pictured participating with PLO chief Yaser Arafat in celebrations in Beirut, while Israel buried five victims of a PLO terrorist bomb attack.

"Jesus Christ Superstar": Alan Rich, "The Selling of the Savior," *New York Magazine*, October 25, 1971; see also reports on criticism by Jewish groups in *New York Times*, especially October 14 and 31, 1971; and *Newsday*, October 12, 1971.

Sandy Duncan: Foster-Epstein, op cit.

New York Times ad: *Publishers Weekly*, September 1, 1971; *Jewish Telegraphic Agency Daily Bulletin*, August 17, 1971.

Kissinger profile: Foster-Epstein, op cit.

Other media, football chaplain, *New York Times* incidents: Author's notes; Foster-Epstein, op cit.

C. W. Post incident: Reports in *Post Pioneer* (student newspaper), August 24, September 14, 1977.

DeSica film review: "Anti-Semitism Charged," *Christian Century*, July 19, 1972.

Local elections: *New York Times*, August 16, 1981; March 18, 1973.

Rock music groups: Author's notes; "when Marianne Faithful Sings, Life Is a Four-Letter Word," *Esquire*, June 1981.

Nixon: Reports, *New York Times*, especially May 12, 1974; May 19, 1974; August 26, 1976.

Spiro Agnew: "I Am Not a Bigot" *Newsweek*, May 24, 1976.

General Brown: Meg Greenfield, "The General and the Jews," *Newsweek*, December 9, 1974; "The General and the Jews," *Newsweek*, November 25, 1974.

Treasury Department letter: *New York Times,* August 26, 1976.

Saxbe: Karnow, op cit.

Anne Frank: Speech, Meyer Levin at Holocaust Remembrance Day, New York, May 25, 1981; author's notes.

Anne Frank Foundation: Edward Alexander, "Stealing the Holocaust," *Midstream*, May 1981. For an effective but short outline of the Holocaust, see the booklet produced by the American Jewish Committee in 1979, *About the Holocaust: What We Know and How We Know It*, by Dorothy Rabinowitz, which has a valuable bibliography.

Chapter Four:
Thunder on the Right

Dietz: Author's notes, based on an investigation during 1979; see also Associated Press report, March 16, 1980.

The right wing in America: *The American Right Wing,* Robert Schoenberger, editor (Holt, Rinehart & Winston, 1969); Richard Hofstadter, *The Paranoid Style in American Politics,* (Knopf, 1965); see also two interesting accounts of the change in American attitudes: Pete Hamill, "The Revolt of the White Lower Middle Class," *New York Magazine,* April 14, 1969; and Gabriel Fackre, "The Blue Collar White and the Far Right," *Christian Century,* May 7, 1969.

Anti-Semitic aspects: George Thayer, *The Farther Shores of Politics* (Simon and Schuster, 1968); Seymour Lipset and Earl Rabb, *The Politics of Unreason* (University of Chicago Press, 1978); for the so-called New Right see Alan Crawford, *Thunder on the Right* (Pantheon Books, 1980).

Wallace: Marshall Frady, *Wallace* (World, 1968); Lewis Chester et al, *An American Melodrama* (Viking, 1969).

Nazis in America: Milton Ellerin, *American Nazis—Myth or Menace?* (American Jewish Committee, 1977) is an especially valuable account; see also remarks, Rep. John J. LaFalce of New York, *Congressional Record,* July 18, 1978; "Neo-Nazi Groups: Artifacts of Hate," *Newsweek,* March 25, 1977; "Nazis in U.S.: Small Bands at War With One Another," *New York Times,* April 19, 1978.

Rockwell: "Interview: George Lincoln Rockwell," *Playboy,* April 1966.

Collin: The Man Behind the Nazis," *New York Daily News,* April 25, 1978.

Hinckley: *Jewish Telegraphic Agency,* April 5, 1981.

Dominica coup attempt: Ken Lawrence, "Behind the Klan's Karibbean Koup Attempt," *Covert Action Information Bulletin,* July-August 1981.

Ku Klux Klan: David M. Chalmers, *Hooded Americanism* (Franklin Watts, 1981); for a broader picture on racism in America, see Thomas F. Gossett, *Race: The History of an Idea in America* (Southern Methodist University Press, 1963).

Klan resurgence: "Klanwatch Intelligence Report," published monthly by the Southern Poverty Law Center, Montgomery, Alabama. These invaluable reports are indispensable for anyone with an interest in the modern Klan. See especially the reports of May, June and July, 1981.

Links with Nazis: Author's files, based on investigation carried out in 1980 and 1981; see also Associated Press reports of September 9, 1981.

Klan violence: "The KKK Goes Military," *Newsweek*, October 6, 1980; "The Klan Rides Again," *Time*, November 19, 1979; see also the various reports of Klan military and firearms training camps, including *New York Times,* September 28 and November 24, 1980; and remarks, Rep. John Conyers Jr. of Michigan, *Congressional Record*, December 4, 1980, which contains much detail on Klan anti-Semitic activities.

National States Rights Party: Thayer, op cit.

Minutemen: J. Harry Jones, *Minutemen* (Doubleday, 1968); The FBI and the Paramilitary Right: Partners in Terror," *Counterspy*, March 1973.

SAO: *Counterspy*, op cit.

Identity: *Counterspy*, Winter 1973.

Posse Comitatus: "The Posse Is Coming," *Counterspy*, Winter 1976.

Christian Patriots Defense League: This section is based on CPDL literature in author's files; see also "Mid-America Plans to Survive," *The Spotlight*, October 29, 1979.

"You should band together": "In Illinois: Festival of the Fed-Up," *Time*, November 5, 1979.

Gerald L. K. Smith: Calvin Trillin, "U.S. Journal: Eureka Springs, Arkansas," *The New Yorker*, July 26, 1969; see also the extensive reports in the *Arkansas Gazette*, especially December 12, 1969, and March 17, 1970; and Jack Anderson column of November 25, 1969.

Liberty Lobby: Charles Bermant, "The Private World of Willis Carto," *The Investigator*, September 1981.

World Anti-Communist League: Paul W. Valentine, "The Fascist Specter Behind the World Anti-Red League," *Washington Post*, May 28, 1981.

John Birch Society: The seminal works of the Birch Society are *None Dare Call It Treason* by John A. Stormer (Liberty Bell Press, 1964), and Dan Smoot's *The Invisible Government* (Western Islands, 1962). For anti-Semitism and the Society, see Neil J. Kressel and Adam J. Brodsky, "Birchers, Anti-Semitism and the New Right," *Reconstructionist,* February, 1981.

Chapter Five:
The Horsemen of the Apocalypse

The Wandering Jew: Tom Burnam, *Dictionary of Misinformation* (Crowell, 1975); Bergen Evans, *Natural History of Nonsense* (Knopf, 1946); M. Hirsh Goldberg, *Just Because They're Jewish* (Stein and Day, 1979).

General Christian anti-Semitism: Fred Gladstone Bratoon, *The Crime of Christendom: The Theological Sources of Christian Anti-Semitism* (Little, Brown, 1969); and Charles Y. Glock and Rodney Stark, *Christian Beliefs and Anti-Semitism* (Harper & Row, 1966) are two valuable works in this field. See also Richard E. Morgan, *The Politics of Religious Conflict* (Pegasus, 1968).

Rise of evangelism: James Morris, *The Preachers* (St. Martins Press, 1973); James A. Haught, "The God Biz," *Penthouse*, December, 1980; Timothy Bay, "Airwave Apostles," *Omni*, August 1980; Robert L. Corn, "God's Little Airwaves," *Inquiry*, June 29, 1981.

Decline in main-line religions: Paul Seabury, "A Failure of Nerve?" *Harper's*, October 1978; Cullen Murphy, "Protestanism and the Evangelicals," *Wilson Quarterly*, Autumn 1981.

"But I do believe in caring..." : Seabury, op cit.

Christian Voice statement: Haught, op cit.

Moral Majority: Ernest Volkman and L. J. Davis, "Jerry Falwell—the Interesting Company He Keeps," *Penthouse*, November 1981; Seymour Martin Lipset and Earl Raab, "the Election and the Evangelicals," *Commentary*, March 1981; William R. Goodman and James J. H. Price, *Jerry Falwell—An Unauthorized Profile* (Paris and Associates, Lynchburg, Virginia, 1981).

Smith statement: *New York Times*, June 11, 1981.

Falwell statement: Goodman and Price, op cit.

"Meet the Press" exchange: Goodman and Price, op cit.

Falwell, evangelicals and Israel: Frances Fitzgerald, "A Disciplined, Charging Army," *The New Yorker*, May 18, 1981; Jere Real, "What Jerry Falwell *Really* Wants," *Inquiry*, August 24, 1981; Stephen Zunes, "Strange Bedfellows," *Progressive*, November 1981.

"The Majority of Americans...": *New York Times*, October 15, 1980.

Smith: Joseph Berger, "Jews and Baptists Act To Heal a Split," *Newsday*, April 22, 1981; *New York Times*, December 14, 1980.

"Funny looking noses...": *Associated Press,* November 13, 1980.

Christian business directories: "Tribulations for Christian Ads," *Business Week*, September 19, 1977.

Jesus revolution: Richard Gelwich, "Will the Jesus Revolution Revive Anti-Semitism?" *Christian Century*, May 10, 1972.

Cults: Allen S. Maller, "Jews, Cults and Apostates," *Judaism,* Fall 1981; "Parents, Children and Cults," *New York Times*, June 8, 1981.

National Council of Churches: "Protestant Liberalism, Consistently Anti-Israel, Fails to Arouse Jews," *Jewish Week-American Examiner*, September 27, 1981; speech, Dr. A. Roy Eckhardt, Third Annual Scholars Conference on the German Church Struggle and the Holocaust, Wayne State University, Detroit, March 20, 1972, author's notes.

Trifa case: Author's notes; based on an extensive investigation during 1974-1977 on accused Nazi war criminals living in the United States.

Sayre incident: Text, Sayre sermon, National Cathedral, March 26, 1972; see also *Religious News Service* reports, April 7, 1972, and September 11, 1972.

Quaker report: Author's notes.

Catholics and anti-Semitism: The complete text of the Vatican Council statement in *New York Times*, January 3, 1975. Insightful accounts of relations between Catholics and Jews include: Eugene Fisher, "Anti-Semitism: A Contemporary Christian Perspective," *Judaism*, Summer 1981; John T. Pawlikowski, "Catholics Look at Jews," *Commonweal*, January 31, 1975; and Dale Stover, "Anti-Semitism: Boundary of Jewish-Christian Understanding," *Christian Century*, June 26, 1974.

Berrigan case: Michael Novak, "The New Anti-Semitism," *Commonweal*, December 21, 1973; "Berrigan and His Critics," *Christian Century*, January 16, 1974.

Meeting of left Christians: *Jewish Week-American Examiner*, June 12, 1981.

"Jesus . . . not a sissy": Price-Goodman, op cit.

Chapter Six
Kristallnacht

Vandalized synagogues on Long Island: Author's notes: "Vandalism Won't Halt Holy Days," *Newsday*, September 28, 1981.

Kristallnacht: Viktor Reimann, *Goebbels: The Man Who Created Hitler* (Doubleday, 1976).

Buber: Otto Friedrich, *Before the Deluge* (Harper & Row, 1972).

Aftermath: Friedrich, op cit.

National problem: "Again, Anti-Semitism," *Newsweek*, January 10, 1981.

Long Island: Author's notes; see also the various reports in *Newsday*, especially May 10, 1981, and August 11, 1981.

Lynbrook incident: the most complete accounts of this nationally publicized incident are found in *Jewish World*, April 9, 1981; and *Newsday*, August 12, 1981.

Police view: Interview, Sergeant Howard Mandell, head, Suffolk County (New York) Police Departmental Task Force on Anti-Semitism, September 22, 1981.

"When a Jewish child...": Seminar on anti-Semitic violence, Suffolk County Police Department, September 26, 1981; author's notes.

Anti-Semitic vandal: "Son's Anti-Semitic 'Prank' Shocks Family on Long Island," *New York Times*, March 19, 1981.

Deficiencies of students: Christopher Lasch, "The New Illiteracy," *New Times*, January 8, 1979.

Textbooks: Frances Fitzgerald, "Rewriting American History," *The New Yorker*, February 26, 1979.

ADL study: *The Treatment of Minorities in Secondary School Textbooks*, Anti-Defamation League, 1961.

AJC study: *New York Times*, May 18, 1969; *Liberty Journal*, September 15, 1969.

Textbook excerpt: ADL study, op cit.

Guidelines: "Guidelines to Jewish History in Social Studies Material" American Jewish Committee, Jewish Communal Affairs Department, September 1971.

1970s textbook revision: *New York Times*, April 28, 1974.

Holocaust and textbooks: "The Treatment of the Holocaust in United States History Textbooks," Glenn S. Pate, Anti-Defamation League, 1980. All quotes from textbooks are from the Pate study.

"Holocaust" series: "America Confronts the Holocaust," American Jewish Committee, 1978.

Failure of educational establishment: "Silence in American Textbooks," in Livia Rotkirchen, editor, *Yad Vashem Studies on the European Jewish Catastrophe and Resist-*

ance (Yad Vashem, Jerusalem, 1970); Susan Jacoby, "Susan, What's Kristallnacht?" *Present Tense,* Autumn 1978; Chaim Schatzker, "The Teaching of the Holocaust: Dilemmas and Considerations," *Annals* of the American Academy of Politics and Social Science, July 1980.

Catholic teaching materials: Pawlikowski, op cit; "Catholic-Jewish Team Reviews Textbooks," *Christian Century,* January 15, 1969.

Higher education: Lucy S. Dawidowicz, *The Holocaust and the Historians* (Harvard University Press, 1981).

Dubonow: Dawidowicz, op cit.

Chapter Seven:
A Loss of Allies

"Harlem on My Mind": Max Geltman, *The Confrontation* (Prentice-Hall, 1970).

Anti-Semitism in catalog: Geltman, op cit.

Black revolution: Lenora E. Berison, *The Negroes and the Jews* (Random House, 1971).

Early black anti-Semitism: Kenneth B. Clark, "What Negroes Think About Jews," *ADL Bulletin,* December 1957; see also his "Candor About Negro-Jewish Relations," *Commentary,* February 1946.

The "Liberator": "Black Anti-Semitism," *Time,* March 17, 1967; "Liberator," May 19, 1967.

"Semitism in Black Ghettos": *Liberator,* January, February, and March 1966.

CORE: Robert G. Weisbord and Arthur Stein, *Bittersweet Encounter: The Afro-American and the American Jew* (Negro Universities Press, 1970).

Black extremists: "Plotting a War on Whitey," *Life,* June 10, 1966; "Black Anti-Semitism," *Time,* March 17, 1967.

Cruse: James Baldwin, et al, *Black Anti-Semitism and Jewish Racism* (R. W. Baron, New York, 1969).

Kerner Commission: Berison, op cit.

School strike: Martin Mayer, *The Teachers Strike: New York, 1968* (Harper & Row 1969).

Anti-Semitic poems: Geltman, op cit.

Baraka: "Black People!" *Evergreen Review*, December 1967.

Failure of black militance, Black Panthers: "Interview: Huey Newton," *Playboy*, May 1973; "Ethnic America," *Inquiry*, October 5, 1981; Earl Raab, "The Black Revolution and the Jewish Question," *Commentary*, January 1969.

Black flirtation with Third World: Murray Friedman, "Black Anti-Semitism on the Rise," *Commentary*, October 1979.

Breakdown of black-Jewish relations: "Disputes Between Blacks and Jews Divide Democrats in Several States," *New York Times*, March 30, 1981. See also two perceptive articles in the Summer 1981 issue of *Judaism*: "Black-Jewish Relations: A Two-Way Street," Nathan Perlmutter, and "Black Anti-Semitism: Diagnosis and Treatment," Sol Roth.

Affirmative action: Walter Berns, "Let Me Call You Quota, Sweetheart," *Commentary*, May 1981; L. H. Gann and Alvin Rabushka, "Racial Classification: Politics of the Future?" *Policy Review* Summer 1981. The classification formulas are taken from this article, the best yet written on the subject

Wise's comment: Mordecai S. Chertoff, editor, *The New Left and the Jews* (Pitman Publishing, New York, 1971).

Left and Jews: Nathan Glazer, "The New Left and the Jews," *Jewish Journal of Sociology,* December 1969; George Lichtheim, "Socialism and the Jews," *Dissent*, July-August 1968.

Old Left: Solomon Bloom, "Karl Marx and the Jews," *Jewish Social Studies*, January 1942; Nathan Glazer, *The Social Basis of American Communism* (Harcourt Brace, 1961).

Soviet anti-Semitism: Ronald I. Rubin, editor, *The Unredeemed: Anti-Semitism in the Soviet Union* (Quadrangle

Books, 1968); Dawidowicz, op cit; C. E. Black, editor, *Rewriting Russian History* (Praeger, 1956).

Modern Soviet "anti-Zionism": William Korey, "Making Anti-Semitism Respectable," *Moment*, December 1978; see also the same author's "Anti-Zionism in the USSR," *Problems of Communism*, November-December 1978.

Effect on other left movements: Daniel P. Moynihan, "Exporting Anti-Semitism," *New Leader*, November 5, 1979.

Deportation of Soviet Jews scheduled: Author's notes, based on interviews with recent Soviet émigrés to this country, 1977 and 1978.

Babi Yar: Lucy S. Dawidowicz, "The Forgotten Victims of Babi Yar," *New York Times*, September 27, 1981.

Chapter Eight:
Anti-Zionism: The Easy Disguise

Defeat of Jewish lobby: Author's notes; see also Jim Klurfeld, "Defeated by a New Era," *Newsday*, May 16, 1978.

Zionism as "religion" of American Jews: Nathan Glazer, "Jewish Loyalties," *Wilson Quarterly*, Autumn 1981.

Golda Meir: Arthur Hertzberg, "Zionism in America," *Jerusalem Post* magazine, July 4, 1976 (special U.S. bicentennial issue).

Jews and relation to Israel: Jacob R. Marcus, "Zionism and the American Jew," *The American Scholar*, May 1933; Max Dimont, *The Jews in America* (Simon and Schuster, 1978).

Zionism: Ben Halpern, *The Idea of a Jewish State* (Harvard University Press, 1961).

Early American Zionists: Stanley Feldstein, *The Land That I Show You* (Anchor Press/Doubleday, 1978).

American Jewish lobby: "'Israeli Lobby' in U.S. Gains Repute for Zeal—and Overzealousness," *Wall Street Journal*, July 7, 1977; Eric Rouleau, "The Jewish Lobby," *Le Monde*, July 11, 1977.

Israel Bonds: "Israel Bonds—Facts and Figures," State of Israel Bonds 1979 fact sheet.

Zionism and anti-Semitism: Jacob Katz, "Zionism vs. Anti-Semitism," *Commentary*, April 1979; J. L. Talmon, op cit; Gershom Schocken, "Revisiting Zionism," *New York Review of Books*, May 28, 1981.

Influence of Jewish lobby: Stephen D. Isaacs, *Jews and American Politics*, (Doubleday, 1974); "Activities of Nondiplomatic Representatives of Foreign Principals in the United States," Hearings, U.S. Senate Foreign Relations Committee, August 1, 1963; Melvin I. Urofsky, *American Zionism from Herzl to the Holocaust* (Anchor Press/-Doubleday, 1976).

Tilt to Saudis: "Growing U.S.-Saudi Bonds," *Washington Post*, December 12, 1976; *Defense Monitor*, April, 1981 (for figures on American military invested in Saudi Arabia.)

Vance meeting with Jews: *New York Times*, October 27, 1977.

Twinam testimony: "Saudi Arabia and U.S. Security Policy," *Current Policy* No. 320, U.S. Department of State, September 25, 1981.

Nixon sideswipe: *New York Times*, September 29, 1981.

"Poisonous" atmosphere: *Los Angeles Times*, October 28, 1981.

AWACS testimony: "AWACS Testimony Elicits Senate Anger," *Aviation Week*, October 5, 1981.

American Jews and Israel: "U.S. Jews' Dilemma," *Manchester Guardian*, September 20, 1981; for reports of torture, see extensive investigation in *London (Sunday) Times*, June 19, 1977.

Nuseibeh speech: Author's notes.

Mathias: Charles McC. Mathias, "Ethnic Groups and Foreign Policy." *Foreign Affairs*, Summer 1981.

Truman recognition of Israel: Clark M. Clifford, "Recognizing Israel: the 1948 Story," *American Heritage*, April 1977.

Talbot: Strobe Talbot, "What to Do About Israel," *Time*, September 7, 1981. Sources have indicated to the author

that the White House photocopied the article and distributed several hundred copies to senators and congressmen,
plus other government officials.

Chapter Nine:
The Power of Oil

Prince Fahd: Author's notes; the incident received extensive
coverage in the European press.
The Arab economic war: Walter Henry Nelson and Terence
Prittie, *The Economic War Against the Jews* (Random
House, 1977).
The oil weapon: Leonard Mosley, *Power Play* (Random
House, 1968).
American acquiescence: Nelson-Prittie, op cit; Kenneth C.
Crowe, *America for Sale* (Doubleday, 1978).
Mobil ad: Crowe, op cit.
Texaco ad: Nelson-Prittie, op cit.
Percy comment: Author's notes.
Business community assertion: *Foreign Direct Investment in
the United States* (five volumes), U.S. Department of
Commerce, April 1976.
Robinson case: Crowe, op cit.
Biases against Jews: Drawn from *ADL Boycott Reports*, pub-
lished continuously since 1974; Nelson-Prittie, op cit.
Army Engineers: Nelson-Prittie, op cit.
Arab investment in United States: Michael Field, *A Hundred
Million Dollars a Day* (Sidgwick and Jackson, London,
1975).
True extent of official figures: Tad Szulc, "Recycling Petro-
dollars: the $100 Billion Understanding," *New York
Times*, September 20, 1981.
Saudis and SAMA: "Squirreling Away $100 Billion," *Time*,
July 13, 1981.
Khashoggi: Crowe, op cit.; "OPEC's Secrets," *Time*, October
5, 1981.

Mason: Crowe, op cit.

Kuwait: "Arab Worldwide Wheeler-Dealer," *Time*, July 13, 1981.

PLO Investments: "The Well-Heeled Guerrillas," *Time*, July 10, 1977.

Boycott: Nancy Turck, "The Arab Boycott of Israel," *Foreign Affairs*, Spring 1977.

Gulf oil, Coca-Cola, bank incidents: Nelson-Prittie, op cit.

Boycott legislation: "Exporting Anti-Semitism," *The New Republic*, March 15, 1975.

Fight over legislation: "Arab Boycott Stirs Anti-Semitism Issue," *National Observer,* May 10, 1975.

Oil company bias: "EEOC Hunts Anti-Jewish Bias at Standard Oil of California," *Washington Post*, October 30, 1976.

Current enforcement of anti-boycott laws: *New York Times,* October 22, 1981.

Continuing Arab enmity toward Israel: Daniel Pipes, "The Politics of Muslim Anti-Semitism," *Commentary*, August 1981.

Chapter Ten:
"Is It Good for Jews?"

Mordecai Noah: Arthur and Lila Weinberg, editors, *Passport to Utopia: Great Panaceas in American History* (Quadrangle, 1978).

Jews and anti-Semitism: John Leonard, "Why Do We Love to Hate the Jews?" *Penthouse*, November 1976; Susan Littwin, "The New Face of Anti-Semitism," *Los Angeles*, June 1981.

Modern Jewish Community: "The American Jew Today," *Newsweek*, March 1, 1971.

Divisions among Jews: "Crisis in Jewish Family to Command Discussion at Major Conventions," *Jewish Week-American Examiner*, June 12, 1981; see also "'Narcissism' a

Threat to Family and Jewish Life in America, Reconstructionists Warned," in same publication, same issue.

Hertzberg: "Is the Jew in Exile?" in *Being Jewish in America* (Schocken Books, 1979).

Isaiah Berlin: *Personal Impressions*, (Harper & Row, 1980).

Toynbee: Oskar Rabinowitz, *Toynbee and Zionism* (Chatto and Windhus, London, 1978).

Jewish Defense League: Janet L. Doglin, *Jewish Identity and the JDL* (Princeton University Press, 1977).

Kahane speech: Englewood, New Jersey, November 10, 1971, author's notes.

Contradictions in Jewish community: Jacob Neusner, *Stranger at Home* (University of Chicago Press, 1980).

Yeshiva dinner: *Jewish Week-American Examiner*, June 7, 1981.

"Kike": Ibid, April 12, 1981.

Tuition tax credits: "Should Jews Support Tuiton Tax Credits?" *Jewish World*, April 30, 1981.

Cult bills: *New York Times*, May 22, 1981.

Timmerman: *Time*, September 10, 1981.

Holocaust show: Letter to author from Simon Wiesenthal Center, May 22, 1981.

Arendt: "Hannah Arendt: The Animus Fades," *New York Times*, October 5, 1981; "Hannah Arendt on Eichmann: A Study in the Perversity of Brillance," *Commentary*, September 1963.

Kahane plan: *Chicago Sun-Times*, June 3, 1981.

Chelm jokes: Testimony of survivor, "They made a pogrom in Chelm right after the war..." *Village Voice*, April 24, 1978.

JEWELS and anti-cult charms: *Jewish Week-American Examiner*, March 8, 1981, and August 9, 1981.

Hirschberg sermon: *New York Times*, October 10, 1981.

The synagogue in Prague: *Jewish Week-American Examiner*, July 19, 1981.

INDEX